On Interest Rates and Asset Prices in Europe

On Interest Rates and Asset Prices in Europe

The Selected Essays of Martin M.G. Fase

Martin M.G. Fase

Deputy Executive Director of
De Nederlandsche Bank, Amsterdam and
Professor of Monetary Economics, University of Amsterdam,
The Netherlands

Edward Elgar
Cheltenham, UK · Northampton, MA, USA

Published by
Edward Elgar Publishing Limited
Glensanda House
Montpellier Parade
Cheltenham
Glos GL50 1UA
UK

Edward Elgar Publishing, Inc.
6 Market Street
Northampton
Massachusetts 01060
USA

A catalogue record for this book
is available from the British Library

Library of Congress Cataloguing in Publication Data

Fase, M. M. G., 1937–
On interest rates and asset prices in Europe: the selected essays of Martin M.G. Fase / Martin M.G. Fase.
"The 16 papers collected in this book cover a quarter of a century of empirical research"—Introd.
Includes bibliographical references and indexes.
1. Interest rates—Europe. 2. Stocks—Prices—Europe. I. Title.
HG1623.E9F37 1999
332.8'2'094—dc21 98-31694
CIP

ISBN 1 84064 020 0

Printed and bound in Great Britain by
Biddles Ltd, Guildford and King's Lynn

Contents

List of Figures

List of Tables

Acknowledgements

The research reported in this book was conducted over a period of more than two decades, while I was Head of the Econometric and Special Studies Department of the Nederlandsche Bank. I have had the privilege of benefiting from the intellectual input of the many colleagues at the Bank with whom I cooperated over the years. This is reflected in the sixteen papers included in this volume, six of which are co-authored. I thank my former colleagues F.A.G. den Butter, A.M. Dongelmans, M. van Nieuwkerk, K. Steel and P.J.G. Vlaar, as well as my former students L.A. van Geylsweijk, W.F.-J. van de Poll and E. Shtrasburg, who have not only been my co-authors but who have also, at appropriate times, provided me with valuable comments on my own papers. I am indebted to them for their cooperation in the past and for allowing me to republish the fruits of our past scholarly work. I also wish to thank the publishers involved for their permission to include the published articles, a few of which appeared only in Dutch, as chapters in this book. Last but not least, I would like to thank C.K. Folkertsma, who shared with me, in such a pleasant way, the burden of editing this book. Furthermore, I am grateful to F.R. Stork and L. Vos, as well as Marianne Brouwer, Gita Gajapersad, Mariëtta Bakker-van den Bol and Vera Roos, for their indispensable help in producing this book.

M.M.G. Fase
Amsterdam, 8 July 1998

Introduction

Ever since I read Conard's magnificent *An Introduction to the Theory of Interest* in the early sixties I have had the feeling that the theory of interest was more or less complete but that the empirics of interest rates was still offering many challenges. This appears to be true and many writers have made their scholarly contributions, some, like Irving Fisher himself, even before Conard wrote his introductory survey. The measurement of interest rates and asset prices became a major topic of my own empirical research in monetary economics. This work of mine was inspired by Fisher's fascinating *The Purchasing Power of Money*, which appeared in 1911, and his admirable *The Theory of Interest* of 1930. Fisher, according to Schumpeter (1954, p. 847) over-anxious to do justice to any predecessors he could find, dedicated the latter book to the main pioneers in the field, the Scottish-American John Rae (1796-1872) and the Austrian Eugen von Böhm-Bawerk (1851-1914). Unlike these classic writers, Fisher did a great deal of empirical work himself. However, once we focus on econometric testing and estimation, a Pandora's box of research challenges and empirical results is opened. Therefore, even in monetary matters, the need to concentrate on a particular viewpoint emerges. The topic of this collection of essays is interest rates and equity or asset prices.

In surveying theories concerning the nature and role of interest 32 years ago, Shackle (1966) — at the time known for his unorthodox views — concludes that interest is the most paradoxical of all economic quantities. On the one hand, it has led to particular views on the desirability of cheap — or dear — money and speculative thoughts of the *justum pretium* type while, on the other, it presents the opportunity of doing calculations. The latter are usually regarded as quantitatively exact and logically inescapable, running as an unbroken thread through the accumulation of wealth, saving and investment. Thus the interest rate is reigning over money holding, economic growth and the general price level. It appears, to paraphrase Shackle again, as the pivot of the entire system, the sun in the economic universe. Nevertheless, when examined closely, these claims dissolve. As Mrs. Joan Robinson (1952, p. 5) has pointed out, there is no such thing as the rate of interest and thus knowledge of interest behaviour is indispensable for understanding the working of monetary shocks.

In the domain of interest rates, empirical research did not really come into its own until the early 1970s when monetarism and large-scale modelling became part of mainstream economics. It was, to the best of my knowledge, Hester (1969) who first took up this challenging question empirically.

In the real world, interest rates and asset prices are as manifold as commodities and services are diverse. The search for a pure interest rate makes it necessary to look for explanations regarding exchange rate uncertainty, risk, liquidity, convenience, inflation premia and perhaps other aspects embodied in the abstract notion of interest, or the rate of interest. This search is extremely useful, as brought out by a number of the empirical examinations reported in this volume.

There is broad agreement today that the main job of central bankers is to protect the stability of the financial system and, as an element of this, to attain price stability. As to the meaning of financial fragility, a consensus among monetary policy makers seems to exist. Less agreement exists on which prices monetary policy makers seek to stabilize; none of the conventional measures of inflation includes asset prices of which interest rates are to some extent a mirror image. According to Irving Fisher almost three-quarters of a century ago, there is a close relationship between money growth and a broadly defined price index including asset prices such as shares, bonds, and property as well as prices of producer and consumer goods. At the same time, interest rates are considered an important means for tightening monetary conditions. Obviously, this type of problem is of great importance from a monetary policy perspective and requires a large amount of research. This book offers examples of empirical research on interest rates, equity prices and asset returns. Moreover, it provides an illustration of the historical development of empirical research methodology on interest rates and equity prices since the early 1970s. This development has been remarkable, indeed.

The 16 papers collected in this book cover a quarter of a century of empirical research on interest rates and a variety of asset prices. They have been organized into two broad categories. The first group is in Part One and includes nine chapters on the measurement of interest rates. The second is in Part Two and contains seven chapters considering equity and asset prices.

Although the nine chapters of Part One offer different messages and focuses, they also have many important elements in common. The first is the emphasis on statistical measurement. The second is the attempt to understand interest rate behaviour through statistical estimation.

The third common element is the attempt to understand the historical interest rate development in the long run, theoretically and empirically. As to measurement, the methods used here show a wide diversity in statistical methodology and coverage. In four of the nine chapters, the main statistical methodology is principal components analysis applied to time series of interest rates. Chapter 1 considers levels and first differences of twenty Dutch market rates which appear to have a very large common variation, suggesting that, Mrs. Joan Robinson's doubts notwithstanding, there is something like the interest rate, but also that the simultaneous use of many interest rates in macroeconomic models is suspect. Similar results show up in Chapters 2 and 3, which consider market interest rates in the major financial centres of the world and the interest rate linkages in the Benelux countries, respectively. Chapter 4 applies the same methodology in examining interest rate convergence in EMU and the major OECD countries. In the four other chapters of Part One, emphasis is on measurement of interest rate behaviour. The Gibson paradox, which Keynes in his *Treatise* (Keynes 1930, II, p. 198) considered ' ... one of the most completely established empirical facts in the whole field of quantitative economics', is studied in Chapters 5 and 6. These two chapters refer to research done in the early seventies when the Gibson paradox was almost forgotten. In spite of Keynes, this relationship, today better known as the Fisher hypothesis, requires much empirical examination as the literature makes clear. Our approach is the Fisher hypothesis in an open economy and in relation to exchange rates in core EMU. This matter is the main topic of Chapter 7. Chapter 8 considers the behaviour of mortgage rates in the framework of a small demand-oriented market model for mortgage credit. The final chapter of Part One reviews the evolution of interest rate theory and empirics over the last three-quarters of the twentieth century, confirming the speculative conjecture that since World War II, apart from term-structure theory, the main innovation has been the econometric estimation of interest rate behaviour.

The chapters in Part One also differ in emphasis and coverage and very often in statistical sophistication. These differences mostly reflect the evolution over time of the shifts in research strategy due to the development of novel econometric techniques, research tools and the widening of the scope of monetary analysis. As to the latter, the shift from closed to open monetary economies, very much fostered by the EMU process, has been an important impetus.

The seven chapters of Part Two examine the behaviour of bonds, stocks as well as investment in art. The latter has been included because I like it; the others are important ingredients of asset price inflation.

Again, the research reported is uncompromisingly empirical, but not devoid of a profound theoretical framework, based on recent insights from the literature. Chapter 10 considers the behaviour of indexed bonds as predictors of inflation expectations in EMU. This knowledge is indispensable for a monetary strategy aiming at inflation targeting. In this chapter, modern econometric technology is used to study long-term and short-term behaviour of bond prices, allowing for temporary deviations from equilibrium by means of the error correction framework with cointegration analysis as an important statistical tool. Chapters 11 to 13 examine stock market behaviour and the interaction between trading in different countries and markets. The famous equity premium puzzle of Mehra and Prescott, introduced in 1985, is examined empirically in detail in two chapters. Chapter 14 considers over 150 years of data for The Netherlands in taking a fresh look at the puzzle which has mainly and one-sidedly been examined with American data. In Chapter 15 the analysis is extended to the major EMU countries, though the sample period is much shorter, with only post-war data. Part Two concludes with a chapter on the analysis of yields on investment in art. The results suggest that purchases of works of art are principally motivated by consumption rather than investment needs. For the consideration of asset price inflation, this is an interesting, although perhaps minor finding.

The research style throughout the sixteen chapters of this volume is to examine a particular aspect of monetary economics, *viz.* what might be called the price of money. Reading the chapters perhaps will lead to an appreciation of a particular aspect of a monetary research tradition at the Dutch central bank. Hopefully, the essays in this book may help to deepen our understanding of asset price inflation, the importance of which Irving Fisher (1933) highlighted so long ago.

PART ONE

On Interest Rates

All of us seek and use simplifications to overcome the frustrating sterility of the cliché that everything depends on everything else. But we all know that we do so at some peril.

Brainard and Tobin (1968, p. 99)

1. A Principal Components Analysis of Market Interest Rates in The Netherlands, 1962–1970

1.1 Introduction

This chapter presents an application of a principal components analysis of 20 market interest rates in The Netherlands. It covers 108 months over the years 1962 until 1970.

The principal motivation of this analysis was our doubts regarding much theoretical reasoning, based on the implicit assumption that interest rates can move independently in a similar way as prices do in a general equilibrium framework. An illustrative example of this view is a recent study by Korteweg (1971). Following the interesting work of Brainard and Tobin (1968), Korteweg introduces a number of interest rates, a subset of which is regarded as instruments of monetary policy. However, in order to be effective instruments, it would be necessary for those rates to move independently. Otherwise they are not expected to be very useful instruments. On the statistical level a problem may arise when various specific interest rates are used as explanatory variables in the reduced form equations of a simultaneous macroeconomic model. A well-known example of this is the FRB-MIT model, which contains even in the simple versions at least 6 different specific interest rates (see, for example, Christ (1971)). There is no doubt that these models do justice to the whole spectrum of investment opportunities open to an investor. However, it may be asked whether movements in the market rates of different assets are sufficiently independent to motivate the inclusion of a large set of interest rates in those models.

The main purpose of the present study is to examine to what extent interest rates in The Netherlands did, in fact, vary independently during the sixties. Although this objective is modest enough, thus we hope to

Reprinted from *European Economic Review* **4** (1973), M.M.G. Fase, 'A principal components analysis of market interest rates in The Netherlands, 1962–1970', 107–134 ©1973 with kind permission from Elsevier Science.

gain some quantitative insight into the actual interdependency among Dutch interest rates.

Formulated in this way, our subject shows some resemblance to a study by Stevers (1963), looking for one single indicator of the whole spectrum of yields on specific government bonds. However, the present investigation differs from Stevers's study, since in this chapter a different method of analysis has been applied and a larger set of rates of return is considered. The present study shows more resemblance, however, to papers by Hester (1969) and Vercruysse, Lavry, and Pirard (1971), who apply similar methods of analysis to American and Belgian data respectively. As a matter of fact, our analysis has been inspired by Hester's paper although our motivation differs, since we are particularly interested in a measure of *the* rate of interest.

The plan of the chapter is as follows. The next section offers some details on the basic data. The statistical method is summarized in section 1.3. The results are discussed in sections 1.4 and 1.5. In the concluding section our results are summarized and compared with the results obtained for the USA and Belgium.

1.2 The Data

To begin we adopt the customary distinction between money and capital market. As to the money market, it is the custom to consider the maturity of the assets and the type of participants as distinctive features. However, some authors add additional criteria to define the money market. For want of a better criterion we follow Jongman (1960, Chapter 2), Polakoff and Ketchum (1970), taking a maturity of one year as the most typical characteristic. In doing so all authors seem to emphasize that the money market, as opposed to the capital market, deals solely with financial assets, being close substitutes for money. It is impossible, however, to cover all intricacies of everyday practice by one or two neatly-worded definitions. By tradition, the Dutch money market includes call money, commercial bills, several types of Treasury paper and short-term loans of different maturities. The latter are usually granted to local authorities and public utilities, but in recent years also to industry.[1] The lenders are banks and others, to whom, however, Euro-dollar deposits offer an alternative. Therefore, our description of the money market should include the Euro-dollar market. Other types of loans by money-creating institutions to the private sector are not counted as belonging to the money market, neither are time deposits. However,

---

1 See *e.g.* De Nederlandsche Bank (1972).

Table 1.1: Means and standard deviations of selected money market interest rates, 1962–1970

i	Debt instrument	Mean (%)	Standard deviation
1	Call money	3.80	1.77
2	3-month Treasury paper	4.14	1.45
3	1-year Treasury paper	4.48	1.59
4	2-year Treasury paper	4.65	1.50
5	3-year Treasury paper	4.81	1.45
6	5-year Treasury paper	5.09	1.41
7	Loans to local authorities 3-month	5.27	1.93
8	Loans to local authorities 1-year	5.65	1.78
9	Euro-dollar deposits	5.25	1.86
10	Nederlandsche Bank official discount rate	4.86	0.84

the interest rates for these debt instruments are strongly related to the official discount rate.

Table 1.1 shows the mean and standard deviation of each of the interest rates considered. The table shows the largest mean for short-term loans with a maturity of one year, and the smallest for call money. The standard deviation, too, varies with the various debt instruments. A notable feature is the significantly larger variability for debt instruments with an active market; it is the smallest for the official discount rate. This illustrates the institutional character of this rate, which sometimes remained constant for a considerable period of time.

An alternative way of looking at the money market data is by graphical representation, as has been done in Figures 1.1, 1.2 and 1.3. From those figures it may be seen that the various interest rates are highly interrelated, resulting in largely parallel trends.

By contrast to the money market, the capital market is more clearly structured. The capital market is usually defined as that segment of the financial asset market where debt instruments are traded with a maturity of more than one year.[2] The major difference between these various instruments is the distinction between risk-bearing capital and fixed-interest-bearing securities. The two groups may show substantial differences in yield, particularly in periods of considerable price fluctuations.

Table 1.2 summarises the capital market figures used. The first 8 series represent yields on non-risk-bearing, the last 2 on risk-bearing

[2] See *e.g.* Polakoff and Ketchum (1970).

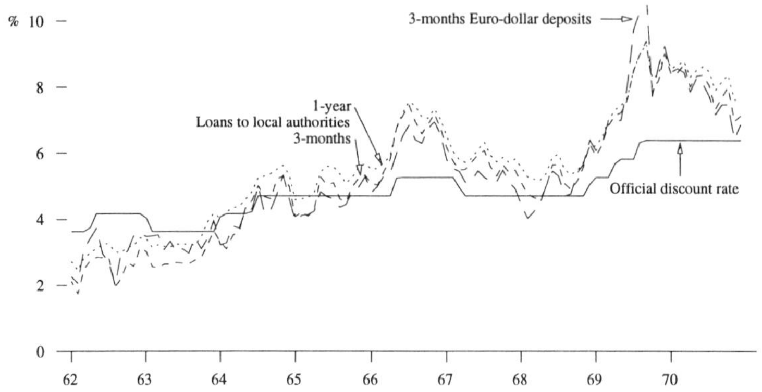

Figure 1.1: Three money market rates and the official discount rate, 1962–1970

capital. The main criterion for selecting the debt instruments has been the availability of time series. The figures are based on monthly averages of yield in the 1962–1970 period. For each series the mean and standard deviation have been calculated. As might be expected, there is a substantial difference between the yield on investments in local and international shares on the one hand and the yield on investments in other securities on the other. Another notable feature is that the dispersion is the smallest with the yield on shares. Lastly, mortgages score the highest

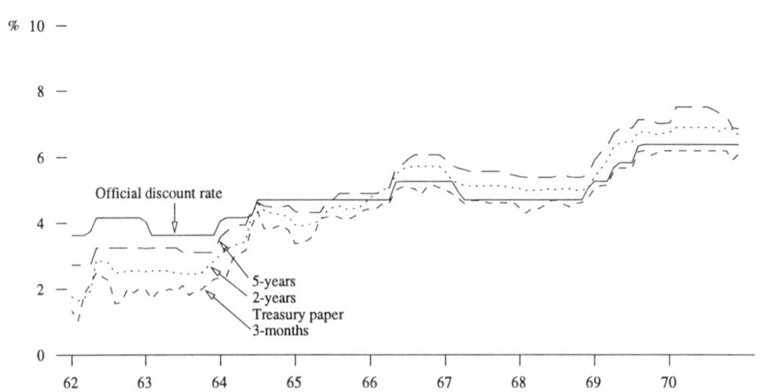

Figure 1.2: Three money market rates and the official discount rate, 1962–1970

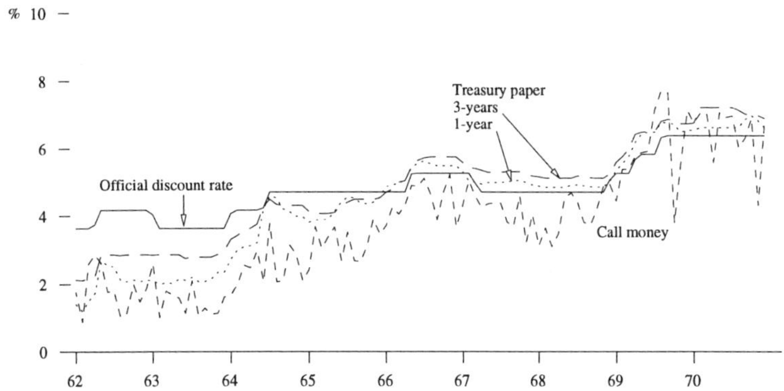

Figure 1.3: Three money market rates and the official discount rate, 1962–1970

mean and mortgage bank bonds the highest standard deviation. The overall movement of various capital market rates is shown by Figures 1.4 and 1.5. Both include the Bank's official discount rate to link capital market rates to the money market. This graphical representation shows once more that yield on shares is markedly lower than the yield on fixed-interest-bearing securities.

1.3 Method of Analysis

As our principal concern is to account for the variance among interest rates the method of principal components analysis, mainly due to Hotelling (1933), seems an appropriate tool of analysis. This method is rather well-known; we recall, therefore, only a few points that are relevant to understand our results.[3]

Let z_{it} denote the standardised ith rate of interest at time t. If all interest rates observed move proportionally, we have

$$z_{it} = \alpha_{i1} f_{1t}, \tag{1.1}$$

for all i and t, with α_{i1} denoting a set of constants to be determined and f_1 the non-observable first principal component. In general, (1.1) will only hold approximately. We therefore seek to determine those α_{i1} and

[3] For details we refer to Harman (1968) or Lawley and Maxwell (1971). A classic reference for the economist is Stone (1947). Of other applications we mention: Cramer (1966), Kloek and Bannink (1962), Sommermeijer (1962) and Theil (1962).

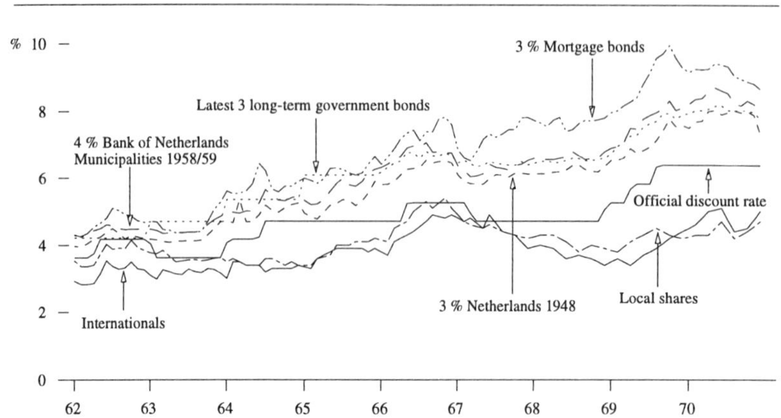

Figure 1.4: Six capital market yields and the official discount rate, 1962–1970

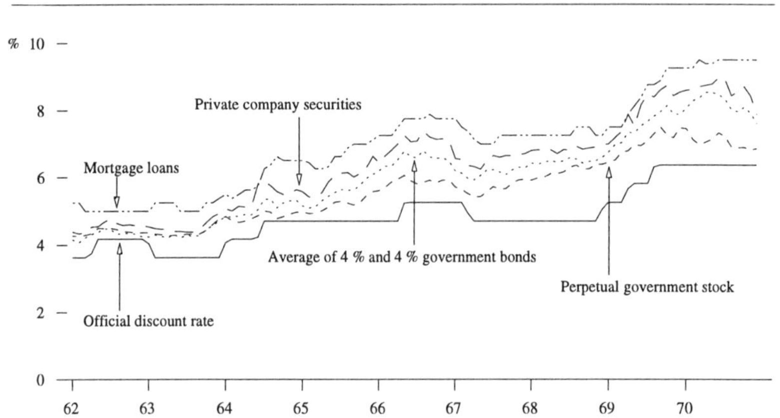

Figure 1.5: Four capital market yields and the official discount rate, 1962–1970

Table 1.2: Means and standard deviations of selected capital market rates, 1962–1970

i	Debt instrument	Mean (%)	Standard deviation
1	Perpetual government debt	5.62	0.98
2	3.25% Netherlands 1948	5.77	1.19
3	Average of three 4.25% and 4.50% government loans	6.02	1.28
4	Latest three long-term government bonds	6.02	1.27
5	4.50% Bank for Netherlands Municipalities 1958/59	6.17	1.30
6	Private company securities	6.39	1.38
7	3% mortgage bank bonds	6.82	1.60
8	Mortgage loans	6.99	1.41
9	Local shares	4.08	0.49
10	International shares	3.85	0.61

f_{it} which will minimize residual sum S_1, with

$$S_1 = \sum_t \sum_i (z_{it} - \alpha_{i1} f_{1t})^2 . \tag{1.2}$$

Because (1.2) is determined up to a constant factor we impose the normalisation $\sum_i f_{1t}^2 = 1$. It can be shown that (1.2) has its minimum value when

$$f_{1t} = \frac{1}{\lambda_1} \sum_i z_{it} \alpha_{i1} , \tag{1.3}$$

where λ_1 denotes the largest eigenvalue of the $(p \times p)$ matrix (m_{ih}) with

$$m_{ih} = \sum_i z_{it} z_{ih} ,$$

and i, $h = 1, 2, \ldots, p$ while the α_{i1} are derived from the elements of the corresponding eigenvector by multiplying with $\sqrt{\lambda_1}$. It may furthermore be shown that

$$\lambda_1 = \sum_i \alpha_{i1}^2 .$$

The expression (1.3) implies that f_1 is a linear function of the observed variables with coefficients proportional to the elements from the eigenvector corresponding to the largest eigenvalue λ_1.

The second principal component may be taken in the same way from the resulting residuals. In general, the kth principal component is obtained as

$$f_{kt} = \frac{1}{\lambda_k} \sum_i z_{it} \alpha_{ik}. \tag{1.4}$$

It may be easily proved that each principal component is orthogonal to all others. In equation (1.4) λ_k denotes the kth eigenvalue of the matrix (m_{ih}) ranked in descending order of magnitude. The factor loadings α_{ik} are computed from the corresponding eigenvector. Finally as before, we have

$$\lambda_k = \sum_i \alpha_{ik}^2.$$

It is obvious that for standardised variables the matrix (m_{ih}) turns into a correlation matrix. In that particular case, the factor loadings correspond to simple correlation coefficients between the ith variable z_i and the kth principal component f_k.

Note that the sum of the eigenvalues λ_k equals the trace of the matrix (m_{ih}), denoted by $\mathrm{tr}(m_{ih})$. $\mathrm{tr}(m_{ih})$ equals p if standardised variables are used. Each factor f_k therefore accounts for a fraction ϕ_k of the total variation in z_i, with

$$\phi_k = \frac{\lambda_k}{\mathrm{tr}(m_{ih})}.$$

The quantity ϕ_k is an unweighted average of the R^2 of the interest variables with f_k. It is used as R^2 in regression analysis, indicating goodness of fit.

In particular situations, the interpretation of principal components is simplified if the computed matrix of factor loadings is transformed. The varimax rotation is a frequently-used method to achieve such a transformation. The point is to construct an orthogonal transformation matrix in such a way that the function

$$V = p \sum_j \Big(\sum_i \beta_{ij}^4 - \Big(\sum_i \beta_{ij}^2 \Big)^2 \Big), \tag{1.5}$$

where

$$\beta_{ij} = \frac{\alpha_{ij}}{\sqrt{\sum_j \alpha_{ij}^2}}$$

and $j = 1, \ldots, q$, $i = 1, \ldots, p$ is maximised. The required factor loadings are a function of the angle of rotation, which is obtained by iteration from the factor loadings derived from each rotation, until (1.5) attains a maximum.

1.4 The Principal Components of Money and Capital Market Rates

In the present application, the basic interest variables z_i have been normalized so that the starting point of our computations has been the correlation matrix. In one case we did not normalize to unit variance. In this case the matrix (m_{ih}) turns into a covariance matrix. This section discusses the main results of our principal component analysis of the money and capital market. Throughout this discussion we use the notation introduced in the preceding section.

1.4.1 Results of the Money Market

Table 1.3 shows that the first factor, corresponding to the largest eigenvalue λ_1, explains more than 95% of the total variation of money market interest rates. If the computation is repeated for two sub-periods or with monthly figures pooled into quarterly figures, the outcome hardly changes. If the computation is based on the covariance matrix, the total variation explained by the first factor does not change substantially, either.

These results clearly indicate that the first principal component suffices to describe the common variation in money market interest rates, although the second will still be of some interest. Meanwhile, it may be asked whether it is possible to define the first two principal components more narrowly. Therefore we have to look at the α_{i1} and α_{i2} shown in Table 1.4, which go with the two largest eigenvalues of the correlation matrix of monthly interest rates for the money market, 1962–1970.

If the variables have been normalized to unit variance, the α_{ik} of Table 1.4 may be regarded as coefficients of correlation among the ith interest rate and the kth principal component. The most notable feature of Table 1.4, therefore, is the persistently high degree of correlation with the first principal component: even at its lowest it is still 0.95. So, the conclusion is warranted to regard the first principal component as 'the' money market interest rate. The second component, which by itself is of much less importance but still significant, shows a striking factor-loading pattern: positive correlation for Treasury paper, negative correlation for the other money market instruments (of course, the signs may be reversed!).

It is certainly striking that this difference in sign distinguishes Treasury paper from the other money market instruments. It should be noted that since the 1948 Treasury paper is not quoted daily, it mainly serves as a short-term investment which does not very often change hands, and

Table 1.3: Three largest eigenvalues for 10 money market interest rates, January 1962–December 1970

	Correlation matrices with monthly figures			Correlation matrix with	Covariance matrix with
	1962– 1970	Jan. '62 Jun. '66	July '66 Dec. '70	quarterly figures whole period	monthly figures whole period
λ_1	9.57	9.31	9.32	9.67	24.08
λ_2	0.20	0.31	0.40	0.16	0.57
λ_3	0.09	0.20	0.17	0.07	0.28
$\mathrm{tr}(m_{ih})$	10	10	10	10	24.14
ϕ_1	95.7%	93.1%	93.2%	96.7%	95.8%

as collateral with certain call money transactions. The risk stems from the fact that rising interest rates result in a decline of security prices, and transaction costs are low. Not so with call money, short-term loans and Euro-dollar deposits, where particularly the first and the third are investment alternatives very sensitive to changes in interest rates. The ensuing interest arbitrage involves cost as well. We see from Table 1.4 that it is particularly for these instruments that the α_{i2} stand out very clearly with relatively high correlation coefficients. It seems warranted, therefore, to regard the second principal component as related to default risk and to the cost of transaction.

Table 1.4: Factor loadings of the first and second principal component of money market interest rates, 1962–1970

i	Debt instrument	α_{i1}	α_{i2}
1	Call money	0.95	−0.22
2	3-month Treasury paper	0.98	0.12
3	1-year Treasury paper	0.99	0.15
4	2-year Treasury paper	0.99	0.13
5	3-year Treasury paper	0.99	0.11
6	5-year Treasury paper	0.99	0.09
7	Loans to local authorities 3-month	0.99	−0.08
8	Loans to local authorities 1-year	0.99	−0.04
9	Euro-dollar deposits	0.96	−0.26
10	Nederlandsche Bank official discount rate	0.96	−0.03
Eigenvalue λ_k		9.57	0.20
ϕ_k		95.7%	2.0%

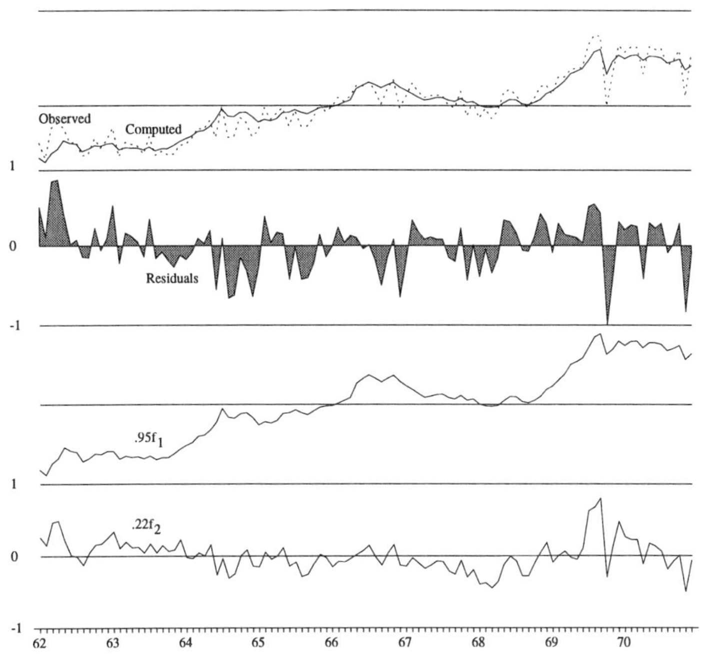

Figure 1.6: First and second principal component of call money rate, 1962–1970

The conclusion to be drawn from our analysis is that there are apparently two factors that account for almost all variation among money market interest rates. The first component reflects the true interest rate, the rate which completely abstracts from the credit or default risk. It stands for compensation for sacrificed liquidity. The second principal component may be interpreted as a reflection of the transaction cost and risk element, which turns out to be of minor importance. Both factors show up best with the call money rates and the interest rates for Euro-dollar deposits. This suggests that either of these two series is the most suitable for use when investigating interest behaviour on the money market.

To conclude our analysis of the money market, Figure 1.6 shows the call money rates observed in the market with contributions made by the first two principal components. The figure plots what in our notation is z_1, that is the standardised call money rate. This rate has been compared with the value computed from $0.95f_1 - 0.22f_2$. The graphs confirm once more that the first principal component dominates the call money rates.

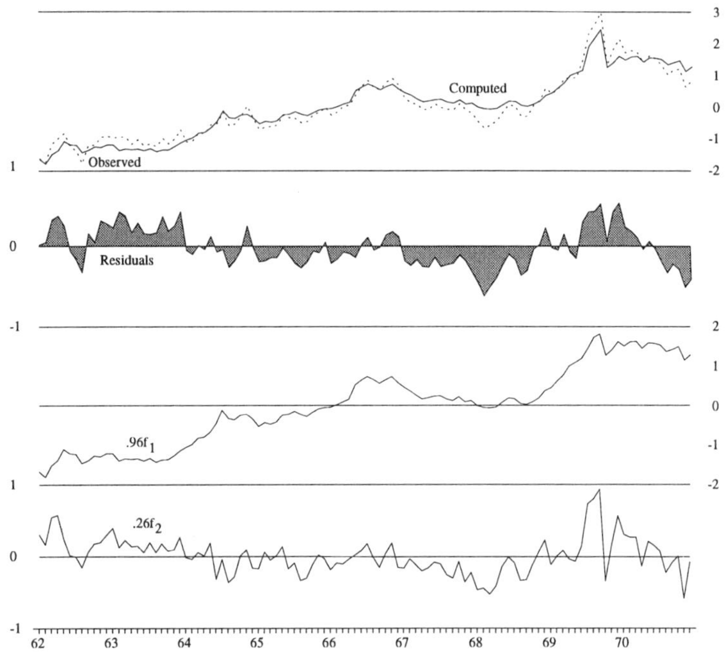

Figure 1.7: First and second principal component of net Euro-dollar rate, 1962–1970

From Figure 1.7 it appears that the same holds for a description of 3-month Euro-dollar deposit rates, z_9 in our notation. In this case too, the overall picture is determined by movements in f_1. At first sight the goodness of fit for $z_9^* = 0.96f_1 - 0.26f_2$ even seems to be slightly better. This result is entirely due to the somewhat larger contribution of the second principal component f_2.

1.4.2 Results of the Capital Market

Similar to our analysis of the money market, the three largest eigenvalues for 10 capital market rates have been reported in Table 1.5. It appears that for monthly figures and the whole sample period the first principal component accounts for almost 90% of the variation among the capital market interest rates. This percentage is somewhat lower than the almost 96% found for the money market. The second principal component, however, which accounts for another 8%, is considerably more important than with the money market. Thus, more than 97.5%

Table 1.5: Three largest eigenvalues for 10 capital market interest rates, January 1962–December 1970

	Correlation matrices with monthly figures			Correlation matrix with quarterly figures whole period	Covariance matrix with monthly figures whole period
	1962–1970	Jan. '62 Jun. '66	July '66 Dec. '70		
λ_1	8.97	9.09	7.68	9.01	13.90
λ_2	0.81	0.65	1.87	0.79	0.29
λ_3	0.14	0.13	0.25	0.13	0.10
$\mathrm{tr}(m_{ih})$	10	10	10	10	14.39
ϕ_1	89.7%	90.9%	76.8%	90.1%	96.6%

of the total variation is accounted for by the first and second components together. For the money market we obtained the same percentage. If the sample period is split up into two sub-periods, it appears that for each of the sub-periods the first and second principal components explain slightly less of the total variation than for the period as a whole: 97.4% and 95.5%. An interesting feature is the shift which may be observed in the values for the individual components. In the second half of the 1962–1970 period the first principal component appears to have dropped considerably in value in favour of the second component: from 90.9% to 76.8%. The third component also shows a small difference for the two sub-periods.

Table 1.5 shows that the eigenvalues of the correlation matrix are hardly affected by pooling the monthly data into quarterly figures. Taking the covariance matrix does increase the importance of the first principal component substantially. In that case the first and second principal components together explain more than 98% of the total variation — a percentage again equal to the corresponding money market figure. It has to be concluded, therefore, that for the capital market the method of standardisation does to some extent affect the results. Further, and even more than with the money market, there is reason for a closer examination of the second principal component. To that end a number of factor loadings and correlation coefficients $R(f_k, z_i)$ have been brought together in Table 1.6. As already mentioned, the two coincide if the latent roots are computed of correlation matrices. For each of the four cases the first column shows very high correlation between yield and first principal component for the first eight capital market instruments. For yield on shares the correlation is significantly lower. The correlation pattern of the second principal component is also striking: small negative correlations for yields on non-risk-bearing securities and relatively large

Table 1.6: Factor loadings of the first and second principal component of capital market interest rates

i	Debt instrument	Whole period		First half		Second half		Covariance matrix whole period[a]	
		α_{i1}	α_{i2}	α_{i1}	α_{i2}	α_{i1}	α_{i2}	$R(f_1, z_i)$	$R(f_2, z_i)$
1	Perpetual government debt	0.97	−0.21	0.99	−0.05	0.93	−0.30	0.98	−0.14
2	3.25% Netherlands 1948	0.99	−0.09	0.99	0.09	0.98	0.06	0.99	0.01
3	Average of three 4.25% and 4.50% government loans	0.99	−0.12	0.99	−0.08	0.99	−0.02	0.99	−0.03
4	Latest three long-term government bonds	0.99	−0.07	0.99	−0.09	0.99	0.03	0.99	0.02
5	4.50% Bank for Netherlands Municipalities 1958/59	0.99	−0.11	0.99	−0.07	0.99	0.01	0.99	−0.02
6	Private company securities	0.99	−0.09	0.99	−0.08	0.99	0.03	0.99	0.00
7	3% mortgage bank bonds	0.98	−0.15	0.96	−0.15	0.95	−0.17	0.99	−0.08
8	Mortgage loans	0.98	−0.07	0.96	−0.17	0.97	0.17	0.99	0.05
9	Local shares	0.72	0.65	0.71	0.67	−0.06	0.93	0.66	0.66
10	International shares	0.82	0.51	0.90	0.30	0.23	0.92	0.77	0.61
Eigenvalue λ_k		8.97	0.81	9.09	0.65	7.68	1.87	13.90	0.29
	ϕ_k	98.7%	8.1%	90.9%	6.5%	76.8%	18.7%	96.6%	2.0%

Note: [a] In this case the α_{ik} and $R(f_k, z_i)$ do not coincide.

positive correlations for yield on shares. The pattern is similar if the computation is based on the covariance matrix.

Quite remarkable, lastly, is the difference between correlation patterns for the two sub-periods, which, however, should have been expected from the values of ϕ_k shown in Table 1.6. We note that particularly in the period July 1966–December 1970, the correlations among yield on shares and the first principal component are slight.

In order to find out whether the dominance of the second principal component in yield on shares is systematic, we have applied a varimax rotation to the loadings of Table 1.6. The result of the varimax rotation confirms the interpretation given above. The results for the whole sample period and the first sub-period are similar. The pattern for the period 1966–1970 is even more striking: the loadings on the first principal component are very low for the two share yields, *viz.* −0.09 and 0.17; for the remaining variables the loadings on the first component exceed 0.95 in all cases. This pattern contrasts the pattern of loadings on the second principal component: the loadings of yield on shares are 0.97 and 0.87; the others range between −0.24 and 0.19.

The above analysis suggests the existence of two long-term interest rates on the capital market, which move independently. They might be identified by the rate of return on non-risk-bearing and risk-bearing assets, respectively. Our results indicate that during the second half of the sixties the risk feature has become more important. It is not clear what has caused this change.

Summarizing, we may conclude that we have found evidence for distinguishing two independently moving interest rates on the capital market. The first is described by the first principal component and is related to the rate of interest on non-risk-bearing instruments. It might be identified as the true interest rate, that is the rate of substitution between money today and money tomorrow. The second is dominated by the second principal component and is markedly related to the rate of return on shares. It is probably a risk premium, and as such it is naturally more evident with investments in shares than with fixed interest bearing securities. It could not be ascertained to what extent the interest rate reflects a premium for inflation. We return to this question in the next section.

Lastly Figures 1.8 and 1.9 show the first and second principal components for the whole sample period for the yields on the latest three government loans, and on local shares. The lay-out of the two figures is the same as with Figures 1.6 and 1.7. The most striking feature is the erratic course of the contribution of the second principal component to the yield on local shares. A much better contrast is obtained when the

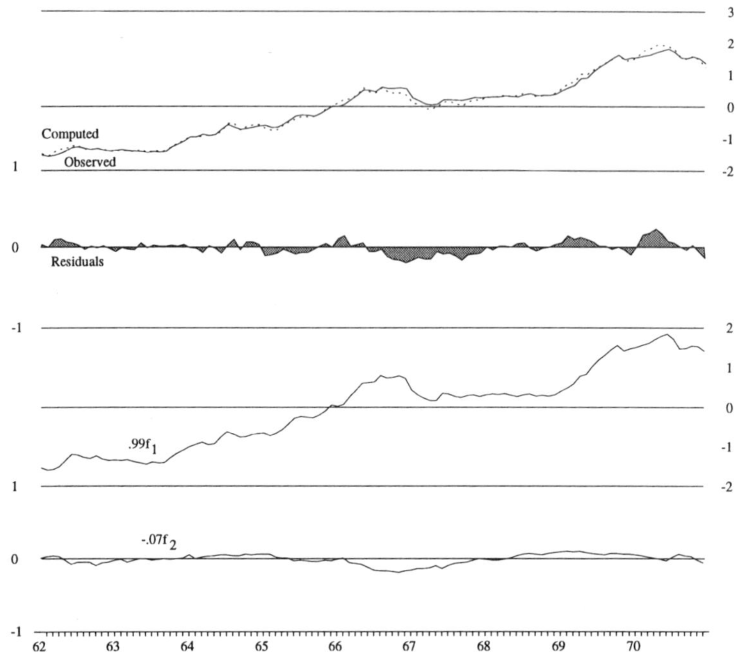

Figure 1.8: First and second principal component of yield on the three latest government loans, 1962–1970

contributions are plotted for the second sub-period alone, as has been done in Figure 1.10. These figures show very clearly that the changes in the yield on the latest three government loans are determined first of all by f_1, while the yield on local shares is best described by f_2. It should be noted that the figures show once more that the two series vary independently of one another.

1.5 A Closer Examination of the Results

In the preceding section, we calculated principal components for the money and capital market separately, adopting the custom to draw the line between both markets of financial assets at a maturity of about one year. However, it should be kept in mind that the basic function of the two markets is identical. That is to say, participants in both markets are assumed to maximize the utility of holding financial assets or of issuing debt instruments. Sometimes it is suggested that the money market, as opposed to the capital market, is a minimum risk market since it

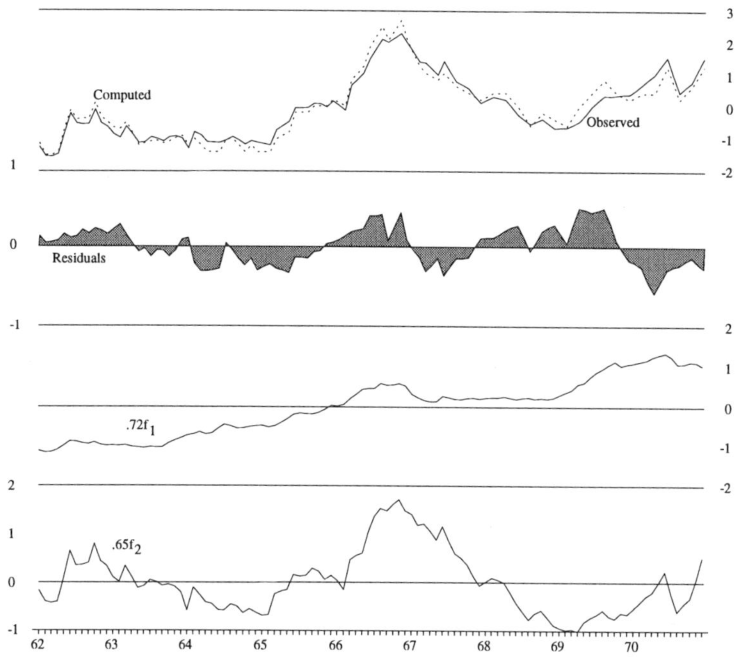

Figure 1.9: First and second principal component of yield on local shares, 1962–1970

deals solely with near-money assets. This is in accordance with the view describing the market for financial assets as a market which consists of many separate but interrelated markets where instruments of varying degree of moneyness are traded.[4] It is interesting to examine whether in a principal component analysis of the 20 market rates used in section 1.4, this idea does show up.

To that end, the last two rows of Table 1.7 show the eigenvalues of the monthly figures for the whole sample period and for the two sub-periods. The eigenvalues present the same picture as in the preceding section. For the whole sample period, more than 90% of the total variation is accounted for by the first principal component; for the second sub-period, in which also the second principal component explains a considerable part of the variation, the figure is considerably lower, namely 83%. We noted the same feature with the principal components analysis of the capital market, whereas it was absent in the money market. The change, therefore, has to be ascribed to developments in the capital market.

---

4 See Goedhart (1947, p. 177) or Polakoff and Ketchum (1970, p. 407).

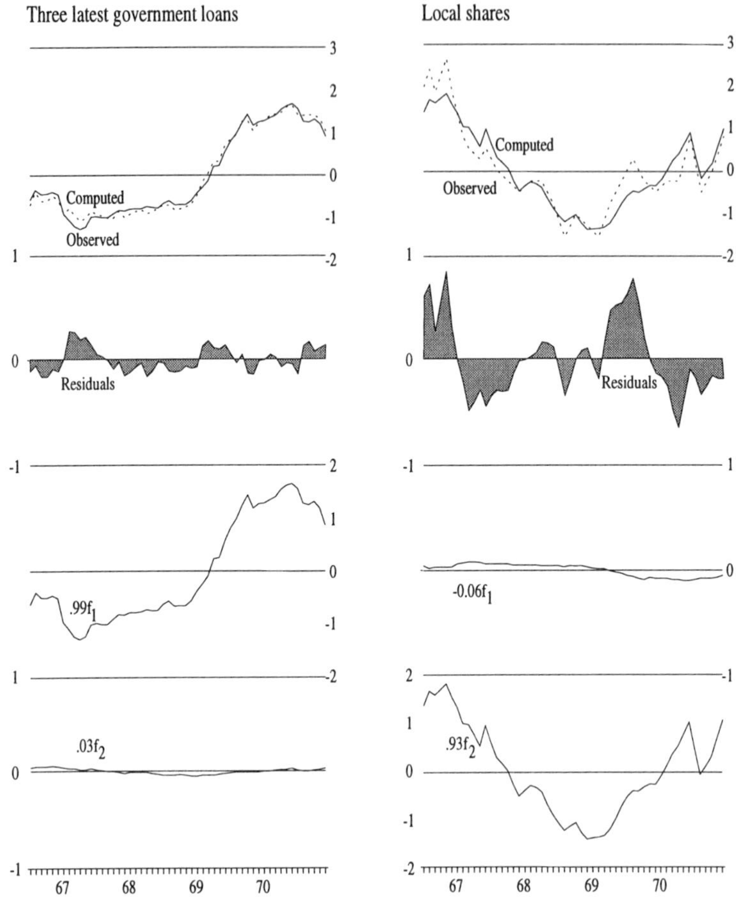

Figure 1.10: First and second principal component of yield on the three latest government loans and on local shares, July 1966–December 1970

As before, the factor loadings, also shown in Table 1.7, indicate a high degree of correlation between the yields and the first principal component. The same result was previously obtained for the two submarkets. The fact that the correlation matrices used for the computations yielded high positive correlation coefficients had already been indicative of the existence of an abstraction like *the* rate of interest. This rate of interest may apparently be identified as the first principal component. The second principal component very adequately separates the first 18

Table 1.7: Factor loadings of the first four principal components on rates of the market of financial assets, 1962–1970

i	Debt instrument	Whole period α_{i1}	α_{i2}	α_{i3}	α_{i4}
1	Call money	0.94	−0.09	0.22	−0.06
2	3-month Treasury paper	0.98	−0.02	−0.03	0.07
3	1-year Treasury paper	0.98	−0.02	−0.05	0.06
4	2-year Treasury paper	0.99	0.00	−0.05	0.05
5	3-year Treasury paper	0.99	−0.01	−0.06	0.05
6	5-year Treasury paper	0.99	−0.01	−0.04	0.03
7	Loans to local authorities 3-month	0.98	−0.03	0.16	0.06
8	Loans to local authorities 1-year	0.98	−0.03	0.12	0.09
9	Euro-dollar deposits	0.94	−0.11	0.30	0.00
10	Nederlandsche Bank official discount rate	0.96	−0.09	0.04	0.13
11	Perpetual government debt	0.97	−0.16	−0.05	−0.16
12	3.25% Netherlands 1948	0.99	−0.04	−0.11	−0.04
13	Average of three 4.25% and 4.50% government loans	0.99	−0.07	−0.07	−0.06
14	Latest three long-term government bonds	0.99	−0.02	−0.08	0.06
15	4.50% Bank for Netherlands Municipalities 1958/59	0.99	−0.06	−0.07	−0.06
16	Private company securities	0.99	−0.05	−0.05	−0.06
17	3% mortgage bank bonds	0.98	−0.10	−0.08	−0.10
18	Mortgage loans	0.98	−0.03	0.08	0.04
19	Local shares	0.69	0.68	0.10	−0.19
20	International shares	0.80	0.55	−0.08	0.18
	λ_k	18.36	0.85	0.25	0.17
	ϕ_k	91.8%	4.2%	1.3%	0.8%

variables from the last two: yield on shares. This outcome has also been found before. As the yield on shares still shows considerable correlation with the first factor, which may be regarded as more or less isolating the interest component, the second factor might be identified as the risk component of the interest rate. It seems likely, therefore, that this element has gained in significance in the second half of the sixties. The most evident conclusion to be drawn from Table 1.7 is that the data do not offer support for the customary segmentation of the financial asset market into a money and a capital market. It turns out to be meaningful to distinguish two separate interest rates in the financial asset market, being related to the first and second principal component respectively.

We believed that the third principal component slightly correlates

Table 1.7: (continued)

First half				Second half			
α_{i1}	α_{i2}	α_{i3}	α_{i4}	α_{i1}	α_{i2}	α_{i3}	α_{i4}
0.87	0.00	0.45	0.15	0.85	−0.03	−0.37	−0.33
0.98	−0.16	0.01	0.05	0.99	0.04	0.00	−0.05
0.98	−0.14	−0.09	0.05	0.98	0.03	0.00	0.03
0.98	−0.11	−0.10	0.04	0.99	0.08	0.03	0.01
0.98	−0.11	−0.12	0.00	0.99	0.07	0.08	−0.06
0.98	−0.09	−0.11	0.06	0.98	0.06	0.04	−0.05
0.97	−0.14	0.06	0.01	0.94	0.14	−0.29	0.05
0.97	−0.15	−0.04	−0.02	0.96	0.16	−0.20	0.06
0.94	−0.09	0.18	0.02	0.89	0.02	−0.42	0.06
0.91	−0.11	−0.10	0.32	0.98	0.06	0.05	−0.02
0.98	0.10	0.02	−0.13	0.90	−0.39	−0.03	0.06
0.99	0.03	0.00	−0.11	0.96	−0.05	0.24	0.01
0.99	0.05	0.02	−0.11	0.98	−0.12	0.13	0.02
0.99	0.04	−0.05	−0.12	0.99	−0.07	0.11	−0.03
0.99	0.06	0.01	−0.11	0.98	−0.09	0.13	0.04
0.99	0.05	0.00	−0.09	0.98	−0.07	0.07	0.08
0.97	−0.04	−0.04	−0.03	0.92	−0.27	0.05	0.17
0.97	−0.05	−0.03	−0.10	0.96	0.06	0.20	−0.03
0.63	0.75	0.02	0.07	0.05	0.94	−0.14	0.23
0.87	0.37	−0.15	0.11	0.30	0.87	0.26	−0.18
18.02	0.87	0.33	0.24	16.58	1.99	0.69	0.26
90.1%	4.4%	1.6%	1.2%	82.9%	10.0%	3.5%	1.3%

with the percentage changes in the cost-of-living index. For the whole sample period the correlation coefficient amounts to 0.20, for the second sub-period 0.37. If the price changes are taken with a time-lag of one year, the coefficient rises to 0.22 and 0.41 respectively.

It is interesting to note that the dichotomy of the financial assets market suggested by our analysis coincides with the popular distinction of investments into those representing nominal and real assets, the latter offering protection against losses due to inflation. It may be asked whether it is possible to find a common component representing the real rate of interest. To investigate this point, the 20 rates of interest used and the 12-month percentage changes in the cost-of-living index have been subjected to a principal components analysis. Some of the outcomes of this analysis are shown in the two bottom rows of Table 1.8.

There is no significant deviation from the picture presented by Table 1.7. The first principal component nowhere explains less than 80% of the total variation; the second principal component doubles to 10% in the second sub-period, while in the same period the third principal component accounts for almost another 5%. The initially computed factor loadings are not as easy to interpret as in the previous cases. An orthogonal varimax rotation has therefore been applied to the matrix of factor loadings obtained. It gives the results shown in the upper part of Table 1.8.

With the first principal component, the loadings on the first 18 interest rates dominate. With the second principal component, the loadings on the share yields dominate, and it is with the third principal component that the loadings on the price variable is most pronounced. It should also be noted that the loading of this last variable is very small on the second principal component.

The main lesson from this exercise is that in the financial assets market, a segmentation of two sub-markets with their own rates of interest seems to exist. The first corresponds to the rate of interest with most of the price changes removed and is related to the first principal component, it seems to be related to the risk premium which is inherent in any interest rate. Apparently this premium is sufficiently large to justify a particular market rate. We suspect that the third principal component is related to inflation. It is meaningful therefore to interpret this component as the inflation compensation in the rate of interest. This inference is further supported by the fact that the factor loading of this component is virtually zero on each of the two share yields. The higher value for λ_3 in the second sub-period might then indicate a decreasing belief among the public in the stability of the value of money.

To illustrate these conclusions, the first three principal components of the 21 variables of Table 1.8 have been plotted in Figure 1.11. The left-hand figure refers to the first half of the 1962–1970 period, the right hand figure to the second half. For the sake of comparability, the standardised observed yields on the latest three government loans and on local shares have been plotted, as have the standardised percentage changes in the cost-of-living index. The figure shows that the movements of f_1 and f_2 do in fact follow different patterns. We may also observe that the goodness of fit of the first three principal components to the three variables is rather high.

Table 1.8: Varimax rotation of factor loadings on 20 market interest rates and price changes, 1962–1970

i	Debt instrument	Whole period			First half			Second half		
		α_{i1}	α_{i2}	α_{i3}	α_{i1}	α_{i2}	α_{i3}	α_{i1}	α_{i2}	α_{i3}
1	Call money	0.82	0.30	0.16	0.58	0.30	−0.19	0.62	0.00	0.08
2	3-month Treasury paper	0.86	0.37	0.26	0.86	0.22	0.27	0.89	0.12	0.16
3	1-year Treasury paper	0.86	0.38	0.28	0.88	0.25	0.28	0.89	0.13	0.27
4	2-year Treasury paper	0.86	0.40	0.25	0.87	0.28	0.30	0.90	0.17	0.21
5	3-year Treasury paper	0.88	0.38	0.22	0.87	0.28	0.30	0.92	0.15	0.14
6	5-year Treasury paper	0.88	0.38	0.20	0.87	0.29	0.25	0.90	0.14	0.16
7	Loans to local authorities 3-month	0.82	0.37	0.28	0.82	0.25	0.32	0.72	0.22	0.23
8	Loans to local authorities 1-year	0.83	0.37	0.27	0.86	0.24	0.31	0.78	0.24	0.22
9	Euro-dollar deposits	0.79	0.29	0.28	0.71	0.29	0.37	0.64	0.10	0.27
10	Nederlandsche Bank official discount rate	0.86	0.29	0.19	0.79	0.25	0.17	0.90	0.15	0.18
11	Perpetual government debt	0.93	0.25	0.19	0.80	0.44	0.23	0.85	−0.30	0.19
12	3.25% Netherlands 1948	0.91	0.35	0.16	0.82	0.40	0.28	0.97	0.03	0.05
13	Average of three 4.25% and 4.50% government loans	0.92	0.33	0.18	0.82	0.41	0.26	0.96	−0.03	0.08
14	Latest three long-term loans	0.90	0.37	0.19	0.82	0.40	0.28	0.95	0.01	0.10
15	4.50% Bank for Netherlands Municipalities 1958/59	0.91	0.33	0.19	0.82	0.42	0.25	0.96	0.00	0.10
16	Private company securities	0.90	0.35	0.20	0.82	0.41	0.26	0.94	0.03	0.12
17	3% mortgage bank bonds	0.92	0.30	0.19	0.85	0.32	0.24	0.89	−0.16	0.17
18	Mortgage loans	0.89	0.36	0.18	0.85	0.31	0.25	0.95	0.14	0.05
19	Local shares	0.34	0.92	0.07	0.25	0.95	0.07	−0.08	0.98	0.06
20	International shares	0.54	0.77	−0.08	0.69	0.66	−0.01	0.29	0.83	−0.36
21	% change in the price index [a]	0.29	0.00	0.95	0.35	0.04	0.92	0.28	−0.16	0.93
	λ_k	18.58	1.12	0.57	18.38	1.06	0.53	16.80	2.14	1.00
	ϕ_k	88.5%	5.3%	2.7%	87.5%	5.0%	2.5%	80.0%	10.2%	4.7%

Note: [a] Taken over 12 month

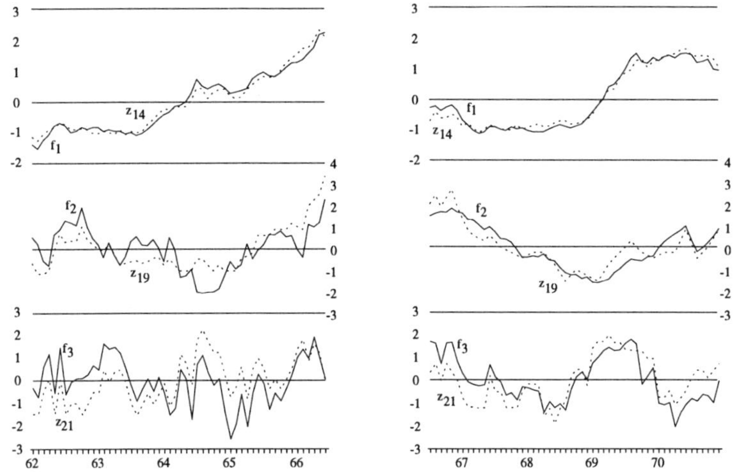

Figure 1.11: The first three principal components and the normalized yields on the latest three government loans (z_{14}), on local shares (z_{19}) and the percentage price change (z_{21})

1.6 Conclusions and Final Remarks

Our analysis suggests three main conclusions. The first is that we found the total variation in the whole spectrum of specific interest rates in the Dutch money and capital markets rather well accounted for by the first principal component. It would seem that the identification of this first principal component with the 'true' interest rate has been reasonable. In our opinion, the true interest rate reflects the time preference of lenders and borrowers on the financial markets.

Our second conclusion is that we have found some empirical evidence for the theoretical conjecture that the observed interest rates show various aspects. Besides the 'true' interest rate, we have found two other components, presumably related to the inflation and default risk, respectively. It should be noted, however, that the importance of those aspects as reflected by the values of ϕ_2 and ϕ_3, is less than the time preference aspect. A problem is that the first principal component does still show some correlation with price changes, indicating that *the* rate of interest may yet contain an inflation premium. Unfortunately the method applied is not suitable for an exact breakdown of the nominal rate of interest into its components.

Thirdly, the analysis shows that the traditional distinction between money and capital markets is not reflected in the outcomes of our principal components analysis. It suggests, however, a distinction between a market for non-risk-bearing securities and one for risk-bearing investments. The yield on each of these two categories of securities may be described by the first and second principal component respectively, which, of course, vary independently of one another. In this view it is meaningful, therefore, to distinguish two (representative) rates of interest. It is our belief that this point may be useful for further econometric investigations of monetary problems.

Concluding this chapter we should like to say a few words about similar investigations in the literature. Hester (1969) has applied a principal components analysis for US interest rates, and Vercruysse, Lavry, and Pirard (1971) for Belgian rates. Hester analyses 11 interest rate series, 5 of which relate to the money market and the others to medium and long-term rates. He employs observations over the period January 1958–January 1969. In the several variants discussed, the first principal component nowhere explains less that 83% of the total variation, the next two components account for about 11% and 3%. The first component is regard as *the* rate of interest, the second is in Hester's view related to maturity, but for the third he offers no interpretation. In the spirit of Theil (1962), Hester uses his results to investigate the relationship between the rate of interest as represented by the first three principal components and a price index which has also been constructed with the help of principal components. He finds a fairly high degree of correlation. This means that econometric investigations have to differentiate between the nominal and the real rate of interest. In a different context, Feldstein (1970) has pointed out that this distinction, which is, incidentally, also suggested by our analysis, is useful for avoiding specification bias.

The Belgian study by Vercruysse *et al.* is based on 12 interest rates, ranging from the interest on call money to the yield on long-term government bonds. The authors use monthly figures for the sample period 1957–1969 and there is a striking resemblance between their findings and the outcomes of our own investigation, albeit their principal components analysis of interest rates had a different objective. The first principal component accounts for 90% of the total variation, the second and the third account for 5% and 2% respectively. If the interest rates are classified according to maturity (short, medium, and long-term), the first principal component even explains as much as 97%, 91% and 94% respectively. The authors do not speculate upon the interpretation of this outcome. The results are used for an economic explanation of the rate of interest, in order to be able to forecast Belgian interest rates a couple of months ahead. From a Dutch point of view, this study is of particular interest because of the open character of both the Belgian and the Dutch economies. We did attempt to account for this by linking the domestic rates to the international Euro-dollar rates.

This confirms our own finding that it is not very meaningful, in applied econometric model building, to distinguish a large number of different interest rates as explanatory variables. The influence of interest arbitrage is apparently such that the interdependence is high with only temporary exceptions.

2. The Interdependence of Short-term Interest Rates in the Major Financial Centres of the World: Some Evidence for 1961–1972

2.1 Capital Mobility and Interest Rates

In the last decade the trend has been towards increased capital mobility, which has brought about a climate of financial integration and — at least for the small open economies — a high degree of international interdependence of domestic monetary policies. Capital mobility means that domestic financial assets are perfect substitutes for similar foreign assets. Rational portfolio behaviour implies that financial flows are responsive to interest rate differentials. This suggests equilibrating capital flows resulting in an adjustment of the domestic interest rates to the external interest rates prevailing in the major financial centres of the world.

The theoretical basis for this proposition has been developed for example, by Mundell (1968). In a regime of fixed exchange rates, the argument is that a monetary policy directed at increasing the domestic rate of interest, will result in an inflow of capital and an appreciation of the home currency. The consequent purchase of foreign currency by the central bank expands the domestic money supply and thus, given the demand for money function, lowers the level of interest until the additional money has been absorbed and the inflow of capital, due to interest arbitrage, has ended. So, on balance, domestic assets have been traded for foreign assets, but nothing has really changed. However, several qualifications should be made.

Reprinted from *Kyklos*, **29** (1976), M.M.G. Fase, 'The interdependence of short-term interest rates in the major financial centres of the world: Some evidence for 1961–1972', 63–96, ©1976 with kind permission from Helbing & Lichtenhahn Verlag AG.

The first, mainly empirical, problem is that there is no unique rate of interest, but a whole spectrum of interest rates. Therefore *the* domestic interest rate is a rather vague concept. Theories concerning the term structure of interest rates, as well as empirical evidence for various countries, show, that on the domestic level one may expect strong parallel movements among the rates of return on financial assets of varying maturity. For that reason it seems theoretically legitimate to select for each individual country one single rate of interest as the dominant instrument of financial integration among countries, which assumption is sufficiently buttressed by empirical evidence (see Fase (1973) and the references given there). On this basis, perfect capital mobility may be taken to mean perfect substitutability among short-term assets, like treasury bills or demand deposits of different currency denominations. Apart from the political sovereignty of each single country, it is only because of the existence of these different currencies and their exchange rates that differentials between interest rates can persist. To avoid exchange rate risks, covered interest arbitrage is common practice among arbitrageurs, who dislike net open positions. This implies that international interest rates should be compared after adjustment for forward premiums or discounts. Of course, this does not answer the question of whether forward premiums exist because of interest rate differentials among countries or the other way around. This leads to the next question of whether the implications for monetary policy of perfect substitutability, as indicated above, are independent of the size of the country. Large countries seem to have much more power than small countries to pursue an independent monetary policy, given a fixed exchange rate. It would be interesting to find out whether it is possible to classify them into leaders and followers.

This chapter deals with some of the questions raised above. The main purpose is to examine empirically to what extent there is common variation among the short-term interest rates quoted in eleven major financial centres. If enough common variation exists this may suggest a measure for an abstraction like the concept of the world rate of interest or, at least, it may offer some aid to select a representative time series for this world interest rate. The data used are monthly observations on short-term interest rates for the sample period 1961–1972. The technique employed is the method of principal components analysis. The use of this method for the present analysis has been inspired by earlier work (see Fase (1973)) in which we examined whether interest rates in The Netherlands did vary independently during the sixties.

2.2 Data and Method of Analysis

The data employed in the present analysis are the short-term interest rates of member countries of the Group of Ten and Switzerland. The data are, in most cases, end-of-month quotations and span the period from January 1961 to December 1972. Accordingly, periods of expected devaluations or revaluations are encompassed, and such expectations are presumably reflected in the quotations of certain countries. Similarly, variations in institutional arrangements would have affected the observed behaviour of international interest rates.

As shown in Table 2.1, the means of covered and uncovered interest rates vary between countries. Since the US money market happens to be a convenient point of reference, there is no differential between covered and uncovered interest rates in the USA. We also note the extremely high means for Japan. This might reflect the ability of the Japanese authorities to insulate, at least until quite recently, the domestic money market from foreign influence. However, we note that also for Belgium, with its two tier system, Italy and France the means diverge somewhat, indicating the existence of restrictions on capital flows.

Table 2.1 also reports that the standard deviation does not vary greatly between countries, with the lowest for Switzerland. Adjustment for forward premiums or discounts widens the standard deviation for all countries except, of course, for the USA. For countries like Germany,

Table 2.1: Means and standard deviations of short-term interest rates in 11 countries, 1961–1972 (percentages)

	Uncovered		Covered	
Country (i)	Mean	Standard deviation	Mean	Standard deviation
USA	4.32	1.35	4.32	1.35
The Netherlands	3.66	1.57	4.64	1.67
Belgium	4.84	1.43	5.05	1.61
UK	3.72	1.33	4.12	1.42
Canada	4.53	1.38	4.36	1.50
W. Germany	3.53	1.33	4.75	2.27
Switzerland	3.38	1.15	4.78	1.47
Italy	4.33	1.23	3.67	2.19
Sweden	5.35	1.56	4.48	1.74
France	5.28	1.79	5.37	2.13
Japan	7.27	1.44	7.01	2.16

Italy and France, the spread becomes even larger than 70%, indicating recurrent speculation against these currencies. We excluded the Euro-dollar rate on purpose in order to keep some outside information to identify the results. We return to this point in due course.

With a few exceptions, the observed rates of interest are those on three-mont treasury bills. However, for Italy only twelve-month treasury bill rates were available, and for Switzerland short-term deposit rates at the major commercial banks in Zürich were used. For Japan and France call money rates were employed because over the sample period no data on three-month rates are available. All figures were calculated on an annual basis; the forward adjustment always refers to three-month forward contracts rather then one- or six-month forward rates since three-month forward rates are considered more indicative by te market than one-month rates while six-month rates are particularly interesting for roll-over credits.

As our main concern is to account for the common variation among interest rates in various countries, the method of principal components analysis seems an appropriate tool. As this method is rather well-known, we summarize only a few points that are relevant to understand our results.[1]

Let z_{it} denote the standardised rate of interest in country i at time t, with $i = 1, \ldots, p$ and $t = 1, \ldots, T$. If all interest rates observed move proportionally, we have

$$z_{it} = \alpha_{i1} f_{1t} \tag{2.1}$$

for all i and t, with α_{i1} denoting a set of constants to be determined and f_1 the non-observable first principal component. In general, (2.1) will only hold approximately. We therefore seek to determine those α_{i1} and f_{1t} which will minimize the residual sum S_1, with

$$S_1 = \sum_t \sum_i (z_{it} - \alpha_{i1} f_{1t})^2 . \tag{2.2}$$

Because (2.2) is determined up to a constant factor, we impose the normalisation rule

$$\sum_i f_{1t}^2 = 1.$$

It can be shown that (2.2) attains a minimum value when

$$f_{1t} = \frac{1}{\lambda_1} \sum_i z_{it} \alpha_{i1} , \tag{2.3}$$

[1] For details we refer to Lawley and Maxwell (1971). The classic reference for economists is Stone (1947).

where λ_1 denotes the largest latent root of the $(p \times p)$ sample matrix (m_{ih}) with

$$m_{1h} = \sum_i z_{it} z_{ih},$$

and $i, h = 1, 2, \ldots, p$, while α_{i1} are derived form the elements of the corresponding latent vector by multiplying with $\sqrt{\lambda_1}$. It may furthermore be shown that

$$\lambda_1 = \sum_i \alpha_{i1}^2.$$

Expression (2.3) implies that f_1 is a linear function of the observed variables with coefficients proportional to the elements of the latent vector corresponding to the largest latent root λ_1.

By the same token, the second principal component may be taken from the resulting residuals. In general the k-th principal component is obtained as

$$f_{kt} = \frac{1}{\lambda_k} \sum_i z_{it} \alpha_{ik}. \tag{2.4}$$

It may be easily proved that each principal component is orthogonal to all others. In equation (2.4) λ_k denotes the k-th latent root of the sample matrix (m_{ih}) ranked in descending order of magnitude. The factor loadings α_{ik} are computed from the corresponding latent vector. Finally, as before, we have

$$\lambda_k = \sum_i \alpha_{ik}^2.$$

It is obvious that for standardised variables the matrix (m_{ih}) turns into the sample correlation matrix (r_{ih}). In that particular case, the factor loadings correspond to simple correlation coefficients between the ith variable z_i and the k-th principal component f_k.

Note that the sum of the latent root λ_k equals the trace of the matrix (m_{ih}), denoted by $\mathrm{tr}(m_{ih})$. Of course, $tr(m_{ih})$ equals p if standardised variables are used. Each factor f_k therefore accounts for a fraction ϕ_k of the total variation in z_i, with

$$\phi_k = \frac{\lambda_k}{\mathrm{tr}(m_{ih})}.$$

The quantity ϕ_k is an unweighted average of the R^2 of the interest variables with f_k. It is used as R^2 in regression analysis, indicating goodness of fit.

In particular situations, the interpretation of principal components is simplified if the matrix of factor loadings is transformed. The varimax rotation is a method frequently used to achieve such a transformation. The point is to construct an orthogonal transformation in such a way that the function

$$V = p\sum_j\Big(\sum_i \beta_{ij}^4 - \big(\sum_i \beta_{ij}^2\big)^2\Big), \tag{2.5}$$

with

$$\beta_{ij} = \frac{\alpha_{ij}}{\sqrt{\sum_j \alpha_{ij}^2}}$$

and $j = 1, \ldots, q$, $i = 1, \ldots, p$ is maximised. The required factor loadings are a function of the angle of rotation, which is obtained by iteration from the factor loadings derived from each rotation until (2.5) attains a maximum.

Although we are mainly interested in the quantity ϕ_k, we have also to decide how many components should be retained. To study this problem Bartlett (1951) designed a test for the hypothesis that the $p-q$ smallest latent roots of the sample correlation matrix (r_{ih}) are equal, indicating that it makes no sense to compute more than q components. In the case of the sample correlation matrix, the suggested test statistic is

$$T\Big(-\ln|r_{ih}| + \ln(\lambda_1\lambda_2\ldots\lambda_q) + (p-q)\ln\lambda\Big), \tag{2.6}$$

where $|r_{ih}|$ is the determinant of the correlation matrix, $p-q$ the number of smallest latent roots of this matrix,

$$\lambda = \frac{p - \lambda_1 \cdots - \lambda_q}{p-q}$$

and T the number of observations. Under the null hypothesis, we may treat expression (2.6) as an approximate χ^2 statistic with

$$\frac{1}{2}(p-q+2)(p-q-1)$$

degrees of freedom. A similar criterion holds when we start from the sample covariance matrix (see Lawley and Maxwell (1971, pp. 20–22)).

2.3 The Principal Components for Eleven International Interest Rates

With a few exceptions, the interest rates employed in the present analysis have been standardised to unit variance so that the latent roots have been computed from the sample correlation matrix. In view of the fairly large spread of the standard deviations reported in Table 2.1, we have in two cases also computed the latent roots from the covariance matrix in order to assess how standardisation affects the principal components. The five largest latent roots have been reported in Table 2.2; the symbols used in this table, and in the following, correspond to the notation introduced earlier.

First of all, the table shows that standardisation does not substantially affect the results. Both for the correlation matrix and the covariance matrix, the first principal component of uncovered interest accounts for nearly two-thirds of total variation, indicating that standardization hardly affects ϕ. A similar pattern of the ϕ emerges for the other components. Therefore we confine our discussion to the results based on the correlation matrix. However, from a comparison between uncovered and covered interest rates, notable differences emerge. The first principal component, corresponding to the largest latent root λ_1, accounts for almost 65% of the total variation among the uncovered interest rates. For covered interest rates this proportion amounts to 58%.

For both uncovered and covered interest rates, Bartlett's statistic suggests that at the 5% significance level the fifth and subsequent principal components are genuinely equal. We are thus inclined to ignore them. However, it should be noted that the retained components are not always equally important for covered and uncovered interest rates. This is one reason to analyse covered and uncovered rates separately. In view of interest arbitrage it is meaningful to treat covered rates first.

2.3.1 Results for Covered Interest Rates

Interest arbitrageurs usually seek to hedge against exchange rate risk by supplying forward contracts. Therefore the covered interest rate, that is the local yield adjusted for forward premium or discount, is the most relevant rate of return. In view of the interest rate parity theorem, parallel movements between these rates of return may be predicted. Departures from parallel movements indicate unexploited profit opportunities for interest arbitrage which require explanation for example, by increasing risk associated with the size of past commitments or the opportunity cost of holding foreign short-term assets. Table 2.3 shows the outcomes

Table 2.2: Five largest latent roots of 11 international interest rates, January 1961–December 1972

	Correlation matrix		Covariance matrix	
	Covered	Uncovered	Uncovered	Covered
λ_1	6.39	7.07	19.08	14.74
λ_2	1.20	1.29	5.12	2.38
λ_3	1.01	0.97	4.39	1.81
λ_4	0.86	0.52	2.90	1.09
λ_5	0.55	0.39	1.58	0.73
$\mathrm{tr}(m_{ij})$	11.00	11.00	35.83	22.29
ϕ_1	58.10%	64.30%	53.30%	66.10%
ϕ_2	10.90%	11.70%	14.30%	10.70%
ϕ_3	9.20%	8.80%	12.30%	8.10%
ϕ_4	7.80%	4.70%	8.10%	4.90%
ϕ_5	5.00%	3.50%	4.40%	3.30%

of our computations for covered interest rates in five sub-periods.

A comparison with the latent roots of Table 2.2 shows that in most of the sub-periods the first principal component accounts for less of the total variation than in the whole period; for the first half of the entire period, however, the percentage is considerably higher. Another notable difference is that although Bartlett's test statistic indicates four significant principal components for the whole period, only two actually show up if two sub-periods are distinguished. Dividing the whole period into three sub-periods, only one princpial component remains for 1961–1964 and

Table 2.3: Three largest latent roots of 11 covered money market interest rates in five sub-periods of the period January 1961–December 1972

	1961–1966	1967–1972	1961–1964	1965–1968	1968–1972
λ_1	7.56	4.99	5.62	5.89	4.99
λ_2	1.59	1.76	1.71	1.61	1.94
λ_3	0.58	1.11	0.96	1.16	1.19
ϕ_1	68.70%	45.40%	51.10%	53.50%	45.40%
ϕ_2	14.50%	16.00%	15.50%	14.60%	17.60%
ϕ_3	5.30%	10.10%	8.70%	10.50%	10.80%

1965–1968. For the years 1969–1972, two components should be retained. Although the statistical justification for using Bartlett's test statistic in the present application is rather weak (see Lawley and Maxwell (1971, p. 21)) this finding is noteworthy, particularly because the last sub-period differs from the others by severe international monetary disturbances, as the recent foreign exchange history shows.

To facilitate the interpretation of our results, Table 2.4 shows the factor loadings for each of the periods. Since the variates have been normalised to unit variance, the reported α_{ik} may be regarded as correlation coefficients among the interest rate in country i and the k-th principal component.

For the whole period, the first principal component is strongly correlated with the interest rates in the US and five other countries. A varimax rotation (see Table 2.A.1 in Appendix 2.A) reveals a close relationship between the first principal component and short-term interest rates in the US and Canada respectively. This finding agrees with the fact that the financial markets in Canada are highly dependent on the financial developments in the US. In view of these results, it seems justified to regard the first principal component as representing *the* international or world short-term rate of interest which, incidentally, shows a close correlation with the US money market rate of interest.

The period considered is far from homogeneous; particularly, the last few years are characterised by sharp movements in foreign exchange rates. It is meaningful, therefore, to investigate whether the above conclusion is supported by an analysis of the sub-periods. If the whole sample period is divided into two, it appears that in the first half there is a high degree of correlation between the first principal component and all interest rates considered, except those of Italy and Japan. This is borne out by the factor loadings that result from a varimax rotation. Figures for the second half suggest a high degree of correlation between the first principal component and short-term interest rates in the US and again five other countries. Application of a varimax rotation again shows the first principal component to be closely related to interest rates in the US and Canada. It may be concluded, therefore, that particularly in the latter half, interest rate developments in the US have dominated international interest rate behaviour. This is in accordance with the findings of Argy and Hodjera (1973) and seems to support the untested hypothesis of Hernandez-Lopez (1973) of a dominant US influence on domestic interest rate behaviour in Belgium. If the sample period is divided into three sub-periods, the picture is slightly different. The dominant position of the US, expressed by the relatively high factor loadings for the first principal component, is retained. But in addition to Canada,

Table 2.4: Factor loadings of the first and second principal component of 11 covered market interest rates, January 1961–December 1972

Variates	1961–1972		1961–1972		1961–1972	
Country (i)	α_{i1}	α_{i2}	α_{i1}	α_{i2}	α_{i1}	α_{i2}
USA	0.93	−0.25	0.95	−0.20	0.86	−0.34
The Netherlands	0.88	−0.14	0.92	−0.09	0.69	−0.32
Belgium	0.91	0.00	0.96	0.09	0.81	0.10
UK	0.63	0.22	0.91	−0.23	0.40	0.47
Canada	0.88	−0.31	0.91	−0.23	0.86	−0.34
West Germany	0.77	−0.17	0.77	0.26	0.64	−0.28
Switzerland	0.89	0.13	0.91	−0.11	0.73	0.28
Italy	0.20	0.63	0.33	0.84	−0.15	0.62
Sweden	0.60	−0.08	0.84	−0.02	0.60	0.07
France	0.93	0.21	0.94	−0.05	0.85	0.35
Japan	0.32	0.70	−0.38	−0.80	0.38	0.73
Variates	1961–1964		1965–1968		1969–1972	
Country (i)	α_{i1}	α_{i2}	α_{i1}	α_{i2}	α_{i1}	α_{i2}
USA	0.92	−0.19	0.90	0.09	0.88	−0.30
The Netherlands	0.67	0.59	0.91	−0.05	0.66	−0.40
Belgium	0.59	−0.19	0.76	0.42	0.80	0.12
UK	0.85	−0.19	−0.17	0.72	0.53	0.51
Canada	0.90	−0.18	0.86	0.10	0.89	−0.28
West Germany	−0.13	0.92	0.93	−0.23	0.54	−0.31
Switzerland	0.72	0.51	0.85	−0.17	0.64	0.36
Italy	−0.80	−0.05	0.58	0.50	−0.23	0.52
Sweden	0.56	−0.30	−0.38	0.39	0.80	−0.03
France	0.74	0.00	0.84	0.13	0.80	0.44
Japan	0.62	0.13	0.35	−0.62	0.15	0.81

high factor loadings now also occur with the United Kingdom (1961–1964), The Netherlands and Germany (1965–1968), Belgium, Sweden and France (1969–1972). In this case the varimax rotation does not add much new information. It is interesting to note, however, that Japan — and sometimes Italy — invariably shows a very low factor loading for the first principal component and a very high one for the second. It should be recalled, however, that for both countries we employed rather different interest rates.

As noted earlier, two principal components suffice to describe changes in interest rates in the sub-periods. The second component accounts for about 15% of the total variation. It may be asked whether the second component represents any particular aspect. Application of a varimax rotation did not yield any specific information. Strictly speaking, the second component was hardly significant in the periods 1961–1964 and 1965–1968. For the period 1969–1972, when measured by the magnitude of ϕ_2, it has gained in importance compared with the earlier two periods. The same situation arises if the sample period is divided into two sub-periods. This provides an indication of how the second principal component may be interpreted, for it was at the end of the sixties that pressures in the foreign exchange markets increased. As we are considering covered interest rates, the only remaining risk involved in investment abroad is — to borrow a phrase of Aliber (1973) — a political risk. That is the risk caused by disturbing institutional measures, such as a sudden adjustment of exchange rates, suspension of convertibility, or restriction on capital movements; in short, measures that represent the existence of national sovereignty. If this reasoning is correct, the second principal component might be an indicator of political risk. To investigate this conjecture in more detail, the first three principal components of the interest rates investigated have been plotted in Figure 2.1 for each of the three sub-periods. To visualize our conjectures about the meaning of f_1 and f_2 we have also plotted the standardized US short-term interest rate and the standardized balance on the US current account to account for fear of restrictive measures. The figure shows that the US short-term interest rate runs very much parallel to f_1, confirming our view that the US interest rate dominates world interest rate behaviour. As for the second principal component, we made the conjecture that f_2 is related to political risk and — since we used only short-term forward rates — other expectations beyond a time horizon of three months. In order to support this belief, we compared the balance on current account, lagged and non-lagged, for several major countries and found, as a matter of fact, only parallelism with the non-lagged US figures, although, in all fairness, it must be said that the correlation is not very strong, particularly if we look at the graph for 1965–1968.

To complete the picture, we have also plotted f_3. This component was found to be insignificant but we suspected f_3 to represent white noise. Testing this hypothesis with several devices teaches that it could not be rejected at a 5% level of significance.[2]

---

[2] We applied the run test and, alternatively, Kendall's rank correlation test.

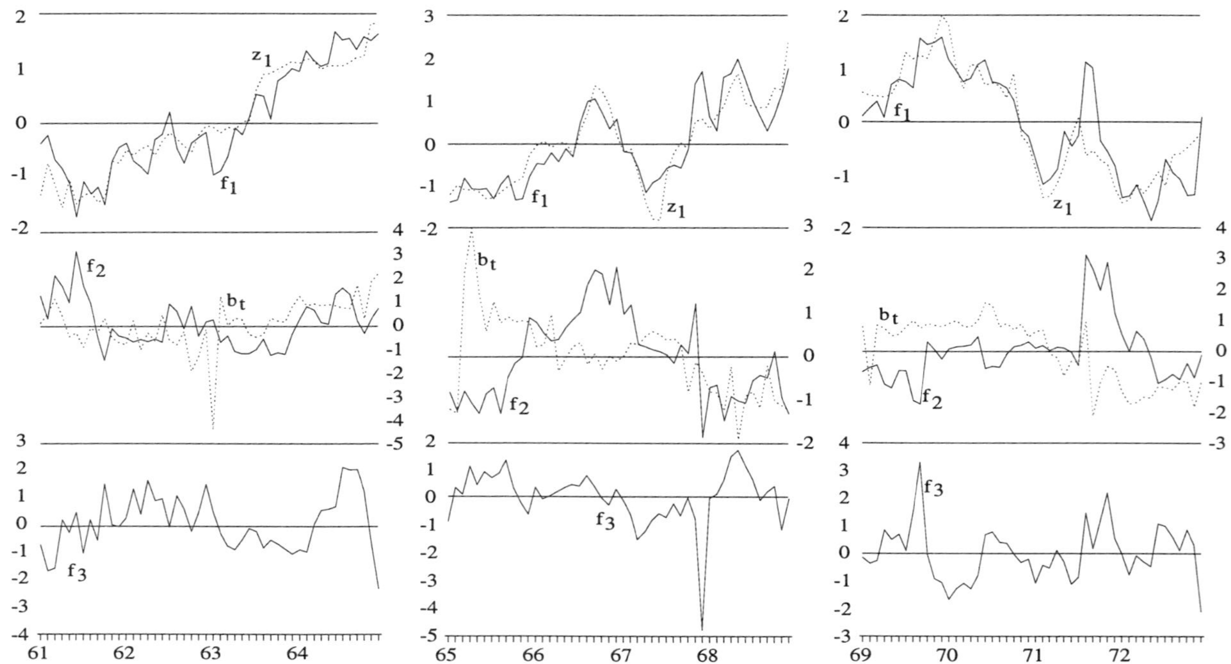

Figure 2.1: The first three principal components of covered international interest rates and the normalized short-term interest rate on the US money market (z_1) and the US balance of payments(b_t)

2.3.2 Results for Uncovered Interest Rates

The main reason for analysing uncovered interest rates separately is to examine whether this approach buttresses the results obtained earlier for covered interest rates. Table 2.5 reports the latent roots for each of the sub-periods that are considered. The most striking feature is the drastic change in magnitude of the first principal component if moved from a division into two sub-periods into one of three. In the case of a dichotomy ϕ_1 is almost 60% and just over 65% respectively. When three sub-periods are considered this percentage varies substantially; it is nearly doubled in 1969–1972 compared with the two earlier sub-periods. The next notable result is that in the case of uncovered interest rates, the second principal component accounts for a much larger percentage of total variation than in previous cases. This is reflected by the numer of significant principal components. For the year 1961–1966 and 1967–1972 four principal components should be retained. When three sub-periods are distinguished, we found three significant components for both 1961–1964 and 1965–1968. However, for the period 1969–1972 only two should be kept. Although the number of significant components has been increased, the pattern is still consistent with our earlier findings.

It would be interesting to know how to interpret the additional principal components. Therefore, the factor loadings for the whole period and the various sub-periods have been set out in Table 2.6. For the whole period, the first principal component shows a high degree of correlation with nearly all interest rates, except those of Italy and Japan. For the period 1961–1966 the situation is roughly the same. For 1967–1972, however, the correlation with the first principal component is much lower. Application of a varimax rotation (see Table 2.A.2 in

Table 2.5: Three largest latent roots of 11 uncovered money market interest rates in five sub-periods of the period January 1961–December 1972

	1961–1966	1967–1972	1961–1964	1965–1968	1968–1972
λ_1	6.54	7.21	4.14	4.13	8.09
λ_2	1.55	1.92	3.07	3.05	1.82
λ_3	0.97	0.6	1.17	1.52	0.43
ϕ_1	59.40%	65.50%	37.60%	37.50%	73.50%
ϕ_2	14.10%	17.50%	27.90%	27.70%	16.50%
ϕ_3	8.80%	5.50%	10.60%	13.80%	3.90%

Table 2.6: Factor loadings of the first, second and third principal component of 11 uncovered market interest rates, January 1961–December 1972

Variates	1961–1972			1961–1972			1961–1972		
Country (i)	α_{i1}	α_{i2}	α_{i3}	α_{i1}	α_{i2}	α_{i3}	α_{i1}	α_{i2}	α_{i3}
USA	0.92	−0.06	−0.25	0.96	−0.12	0.09	0.86	−0.25	0.37
The Netherlands	0.91	−0.06	−0.07	0.93	−0.05	0.23	0.89	0.03	−0.37
Belgium	0.91	0.06	0.18	0.80	0.45	−0.12	0.89	0.28	0.01
UK	0.78	−0.15	−0.31	0.64	0.52	−0.31	0.72	−0.47	0.20
Canada	0.79	−0.38	−0.26	0.69	−0.50	0.15	0.79	−0.53	0.12
W. Germany	0.86	0.35	0.21	0.93	−0.19	−0.20	0.75	0.62	0.02
Switzerland	0.85	−0.20	0.04	0.91	−0.21	0.22	0.87	−0.02	−0.24
Italy	0.53	0.69	0.36	−0.12	0.71	0.29	0.24	0.91	0.20
Sweden	0.89	−0.04	0.18	0.83	0.43	−0.11	0.91	0.17	−0.10
France	0.90	0.00	0.03	0.68	0.06	0.51	0.89	0.04	0.29
Japan	−0.02	−0.69	0.70	−0.60	0.22	0.58	0.86	−0.20	−0.30
Variates	**1961–1964**			**1965–1968**			**1969–1972**		
Country (i)	α_{i1}	α_{i2}	α_{i3}	α_{i1}	α_{i2}	α_{i3}	α_{i1}	α_{i2}	α_{i3}
USA	0.90	−0.25	0.06	−0.67	0.65	0.07	0.87	−0.36	−0.15
The Netherlands	0.94	−0.10	−0.23	0.14	0.89	−0.08	0.92	0.17	−0.11
Belgium	0.39	0.78	0.14	0.80	0.37	−0.12	0.98	0.08	−0.10
UK	0.02	0.81	−0.41	−0.81	0.24	0.22	0.76	−0.44	0.45
Canada	0.32	−0.69	−0.24	−0.79	0.45	0.15	0.86	−0.41	−0.22
W. Germany	0.45	−0.39	0.49	0.60	0.52	0.49	0.81	0.52	0.16
Switzerland	0.87	−0.35	−0.04	0.54	0.64	−0.12	0.94	0.02	0.30
Italy	0.21	0.59	0.19	0.24	−0.46	0.47	0.12	0.96	−0.01
Sweden	0.46	0.74	0.31	−0.18	0.19	0.89	0.93	0.25	−0.03
France	0.76	0.12	0.31	−0.53	0.58	−0.38	0.95	−0.18	−0.13
Japan	0.64	0.24	−0.64	−0.85	−0.42	−0.08	0.95	0.15	−0.08

Appendix 2.A) hardly changes the picture, but again it shows Italy and Japan occupying an obviously different position. This inference is not very explicitly supported by the factor loadings for the three sub-periods. A varimax rotation reveals that in 1961–1964 there was hardly any correlation with the first principal component in the cases of Belgium, the United Kingdom, Italy and Sweden. In 1965–1968 the same held for Germany, Switzerland and Japan, and in 1969–1972 particularly for Italy. The question is, therefore, whether this lack of correlation may not stand in the way of a proper identification of the first principal component. To clarify the position, the first three principal components of each sub-period, along with the normalized US money market rate of interest, have been plotted in Figure 2.2. A comparison with the

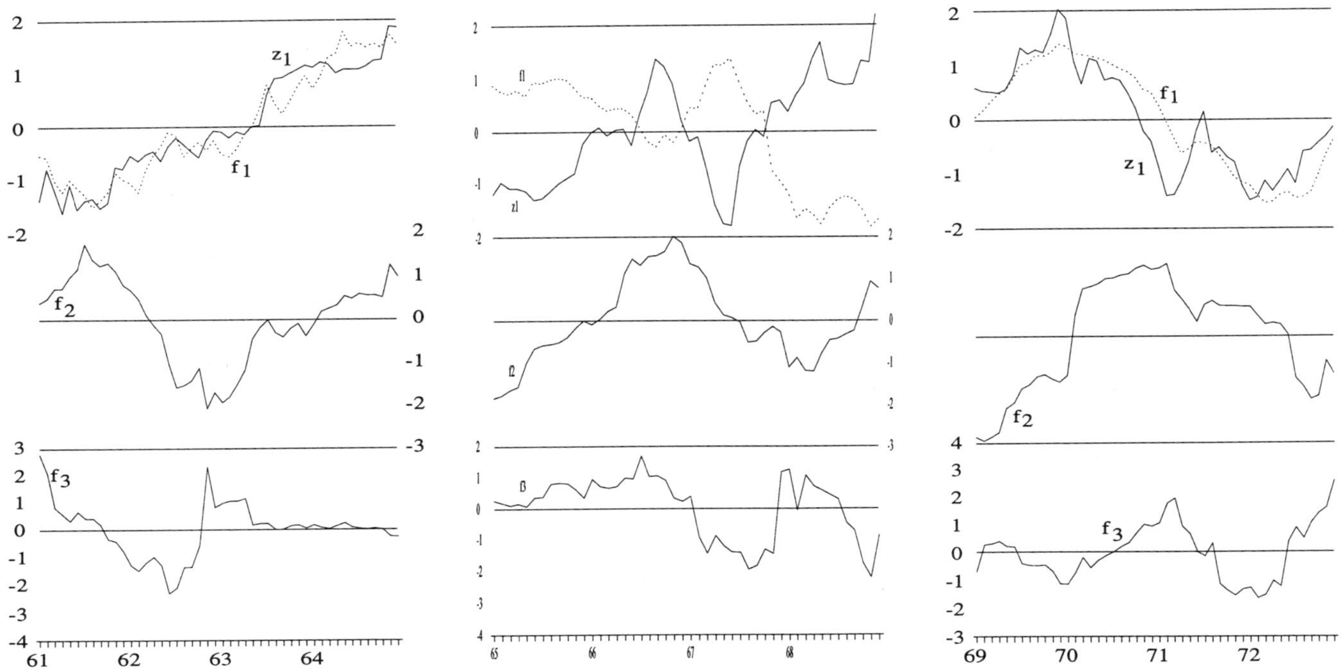

Figure 2.2: The first three principal components of uncovered international interest rates and the normalized short-term interest rate on the US money market (z_1)

corresponding graph in Figure 2.1 shows rather different movements for the 1965–1968 sub-period. This implies that in the other two sub-periods the first principal component identifies the changes in the pattern of US short-term interest rates; no correlation at all can be ascertained for the 1965–1968 period. This is borne out by the factor loading α_{11}, which is -0.67 for 1965–1968. It should be noted, however, that for this period the first principal component is of less importance for the uncovered interest rates than it is for the covered rates, namely $\phi_1 = 37.5\%$ as compared with $\phi_1 = 53.5\%$. Still, it seems reasonable to identify the first principal component as 'the international' or 'world' rate of interest, provided the non-parallelism in the 1965–1968 period, between US short-term interest rates and the first principal component, stems from specific causes.

The year 1966 was characterized by a serious monetary disturbance in the US, which has been canonized sometimes as the 'credit crunch'. A restrictive monetary policy resulted in drastic increases in interest rates and substantial disintermediation. Deleting 1966, however, does not improve the fit of the first principal component to the movements in interest rates.[3] Therefore another explanation is required. To obtain this we recall that from July 1966 to January 1967, and again during the larger part of 1969 (May 1969-June 1970), regulation Q has been effective. Regulation Q imposes interest rate ceilings on deposits at the major banks in the US, and thus encourages US supply of funds at the Euro-dollar market. Of course, this means that interest rate behaviour in the US becomes isolated to some extent and, moreover, that it disturbs interest rate harmonisation with the European countries.

The percentage share of the second principal component in the total variation changes markedly. It averages 15% if two sub-periods are distinguished. In the case of three sub-periods it is nearly 28% in 1961–1964 and 1965–1968, and drops sharply to 16.5% in the third sub-period. This outcome is all the more remarkable as 1965–1968 were the years with the greatest currency upheavals before 1971.

When we consider covered interest rates, we find sufficient arguments for identifying the second principal component as a yardstick for political risk; in doing so, we used the balance on the US current account as a criterion. Figure 2.2 suggests that there is very little relationship between the second principal components of covered and uncovered interest rates. It appears, however, that the degree of correlation among the two components is fairly high: 0.35 for 1961–1964, 0.61 for 1965–1968 and 0.45 for 1969–1972. For the other periods investigated the coefficients are even higher. This suggests again, that f_2 describes political risk.

---

[3] This lack of change is hardly surprising as the 1969 credit crunch does not show up in the graph either. See also Spencer (1973).

Unlike the position with covered interest rates, with uncovered rates the third principal component is nearly always significant, with the 1969–1972 period as the only exception. Uncovered interest rates include an element of added uncertainty about future interest rate changes and the concomitant exchange rate changes. Aliber (1973) speaks in this connection of 'exchange rate risk'. We believe that this suggests an interpretation for the third principal component, which might be termed an indicator for exchange rate risk. It is only for the last four years that it appears to be impossible to distinguish exchange rate risk from political risk. Therefore, in 1969–1972 we believe political and exchange rate risk to be represented by the second principal component.

2.3.3 Comparison of the Results

Summarizing our computational outcomes, we would like to conclude this section with a brief comparison of our results for covered and uncovered interest rates.

First, it is noted that, with one exception, ϕ_1 is always greater for covered than for uncovered rates. The exception is 1969–1972 with $\phi_1 =$ 73.5% for uncovered rates.

Second, for covered rates in most cases two significant principal components were obtained. For uncovered interest rates three principal components were retained, except for 1969–1972. This result is particularly suggestive since it makes f_2 characteristic for uncovered rates. Consequently, we identified f_3 as exchange rate risk, which, for the third sub-period, presumably is merged with political risk.[4]

Third, for covered interest rates ϕ_2 has increased slighly over time. This contrasts sharply with the decline of ϕ_2 for uncovered rates from 27.9% to 16.5%. Our conjecture is that this indicates that political risk has outstripped exchange rate risk at the end of the 1960s.

Fourth, for 1965–1968, the behaviour of the first component of covered rates diverges substantially from the f_1-behaviour of uncovered rates, as is shown again by the relevant figures in Table 2.7.

Fifth, Table 2.7 also shows that the US and the Euro-dollar rate are closely correlated. Since the correlation among the principal component f_1 for covered and uncovered rates is positive and rather strong in only two sub-periods we suspect that, for 1965–1968, the US rate does not move closely with 'world interest rate' behaviour.[5]

[4] This is supported by the simple correlation coefficient between f_2 for covered and f_3 for uncovered rates, which are -0.03 for 1961–1964, -0.00 for 1965–1968 and -0.38 for 1969–1972.

[5] We found 0.95 and 0.86 for 1961–1964 and 1969–1972 respectively. For 1965–1968 the correlation was -0.70.

Table 2.7: Correlation between US Treasury bill rate and the principal component for covered, uncovered, and the Euro-dollar interest rate, 1961–1972

	Covered	Uncovered	Euro-dollar
1961–1964	0.84	0.85	0.86
1965–1968	0.88	−0.45	0.88
1969–1972	0.93	0.86	0.91

Note: The numbers differ slightly from the factor loadings due to rounding.

Sixth, it should be noted that we used the US Treasury bill rate only because it might be representative of US rate behaviour. As to the level of interest rate, we agree perfectly with Coulbois and Prissert (1974), who emphasize the fact that banks consider in their portfolio behaviour other rates as well. For the behaviour of rates we do not share Coulbois and Prissert's view, however.

2.4 Measurement and Theory: Some Reflections

The empirical study of interest rate linkages among financial markets in industrial countries is still in a rudimentary stages and is mostly treated along with efforts to explain international capital flows, surveyed by, for example, Hodjera (1973). A recent contribution, particularly interesting from the viewpoint of monetary policy under fixed exchange rates, has been made by Kouri and Porter (1974).

The narrower issue of interest rate harmonisation in the major industrial countries, dealt with in this chapter, has recently also been examined by Bohi (1972), Hernandez-Lopez (1973) and Argy and Hodjera (1973). Like our approach, Bohi's is entirely empirical but concentrated on the frequency domain rather than on the time domain. Using cross-spectral techniques, he found very low sample coherences, which lead him to the conclusion that short-run movements in international interest rates were not very closely interrelated. Moreover, Bohi did not find evidence for any one country's interest rate to exert a dominant influence.

Hernandez-Lopez' study seeks to estimate the impact of foreign interest rates on the behaviour of the long and short-term interest rates of Belgium. Two aspects of his findings are pertinent here. First, only the impact on the short-term rate appears to be significant.

Second, the foreign rate of interest is represented by the US rate. Hernandez-Lopez discusses this choice at some length but presents no statistical evidence to support it. His main argument for selecting the US rate in preference to, for example, the Euro-dollar rate, is his view that European rates, including the Euro-dollar or Belgian rates, cannot move independently. It is interesting to contrast this view with the one expressed by Argy and Hodjera (1973, p. 10) when they say that 'here is bound to be some simultaneity between the Euro-dollar rate and the European rates, since causation runs not only from the European rates to the Euro-dollar rate but also in reverse'. Moreover, their empirical estimates suggest an almost perfect arbitrage between the US and Euro-dollar markets, and leading to the conclusion that the US interest rate dominates Euro-dollar rate behaviour.

Financial integration would show close parallel movements of interest rates in different countries. Argy and Hodjera present three forms of statistical evidence of the degree of financial integration. They look at interest rate dispersion between a group of ten industrial countries over the year; at behaviour over time of the uncovered interest rate differential (Euro-dollar less domestic rates) for nine countries; and, finally, at the covariation between relevant interest rates. Incidentally, this latter approach comes close to our principal components analysis. Unfortunately, they could not arrive at any firm conclusion about the extent of interest rate harmonisation and financial integration. Therefore, as a last line of attack, Argy and Hodjera regress forward premiums or discounts on a number of variables, including the short-term interest rate differential, trade flows and dummies for capturing destabilizing speculation. Their results indicate a substantial degree of interest rate harmonisation and financial integration. Over the 1960s there has been an increase for Belgium and France and possibly a decline for Canada and The Netherlands. For Germany no tendency could be established while for the United Kingdom no change appears after the late 1950s.

On balance, the reported results show a variety of ways to examine the extent of interest rate interdependence among countries. At the theoretical level our principal components approach seems to be less advanced than Argy and Hodjera's attempt to test the interest parity theorem directly on the basis of a simple model of the forward market. However, contrary to the results of their covariance tests, our principal components analysis produces a much greater number of starting points from which to develop an interpretation, and it leads to answers that are more definite. Despite this advantage one should be aware of the limitations of the technique we have employed, which is, in our particular case, best regarded as a tool for reducing a set of eleven time series of interest rates to a much smaller set, which does away with the interpretation of a vast amount of only seemingly independent information. The principal components technique is a purely descriptive and explorative means which at best may suggest explanatory variables. This view certainly contrasts with the main tradition of econometrics, which cherishes the estimation of relationships emerging from economic theory. Fortunately, as Goldberger (1971) has pointed out, the two approaches have elements in common. We believe that the present analysis offers an example of the usefulness of the two approaches for gaining insight in certain economic problems.

2.5 Conclusion and Final Remarks

The analysis conducted in the this chapter suggests three major answers to our questions.

The first question was to what extent short-term interest rates in different countries were interrelated. With respect to covered interest rates, we found that a rather large proportion of total variation could be accounted for by two principal components. Variation among uncovered interest rates was rather well explained by three principal components. These results mean that it seems reasonable to identify the first principal component with the true 'international' or 'world' rate of interest. The results indicate, however, that perfect substitutability does not prevail.

The second question was whether the remaining principal components indicate particular barriers spoiling strong correlation among the interest rates considered. Our analysis suggests that the second and third principal components are related to two important attributes, which may explain departures form interest parity. In the case of covered rates of interest, we identified the second and last component with political risk, that is risk associated with the political sovereignty of single countries. In the analysis of uncovered interest rates, a third principal component showed up. We assumed that it reflected exchange rate risk. However, we emphasize that the quantitative importance of this aspect, measured by ϕ_3, does not seem to be very substantial, presumably because it has sometimes been absorbed by the first principal component of uncovered interest rates.

The third issue was concerned with the hypothesis that interest rate behaviour in small countries was dominated by interest rate behaviour in large countries. In most cases we found a rather close correspondence between the first principal component and interest rate behaviour in the US money market. This leads us to the conjecture that interest rate behaviour in the US dominates behaviour of the world interest rate, which is in accordance with common practice in some of the literature discussed in this chapter.

APPENDIX 2.A VARIMAX ROTATIONS

Table 2.A.1: Varimax rotation of Table 2.4

Variates	1961–1972		1961–1972		1961–1972	
Country (i)	α_{i1}	α_{i2}	α_{i1}	α_{i2}	α_{i1}	α_{i2}
USA	0.84	0.02	0.90	−0.01	0.84	0.03
The Netherlands	0.61	0.04	0.65	0.07	0.35	0.01
Belgium	0.58	0.13	0.83	0.23	0.32	0.16
UK	0.25	0.12	0.93	0.02	0.09	0.15
Canada	0.90	0.03	0.92	0.03	0.85	−0.01
West Germany	0.51	0.11	0.39	0.22	0.31	0.10
Switzerland	0.54	0.23	0.67	0.02	0.23	0.27
Italy	0.01	0.05	0.06	0.93	−0.13	0.12
Sweden	0.28	0.01	0.60	0.09	0.23	0.06
France	0.66	0.37	0.84	0.18	0.51	0.52
Japan	0.06	0.99	−0.10	−0.33	−0.02	0.96
Variates	1961–1972		1961–1972		1961–1972	
Country (i)	α_{i1}	α_{i2}	α_{i1}	α_{i2}	α_{i1}	α_{i2}
USA	0.30	−0.29	0.94	0.00	0.32	−0.04
The Netherlands	0.14	0.27	0.66	−0.09	0.92	−0.08
Belgium	0.94	−0.08	0.40	0.08	0.16	0.09
UK	0.31	−0.16	−0.07	0.98	0.06	0.18
Canada	0.27	−0.16	0.65	0.00	0.27	−0.03
West Germany	−0.09	0.95	0.83	−0.20	0.10	0.02
Switzerland	0.16	0.27	0.63	−0.09	0.08	0.20
Italy	−0.13	0.01	0.26	0.04	−0.07	0.10
Sweden	0.09	−0.13	−0.14	0.04	0.44	−0.01
France	0.21	0.00	0.65	0.01	0.03	0.52
Japan	−0.02	−0.03	0.17	−0.19	−0.07	0.97

Table 2.A.2: Varimax rotation of Table 2.6

Variates	1961–1972			1961–1972			1961–1972		
Country (i)	α_{i1}	α_{i2}	α_{i3}	α_{i1}	α_{i2}	α_{i3}	α_{i1}	α_{i2}	α_{i3}
USA	0.73	0.25	−0.12	0.76	0.34	−0.29	0.85	0.09	−0.30
The Netherlands	0.49	0.23	−0.04	0.81	0.35	−0.11	0.31	0.16	−0.60
Belgium	0.36	0.39	0.06	0.30	0.73	−0.18	0.46	0.43	−0.27
UK	0.40	0.10	−0.06	0.21	0.97	−0.10	0.40	−0.08	−0.26
Canada	0.91	0.02	0.07	0.49	0.01	−0.22	0.67	−0.19	−0.50
West Germany	0.24	0.58	−0.11	0.52	0.37	−0.50	0.21	0.77	−0.24
Switzerland	0.37	0.11	0.08	0.87	0.19	−0.22	0.26	0.13	−0.34
Italy	0.07	0.98	−0.10	−0.08	0.06	0.08	−0.01	0.99	0.00
Sweden	0.34	0.31	0.10	−0.46	0.58	−0.33	0.34	0.43	−0.64
France	0.60	0.42	0.06	0.39	0.16	−0.04	0.73	0.31	−0.25
Japan	0.01	−0.09	0.99	−0.20	−0.14	0.95	0.33	0.06	−0.85

Variates	1961–1972			1961–1972			1961–1972		
Country (i)	α_{i1}	α_{i2}	α_{i3}	α_{i1}	α_{i2}	α_{i3}	α_{i1}	α_{i2}	α_{i3}
USA	0.93	−0.15	0.04	−0.86	−0.06	0.11	0.84	−0.10	0.33
The Netherlands	0.74	−0.12	0.02	−0.59	0.47	−0.03	0.44	0.19	0.23
Belgium	0.03	0.25	−0.34	0.21	0.93	−0.15	0.63	0.22	0.30
UK	−0.11	0.24	−0.86	−0.46	−0.24	0.19	0.43	−0.20	0.83
Canada	0.28	−0.89	0.22	−0.88	−0.26	0.15	0.83	−0.17	0.29
West Germany	0.27	−0.1	0.16	0.01	0.69	0.45	0.26	0.58	0.32
Switzerland	0.94	−0.12	0.06	0.04	0.38	0.00	0.39	0.15	0.61
Italy	−0.01	0.00	−0.11	0.17	−0.05	0.09	−0.15	0.96	−0.14
Sweden	0.18	0.27	−0.19	−0.15	−0.03	0.98	0.40	0.26	0.25
France	0.43	0.03	0.05	−0.41	−0.14	−0.07	0.74	0.03	0.34
Japan	0.28	−0.09	−0.22	−0.08	−0.69	−0.07	0.45	0.16	0.25

3. On Interest Rates in Belgium and The Netherlands: A Comparative Analysis of Interest Rate Developments and Financial Innovations, 1980–1984

3.1 INTRODUCTION

In his encyclopedic *An Introduction to the Theory of Interest*, Joseph W. Conard notes: "Yet the knowledge is commonplace that there is no such thing as the 'rate of interest'. This is not only an abstraction, but one that most of us have not taken time to relate to the great complex of rates which we meet in the market for money and credit" (Conard 1959, p. 287). This chapter elaborates this notion by attempting to operationalize Conard's abstraction of the rate of interest and to interpret the idea of *the* rate of interest empirically as reflecting marginal productivity of capital and thrift. As such, it is a sequel to, and an amalgamation of, earlier work published in the early 1970s by Fase (1972b, 1973) and Vercruysse, Lavry, and Pirard (1971). Fase reported on a principal components analysis of 20 market interest rates for The Netherlands. Using monthly figures for 1962–1970, he found that for money market rates, 95% of total variation was explained by the first principal component and 2% by the second principal component. On the capital market these percentages were 90 and 8. Vercruysse *et al.* examined 12 interest rates for Belgium, ranging from interest rates on call money to yields on long-term government bonds. Using monthly data for 1957–1969, these researchers found 90% of total variation explained by the first principal component, and 5% and 2% by the second and

Reprinted from *De Economist*, **135**(3) (1987), M.M.G. Fase and K. Steel 'On interest rates in Belgium and The Netherlands: A comparative analysis of interest rate developments and financial innovations 1980–1984', 316–339, ©1987 with kind permission from Kluwer Academic Publishers.

the third principal component respectively. If the interest rates were classified according to maturity: short, medium and long-term, the first principal component even explained as much as 97%, 91% and 94% respectively. Vercruysse *et al.* used their results for predicting the Belgian interest rate a couple of months ahead, but did not attempt to speculate about the economic interpretation of their principal components results as Fase did. Fase concluded that the first principal component could be identified as the true rate of interest, that is the marginal rate of capital and thrift, while the second and third components were interpreted as reflecting portfolio investment risk and inflation expectations. Moreover, he concluded that the conventional distinction between the money and the capital market was not reflected in his empirical results for The Netherlands.

The purpose of this chapter is three-fold. First, we wish to replicate the earlier analysis for both Belgium and The Netherlands, using recent data, and to investigate whether the earlier interpretation of the principal components still holds. Second, we wish to compare the results obtained for the two countries and to make an attempt to interpret them. Third, we wish to examine the question of whether our approach supplies additional statistical evidence for the hypothesis, that domestic interest rates in small open economies are dominated by foreign interest rates as earlier analyses of Fase (1976) and Hernandez-Lopez (1973) have shown.

The organisation of the chapter is as follows. The next section briefly discusses the data and the method of analysis. Section 3.3 presents the results for the two countries separately. The results obtained by pooling the two countries as well as a closer examination and economic interpretation of our findings are presented in section 3.4. Section 3.5 draws the conclusions.

3.2 Data and Method of Analysis

The data used in this analysis are monthly figures of short-, medium- and long-term interest rates for Belgium and The Netherlands, covering the sample period 1980–1984. Details on these rates will be discussed below. Following earlier work for Belgium and The Netherlands, we have used the method of principal components as the tool of analysis. We also adopt the tradition in financial analysis to distinguish between the money and capital market, using the maturity of assets and type of the market participants as distinctive features. In this chapter the money market refers to that segment of the financial market where assets are traded with a maturity of less than one year. Consequently, the capital market refers to the trading of debt instruments with a maturity of over one year.

We use monthly observations on 14 Belgian and 20 Dutch interest rates. Our selection of this sample has been motivated by at least three considerations. First, and in view of our objective, to replicate earlier work, we wanted to be as close as possible to the interest rates used in earlier work of Vercruysse *et al.* for Belgium and Fase for The Netherlands. Second, we believe that the selected interest rates offer an appropriate image of the spectrum of interest rates for both the money and capital market. Third, we have to take into account the availability of data.

As to our choice of sample period 1980–1984, the main motivation has been the fact that since March 1979 the two countries considered existed under the regime of the European Monetary System. This implies fixed exchange rates against the member countries, including the important trading partners for the two countries Germany and France and floating exchange rates against the two important financial centres the US and the UK. The second rationale for this choice is the fact that in October 1979 the US adopted a monetary targeting policy, which caused interest rate volatility all over the world and might have affected the interest rate interdependency within and between the two countries considered here. Finally, and partly as a consequence of increased uncertainty, the period 1980–1984 is interesting as a transition period to the era of financial innovation and deregulation in the two countries, which we expect to take place during the second half of the 1980s.

3.2.1 Data for Belgium

The upper part of Table 3.1 shows the means and standard deviations of 8 rates to be representative for the Belgian money market and the Euromoney market: call money, the official discount rate of the Nationale Bank, the (4-month) certificates of the Security Regulation Fund (Fonds des Rentes), the interbank rates for 1- and 3-month deposits, the 3-month Treasury paper rate, the Euro-dollar rate for 3-month deposits and the prime rate of the commercial bank which, in fact, is indicated as the cash advance rate. There is considerable difference in the ways the rates chosen are formed. The official discount rate, for example, reflects the policy objectives of the Nationale Bank. The rate of the short-term Treasury paper and of the Security Regulations fund certificates tend to vary in accordance with the discount rates of the Nationale Bank. The Security Regulations fund is also an important agent in the call money market. The interbank rates are representative for the 'free' rates in the

Table 3.1: Means and standard deviations of selected money market and capital market rates for Belgium, 1980–1984 (%)

i	Debt instrument	Mean	Standard deviations
1	Call money	10.4	2.0
2	Official discount rate	11.9	1.6
3	4-month certificate of security regulation fund	13.2	2.3
4	1-month interbank rate	12.9	2.2
5	3-month interbank rate	13.1	2.3
6	3-month Treasury paper	13.1	2.3
7	3-month Euro-dollar rate	12.9	3.3
8	Cash-advance rate[1]	15.9	1.8
9	Cash certificate (five years)	12.3	1.1
10	Government bonds: 2-5 years	12.0	1.0
11	Government bonds: > 5 years	12.6	0.9
12	NMKN[2] Investment loans: > 5 years	13.8	1.1
13	GB Mortgage loans[3]	13.8	1.0
14	Shares, total (average monthly yield)	6.6	1.4

Notes:

[1] Continuous credit (prime rate)

[2] NMKN: Nationale Maatschappij voor Krediet aan de Nijverheid, or, Société Nationale de Crédit à l'Industrie (SNCI)

[3] GB: Generale Bank.

money market. As to maturity, and for the sake of convenience, we have included the Euro-dollar in the money market. The largest mean was found for the prime rate and the smallest for call money. The standard deviation, too, varies with the debt instrument. The more active the market the larger the dispersion of the rates. Thus, the official discount rate has the lowest standard deviation, the Euro-dollar rate the highest.

The lower part of Table 3.1 summarises the 6 capital market rates selected for the Belgian sample. Series 10 and 11 concern bonds issued by the central government with a maturity of two years and over. Series 9 are the effective interest rates of 5-year bonds issued by a commercial bank. Rates on long-term investment loans are brought together in series 12 and 13. Series 14 concerns yields on shares (local and international). As might be expected, there is a considerable difference between the yield on portfolio investments in shares on the one hand and on portfolio investments in other securities on the other hand. On the whole, the cash advance rate scores the highest mean and the highest standard deviation. The dispersion is the smallest with government bonds of five years and over.

The time profile of the selected 14 interest rates for Belgium over the sample period is shown graphically in Figures 3.1–3.3 and exhibits a strong parallelism among interest rates in Belgium (the numbers in the graph correspond with the debt instruments of Table 3.1).

3.2.2 Data for The Netherlands

By tradition, the Dutch money market includes call money, several types of Treasury paper, and unsecured time deposits such as 1- and 3-month interbank deposits and short-term loans to local authorities. As in the Belgian case, we consider here Euro-dollar deposits and a money market instrument, too. The upper part of Table 3.2 shows the means and standard deviations of the 10 money market rates selected for this analysis. This upper part of the table shows the highest mean for the Euro-dollar deposits and the lowest for the official discount rate. Figures 3.4–3.5 show the time profiles of the Dutch money market rates which are highly parallel indeed. The other rates vary with maturity. The standard deviation also varies with debt instruments.

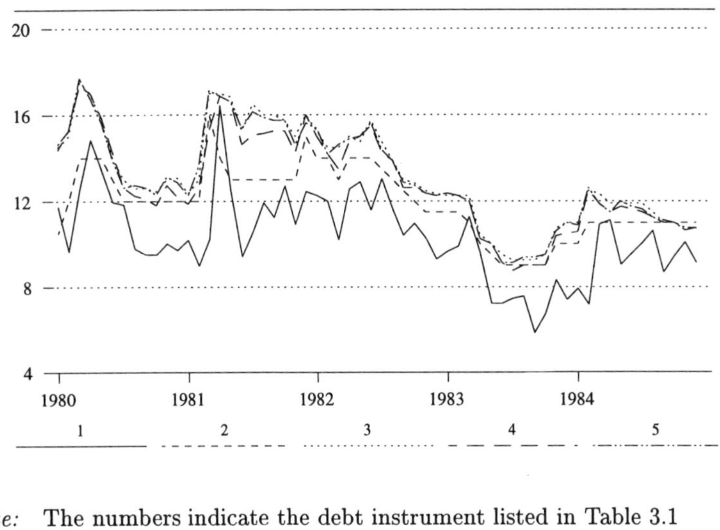

Note: The numbers indicate the debt instrument listed in Table 3.1

Figure 3.1: Interest rates for Belgium 1980–1984

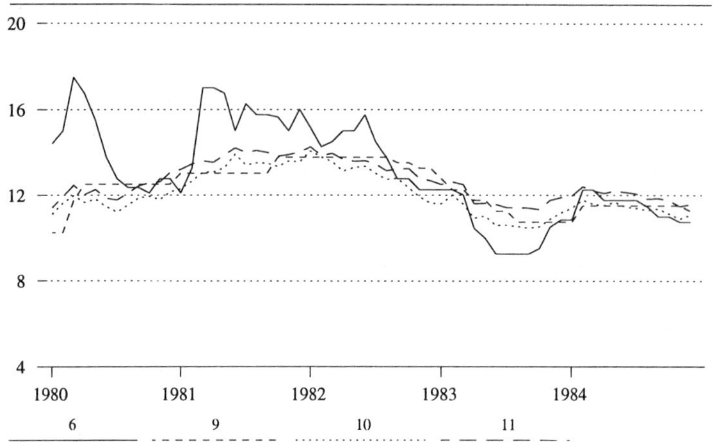

Note: The numbers indicate the debt instrument listed in Table 3.1

Figure 3.2: Interest rates for Belgium 1980–1984

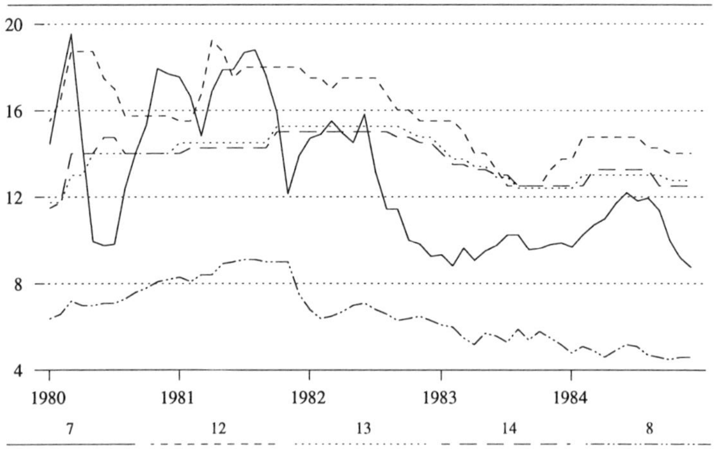

Note: The numbers indicate the debt instrument listed in Table 3.1

Figure 3.3: Interest rates for Belgium 1980–1984

Table 3.2: Means and standard deviations of selected money market and capital market rates for The Netherlands, 1980–1984 (%)

i	Debt instrument	Mean	Standard deviations
1	Call money	8.0	2.5
2	3-month Treasury paper	8.3	2.1
3	1-year Treasury paper	9.4	1.6
4	3-year Treasury paper	9.4	1.6
5	5-year Treasury paper	9.6	1.4
6	1-month interbank deposits	8.3	2.6
7	3-month interbank deposits	8.5	2.6
8	Loans to local authorities: 3-month	8.5	2.6
9	Euro-dollar deposits: 3-month	12.8	3.3
10	Netherlands Bank official discount rate	6.9	2.0
11	Short-term government bonds (3-5 years)	9.5	1.4
12	Medium-term government bonds (5-8 years)	9.6	1.4
13	Latest three long-term government bonds (10.5 years)	9.8	1.3
14	BNG loans	9.6	1.4
15	Commercial bank bonds	9.8	1.5
16	Mortgage bond loans	10.5	1.8
17	Private loans public utilities	10.2	1.5
18	Mortgage loans	10.7	1.6
19	Local shares	6.2	1.6
20	International shares	6.9	1.3

The lower part of Table 3.2 summarises the capital market rates used for The Netherlands. The series 11 to 13 concern bonds issued by the central government and differ only in maturity. Series 15 are rates on bonds issued by the Bank for Netherlands Municipalities (BNG) constituting loans to the local authorities. The commercial bank bonds and the mortgage bond loans are long-term loans by the private sector to the private and mortgage banks to fund their lending activity. The private loans to public authorities and the mortgage loans are two important examples of loans of 20 and 5 years respectively. Unlike the rates of series 11 to 18 the yields on local and international shares represent the rates of return on risk-bearing assets and are, on average, considerably lower than the yields on non-risk-bearing assets. Figures 3.6–3.7 show

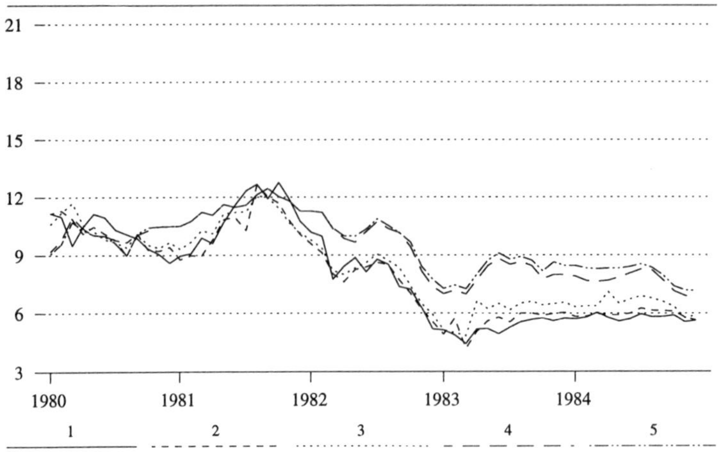

Note: The numbers indicate the debt instrument listed in Table 3.2

Figure 3.4: Interest rates for The Netherlands 1980–1984

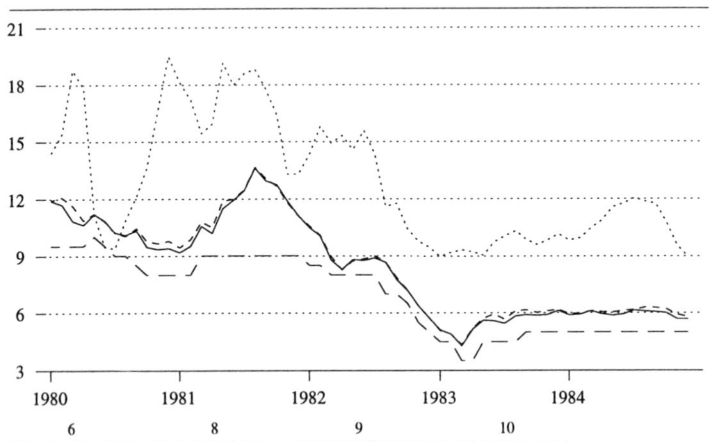

Note: The numbers indicate the debt instrument listed in Table 3.2

Figure 3.5: Interest rates for The Netherlands 1980–1984

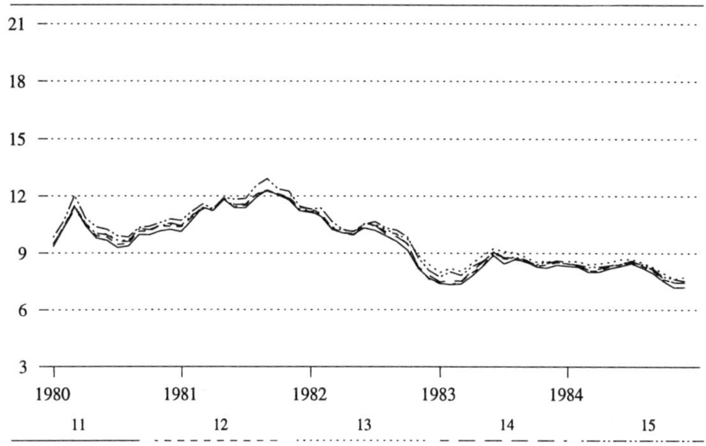

Note: The numbers indicate the debt instrument listed in Table 3.2

Figure 3.6: Interest rates for The Netherlands 1980–1984

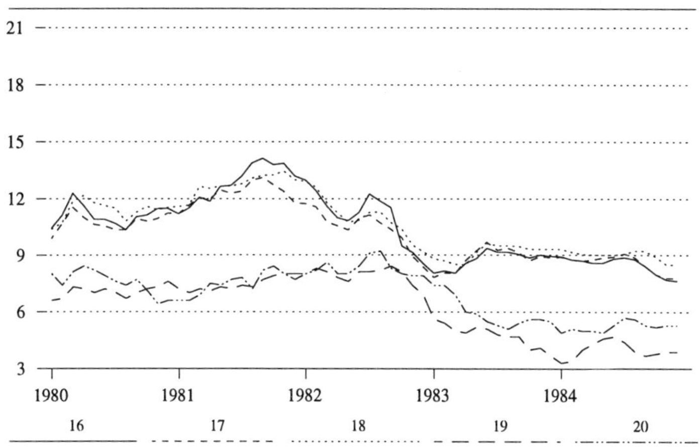

Note: The numbers indicate the debt instrument listed in Table 3.2

Figure 3.7: Interest rates for The Netherlands 1980–1984

graphically the time profiles of the Dutch capital market rates considered here. Again a high degree of similarity may be observed in the time pattern of the interest rates on the two financial markets.

3.2.3 Method of Analysis

As our main concern is to account for the common variation among interest rates in the two countries, the method of principal components analysis seems an appropriate tool. As this method is rather well-known, we summarise only a few points that are relevant to an understanding of our results.[1]

Let z_{it} denote the standardised rate of interest i at time t, with $i = 1, \ldots, p$ and $t = 1, \ldots, T$. If all interest rates observed move proportionally, we have

$$z_{it} = \alpha_{i1} f_{1t} \tag{3.1}$$

for all i and t, with α_{i1} denoting a set of constants to be determined and f_1 the unobservable first principal component. In general, (3.1) will only hold approximately. We therefore seek to determine those α_{i1} and f_{1t} which will minimise the residual sum S_1 with

$$S_1 = \sum_t \sum_i (z_{it} - \alpha_{i1} f_{1t})^2. \tag{3.2}$$

Because (3.2) is determined up to a constant factor, we impose the normalisation rule

$$\sum_t f_{1t}^2 = 1.$$

It can be shown that (3.2) attains a minimum value when

$$f_{it} = \frac{1}{\lambda_1} \sum_i z_{it} \alpha_{i1}, \tag{3.3}$$

where λ_1 denotes the largest latent root of the $(p \times p)$ sample matrix (m_{ih}) with

$$m_{ih} = \sum_t z_{it} z_{ht}$$

and $i, h = 1, 2, \ldots, p$, while α_{i1} are derived from the elements of the corresponding latent vector by multiplying with $\sqrt{\lambda_1}$. It may furthermore be shown that

$$\lambda_1 = \sum_i \alpha_{i1}^2.$$

---

[1] For technical details we refer to Lawley and Maxwell (1971). The classic reference for economists is Stone (1947).

Expression (3.3) implies that f_1 is a linear function of the observed variables with coefficients proportional to the elements of the latent vector corresponding to the largest latent root λ_1.

By the same token, the second principal component may be derived from the resulting residuals. In general the kth principal component is obtained as

$$f_{kt} = \frac{1}{\lambda_k} \sum_i z_{it}\alpha_{ik}. \tag{3.4}$$

It may easily be proved that each principal component is orthogonal to all others. In equation (3.4), λ_k denotes the kth latent root of the sample matrix (m_{ih}) ranked in descending order of magnitude. The factor loadings α_{ik} are computed from the corresponding latent vector. Finally, as before, we have

$$\lambda_k = \sum_i \alpha_{ik}^2.$$

It is obvious that for standardised variables the matrix (m_{ih}) turns into the sample correlation matrix (r_{ih}). In that particular case the factor loadings correspond to simple correlation coefficients between the ith variable z_i and the kth principal component f_k.

As can easily be shown, the sum of the latent roots λ_k equals the trace of the matrix (m_{ih}), usually denoted by $tr(m_{ih})$. The trace equals the number of variables if standardised variables are used. Therefore, each factor f_k accounts for a fraction ϕ_k of the total variation in z_i, with

$$\phi_k = \frac{\lambda_k}{tr(m_{ih})}.$$

The quantity ϕ_k is an unweighted average of the R^2 of the interest variables with f_k. It is used as R^2 in regression analysis, indicating goodness of fit.

In particular situations the interpretation of the principal components is simplified if the matrix of factor loadings is transformed. The varimax rotation is a frequently-used method to achieve such a transformation. The point is to construct an orthogonal transformation in such a way that the function

$$V = p \sum_j \left[\sum_i \beta_{ij}^4 - (\sum_i \beta_{ij}^2)^2 \right], \tag{3.5}$$

with

$$\beta_{ij} = \frac{\alpha_{ij}}{\sqrt{\sum_j \alpha_{ij}^2}}$$

and $j = 1, \ldots, q$; $i = 1, \ldots, p$ is maximised. The required factor loadings are a function of the angle of rotation, which is obtained by iteration from the factor loadings derived from each rotation until (3.5) attains a maximum.

Although we are mainly interested in the quantity ϕ_k we also have to decide how many components should be retrained. To study this problem Bartlett (1951) had designed a test for the hypothesis that the $p-q$ smallest latent roots of the sample correlation matrix (r_{ih}) are equal, indicating it makes no sense to compute more than q components. In the case of the sample correlation matrix, the suggested test statistic is

$$T\left[-\log|r_{ih}| + \log(\lambda_1\lambda_2\ldots\lambda_q) + (p-q)\log\lambda\right], \tag{3.6}$$

where $|r_{ih}|$ is the determinant of the correlation matrix, $p-q$ the number of smallest latent roots of this matrix, $\lambda = (p - \lambda_1 \ldots - \lambda_q)/(p-q)$, and T the number of observations.

Under the null hypothesis, we may treat expression (3.6) as an approximate χ^2 statistic with $\frac{1}{2}(p-q+2)(p-q-1)$ degrees of freedom. A similar criterion holds when we start from the sample covariance matrix (see Lawley and Maxwell (1971, pp. 20–22)). As has been shown by Malinvaud (1964, pp. 39–47) the principal components analysis as a descriptive device fits mathematically and empirically in the regression framework by considering generalised orthogonal regression, although there is still a problem with the stochastic properties of this generalisation.

3.3 Empirical Results

In our application, the interest rates examined have been normalised so that the numerical analysis started with the correlation matrix of interest rates. This section presents the results of our principal components analysis of the interest rates in Belgium and The Netherlands separately. As we consider the rate of inflation as sort of a negative interest rate we have also included the percentage rate of change in the consumer price in our analysis. We note that over the sample period considered here, the inflation rate in Belgium was considerably higher than in The Netherlands.

3.3.1 The Results for Belgium

Table 3.3 shows the results of our analysis of the Belgian data for the first five principal components. The factor loadings are set forth before

Table 3.3: Factor loadings of the first principal components of interest rates and the rate of inflation in Belgium, 1980–1984

		before rotation					after rotation				
		1	2	3	4	5	1	2	3	4	5
1	Call money	0.78	0.23	−0.46	−0.00	0.13	**0.80**	−0.31	0.04	0.03	−0.05
2	Official discount rate	0.94	0.10	−0.17	−0.08	−0.13	**0.79**	−0.53	0.17	−0.01	0.00
3	4-month certificate of security regulation fund	0.94	0.32	−0.05	0.10	−0.01	**0.90**	−0.28	0.32	0.07	0.09
4	1-month interbank rate	0.92	0.34	−0.14	0.11	−0.00	**0.93**	−0.25	0.25	0.07	0.07
5	3-month interbank rate	0.93	0.33	−0.02	0.10	−0.02	**0.89**	−0.27	0.33	0.07	0.10
6	3-month Treasury paper	0.93	0.32	−0.05	0.11	−0.02	**0.90**	−0.28	0.31	0.07	0.08
7	3-month Euro-dollar rate	0.71	0.33	0.54	0.01	0.01	0.46	−0.13	0.86	−0.02	0.07
8	Prime rate	0.95	0.19	−0.14	−0.04	0.08	**0.83**	−0.43	0.23	0.03	0.15
9	Cash certificate and bonds of public credit institutions	0.84	−0.48	−0.08	−0.18	−0.00	0.35	**−0.90**	0.13	0.19	0.07
10	Government bonds: 2-5 years	0.92	−0.18	0.17	0.02	−0.27	0.52	**−0.66**	0.43	0.19	−0.12
11	Government bonds: > 5 years	0.89	−0.27	0.24	0.03	−0.22	0.43	**−0.69**	0.47	0.25	−0.07
12	Investment loans: > 5 years	0.81	−0.55	−0.04	−0.17	−0.01	0.27	**−0.91**	0.14	0.24	0.08
13	Mortgage loans	0.82	−0.46	−0.13	−0.21	0.11	0.35	**−0.87**	0.08	0.18	0.16
14	Shares	0.79	0.05	0.44	−0.13	0.36	0.43	−0.39	**0.58**	0.07	0.55
15	Rate of inflation	0.43	−0.70	−0.01	0.55	0.14	0.03	−0.46	0.02	**0.88**	0.22
ϕ_k (%)		72.30	13.30	5.90	3.10	2.20					
$\sum \phi_k$ (%)		72.30	85.60	91.50	94.60	96.80					

Note: Largest values after rotation of factor loadings are set bold.

and after a varimax rotation. As is known, these factor loadings — α_{ik} in our previous notation with i for the variable and k for the kth principal component — may be interpreted as correlation coefficients among the ith interest rate and the kth principal component. The first principal component accounts for more than 72% of total variation and is highly correlated with short-term debt instruments. The second principal component is highly correlated with the long-term debt and accounts for over 13% of total variation. The third shows a high correlation with both the Euro-dollar rate and the average yield on shares, both risk-bearing debts; while the fourth is highly correlated with the inflation rate. The four components together account for almost 95% of total variation in the rate of interest in Belgium.

An important question concerns the interpretation of these empirical results. The distinction between the money and the capital market is unmistakably evident from the factor loading pattern for the first two principal components. On the other hand, it is equally unmistakable that the second component, accounting for over 13% of total variation, has distinctly less explanatory power than the first principal component and is, consequently, less significant. The first component could thus be viewed as the empirical image of the 'true' rate of interest referred to in Conard's quotation given above. In that case, the second component, which is mainly correlated with long-term rates, may be interpreted as the foregone liquidity or the maturity of the debt. The third component seems to be related to the investment risk which is particularly evident for unsecured Euro-dollar deposits and shares, but could also indicate international interdependency of interest rates in Belgium. The premium for inflation may be represented by the fourth principal component but, measured by its contribution to the explanation of total variation, is of minor significance. It might, incidentally, be noted that an analysis not covering inflation showed the Euro-dollar rate to be highly correlated with the third component, and the yield on shares with the fourth component.

3.3.2 The Results for The Netherlands

Table 3.4 shows the results of our analysis for the Dutch money and capital market rates. Again the factor loadings are presented before and after the varimax rotation. The first principal component accounts for almost 90% of total interest variation, while the second and the third principal component account for only 4.1% and 3.5% respectively.

The factor loadings after the varimax rotation show a totally different pattern when compared with the results for Belgium. As in the Belgian

Table 3.4: Factor loadings of the first principal components of interest rates and the rate of inflation in The Netherlands, 1980–1984

	before rotation					after rotation				
	1	2	3	4	5	1	2	3	4	5
1 Call money	0.96	0.01	−0.26	−0.07	−0.00	0.48	0.32	**−0.80**	0.12	0.09
2 3-month Treasury paper	0.96	−0.06	−0.25	−0.01	−0.04	0.49	0.28	**−0.80**	0.18	0.03
3 1-year Treasury paper	0.97	−0.10	−0.18	0.01	−0.04	0.54	0.26	**−0.76**	0.23	0.03
4 3-year Treasury paper	0.98	−0.05	0.19	−0.06	−0.01	**0.78**	0.34	−0.48	0.19	0.07
5 5-year Treasury paper	0.96	−0.08	0.23	−0.09	−0.02	**0.82**	0.31	−0.44	0.17	0.09
6 1-month interbank deposits	0.97	−0.03	−0.23	−0.03	−0.04	0.50	0.30	**−0.79**	0.16	0.05
7 3-month interbank deposits	0.97	−0.06	−0.22	−0.01	−0.04	0.51	0.28	**−0.79**	0.19	0.04
8 Loans to local authorities: 3-month	0.97	−0.06	−0.22	−0.01	−0.04	0.51	0.28	**−0.79**	0.19	0.04
9 Euro-dollar deposits: 3-month	0.83	−0.26	0.14	0.48	−0.04	0.55	0.16	−0.40	**0.71**	0.05
10 Netherlands Bank official discount rate	0.94	0.12	−0.25	0.05	0.09	0.40	0.41	**−0.76**	0.19	0.19
11 Short-term government bonds (3-5 years)	0.98	−0.11	0.16	−0.03	−0.02	**0.77**	0.29	−0.51	0.23	0.05
12 Medium-term government bonds (5-8 years)	0.98	−0.11	0.16	−0.04	−0.01	**0.77**	0.29	−0.51	0.22	0.06
13 Latest three long-term government bonds (10.5 years)	0.98	−0.07	0.19	−0.04	−0.02	**0.78**	0.33	−0.48	0.22	0.05
14 BNG loans	0.98	−0.11	0.14	−0.03	0.00	**0.77**	0.29	−0.52	0.22	0.07
15 Commercial bank bonds	0.99	−0.06	0.13	−0.02	−0.03	**0.74**	0.34	−0.53	0.23	0.05
16 Mortgage bond loans	0.98	−0.01	0.15	−0.08	−0.03	**0.75**	0.37	−0.50	0.16	0.05
17 Local shares	0.83	0.49	0.20	0.07	0.05	0.47	**0.78**	−0.30	0.14	0.16
18 International shares	0.71	0.66	0.05	0.04	−0.20	0.25	**0.90**	−0.32	0.06	−0.05
19 Private loans public utilities	0.98	−0.10	0.16	−0.06	0.02	**0.78**	0.29	−0.51	0.20	0.08
20 Mortgage loans	0.98	0.00	0.08	−0.09	0.08	**0.71**	0.36	−0.55	0.13	0.17
21 Rate of inflation	0.91	0.25	−0.08	0.09	0.28	0.43	0.52	**−0.58**	0.19	0.40
ϕ_k (%)	89.50	4.10	3.50	1.30	0.70					
$\sum \phi_k$ (%)	89.50	93.60	97.10	98.40	99.10					

Note: Largest values after rotation of factor loadings are set bold.

case, however, it suggests clear segmentation into a market for risk-bearing assets. The first principal component, accounting for almost 90% of total variation is highly correlated with long-term debt. The second and the third principal components, which account for 4% and 3.5% of total variation respectively, are highly correlated with the yield on company shares and the return on short-term debts including the inflation rate. The first principal component accounting for such a high percentage of total variation among the interest rates studied should be interpreted as the true rate of interest. The latter is associated with the marginal productivity of capital or thrift and also with the maturity factor, *i.e.* the rate of substitution between today's and tomorrow's money. The second principal component is highly correlated to the yield on shares and might be identified as the risk premium. The third principal component is related to the short-term interest rates and the rate of inflation. This might not only identify the third component as a measure of the premium for inflation but also as the sacrifice of liquidity, as it is negatively correlated with this factor. The international influence seems to be represented by the fourth principal component, which, however, is of minor importance and statistically insignificant.

3.4 A Closer Look at the Results

In the previous section we presented the main results of the analyses for Belgium and The Netherlands separately. These results support the traditional distinction between money and capital markets for the two countries but also indicate important differences in interest rate structure between Belgium and The Netherlands. This means that the distinction short-long in The Netherlands is less pronounced than in Belgium. A possible explanation of this is that the Belgian money market is not as well developed as the Dutch (cf. Acx *et al.* (1986)). Before further examining the data for the two countries, we shall summarise our results and consider them in the perspective of the results of earlier studies, taken from the cited work by Vercruysse *et al.* and Fase, as well as from Dongelmans and Fase (1975). Table 3.5 presents this summary for both Belgium and The Netherlands, obtained for several sub-periods from 1957 onwards.

For Belgium we note a significant reduction of the explanatory power of the first principal component by 14 percentage points between 1957–1969 and 1980–1984. This reduction is reflected in a substantial increase in the second and the third principal components, which have been interpreted for Belgium as the maturity and risk premium aspect

Table 3.5: Summary of the results of earlier and present studies for Belgium and The Netherlands: explanatory power of the kth principal component ϕ_k (%)

	Belgium			The Netherlands					
	1957–69	1980–84		1962–70		1971–74	1975–82	1980–84	
	(a)	(a)	(b)	(a)	(b)	(a)	(a)	(a)	(b)
ϕ_1	90.0	76.3	72.3	91.8	88.5	87.4	80.6	89.8	89.5
ϕ_2	5.0	11.5	13.3	4.2	5.3	4.7	8.6	3.6	4.1
ϕ_3	2.0	6.3	5.9	1.3	2.7	4.6	5.5	4.1	3.5
ϕ_4		2.5	3.1	0.8			2.0	1.3	1.3
$\sum \phi_k$	97.0	96.6	94.6	98.1	96.5	96.7	96.7	98.8	98.4

Notes:
Column (a) refers to principal components drawn from interest rates only; column (b) refers to the same data augmented with a series of inflation rates. The results for 1975–1982 have been calculated in particular for this table.

respectively. This picture does not show up in the Dutch data, although the explanatory power of the principal components considered shows some variation over time, which however does not seem to be systematic at all and of minor importance. Inclusion of the inflation rate in the period 1980–1984 does effect the explanatory power of the first principal component in Belgium but not in The Netherlands. This might be due to the fact that, over the sample period, the inflation rate and its variability in Belgium was considerably higher than in The Netherlands, *viz.* 7.5% and 4.5% on average and almost 6% and less than 3% at the end of 1984.

The second experiment concerns the calculation of the principal components of the pooled Belgium and Dutch data, including the two domestic inflation rates and the two Euro-dollar deposit rates which as a matter of fact are identical. In addition, we also considered the same data set with the long-term interest rates of the US and Germany added. The estimation results are, after a varimax rotation, set out in Table 3.6. It is seen that for the case exclusive the interest rates for the US and Germany, the first three components explain more than 90% of total variation. This percentage decreases slightly if the two foreign long-term interest rates are taken into account. The results for the factor loading are surprisingly and distinctly different for the two countries. In The Netherlands, all interest rates are highly correlated with the first principal component, while the short-term and long-term interest rates are also correlated with the second and the third principal

Table 3.6: Factor loadings of selected interest rates and inflation rates in The Netherlands and Belgium, 1980–1984

	exclusive foreign interest rate					inclusive foreign interest rate				
	1	2	3	4	5	1	2	3	4	5
The Netherlands:										
1 Call money	0.85		−0.42			0.86		−0.41		
2 3-month Treasury paper	0.88		−0.40			0.90				
3 1-year Treasury paper	0.89					0.90				
4 3-year Treasury paper	0.87					0.85				
5 5-year Treasury paper	0.86					0.84		−0.41		
6 1-month interbank deposits	0.87		−0.41			0.88		−0.40		
7 3-month interbank deposits	0.88		−0.41			0.89		−0.40		
8 Loans to local authorities: 3-month	0.88		−0.41			0.89				
9 Euro-dollar deposits: 3-month	0.67			0.64		0.65		−0.49		
10 Netherlands Bank official discount rate	0.78		−0.49			0.81				
11 Short-term government bond: 3-5 years	0.87					0.84				
12 Medium-term government bonds: 5-8 years	0.87					0.85				
13 Latest three long-term government bonds	0.86					0.84				
14 BNG loans	0.88					0.86				
15 Commercial Bank bonds	0.87					0.85				
16 Mortgage bond loans	0.85					0.83				
17 Private loans to public utilities	0.55	0.63				0.58	0.67			
18 Mortgage loans		0.54	−0.52			0.43	0.60	−0.52		
19 Local shares	0.88					0.86				
20 International shares	0.85					0.83				
21 Inflation	0.68	0.47	−0.41			0.70	0.49	−0.41		

Belgium:										
22 Call money			−0.82					−0.82		
23 Official discount rate		0.52	−0.70				0.50	−0.70		
24 4-months certificates of security regulation fund	0.53		−0.77			0.53		−0.76		
25 1-month interbank rate	0.47		−0.82			0.47		−0.82		
26 3-month interbank rate	0.53		−0.76			0.53		−0.75		
27 3-month Treasury paper	0.52		−0.78			0.51		−0.77		
28 3-month Euro-dollar rate	0.69			0.64		0.67				
29 Prime rate	0.50	0.41	−0.73			0.51	0.41	−0.73		
30 Cash certificates and bonds of public credit institutions		0.91					0.90			
31 Government loans: 2-5 years	0.46	0.66	−0.41			0.42	0.60		0.49	
32 Government loans: over 5 years	0.43	0.71					0.65		0.49	
33 Investment loans: over 5 years		0.94					0.92			
34 Mortgage loans		0.88					0.88			
35 Shares	0.70					0.80				
36 Rate of inflation		0.63			0.75	0.63				0.73
37 US long-term interest rate									0.87	
38 German long-term interest rate						0.72			0.51	
ϕ_k (%)	77.2	9.6	5.0	2.6	1.4	76.1	9.1	5.3	3.5	1.4
$\sum \phi_k$ (%)	77.2	86.8	91.8	94.4	95.8	76.1	85.2	90.5	94.0	95.4

Note: Factor loadings smaller than 0.40 have been omitted.

components respectively. In Belgium, the short-term interest rates are mainly reflected in the first, but the long-term interest rates in the second principal component. As to the third component, the pattern of factor loadings is similar for the two countries. The fourth principal component clearly indicates the foreign influence. However, this clear picture of the foreign influence is corroborated slightly by inclusion of the foreign long-term rates. This reflects the fact that, for Belgium, the rate on government loans represents mainly foreign interest rates. The most striking result of the pooled data analysis, however, is that the number of aspects discovered in Belgian interest rates is larger than for the Dutch. We believe this to indicate the process of financial innovation, that is the creation of new financial instruments, which had already started in the early 1980s in Belgium, and makes it less easy to explain interest variation by one or two components or factors.

It may be argued that the high explanatory power of the first principal component, shown above, is an artefact due mainly to trend correlation. This argument leads Porsius (1977) for example, to employ spectral analysis of interest rates as an alternative to our approach. Another alternative to circumvent this trend correlation problem is offered by Kirchgässner (1985) by using the time series model to filter the series considered before investigating causality patterns. To examine this question we have also applied our method of analysis by taking first differences of the interest rates considered.

The results, set out in Tables 3.8 and 3.9 for Belgium and The Netherlands, indicate a substantial decrease of explanatory power indeed. However, the pattern of the ϕ_k's remains consistent with the earlier results, as does the pattern of factor loading not reported here. A similar result is obtained for the combined results, which are shown in Table 3.7. This includes the US and German long-term interest rate, the two inflation rates, but only one Euro-dollar rate. Therefore, this experiment is not a mere repetition of Table 3.6. However, Table 3.7 supports the conclusions drawn from Table 3.6 and also shows that our findings are not an artefact resulting from trend correlation in the data considered.

Table 3.7: Factor loadings of interest rates in Belgium and The Netherlands plus long-term rate for US and Germany, 1980–1984

	Levels					First differences					
	1	2	3	4	5	1	2	3	4	5	6
The Netherlands:											
1 Call money	0.87							−0.83			
2 3-month Treasury paper	0.90					0.48		−0.82			
3 1-year Treasury paper	0.91					0.75		−0.52			
4 3-year Treasury paper	0.86					0.92					
5 5-year Treasury paper	0.84					0.90					
6 1-month interbank deposits	0.89							−0.93			
7 3-month interbank deposits	0.90					0.49		−0.82			
8 Loans to local authorities: 3-month	0.90					0.49		−0.83			
9 Euro-dollar deposits: 3-month	0.69			0.44		0.57					
10 Netherlands Bank official discount rate	0.82		−0.48					−0.61			
11 Short-term government bonds: 3-5 years	0.85					0.92					
12 Medium-term government bonds: 5-8 years	0.86					0.93					
13 Latest three long-term government bonds: 10.5 years	0.84					0.93					
14 BNG loans	0.87					0.94					
15 Commercial Bank bonds	0.86					0.93					
16 Mortgage bond loans	0.83					0.82					
17 Private loans to public utilities	0.87					0.93					
18 Mortgage loans	0.84					0.66			0.42		
19 Local shares	0.59	0.66				0.48			0.49		
20 International shares	0.43	0.60	−0.52						0.43		0.61
21 Inflation	0.72	0.49							0.48		

Belgium:											
22 Call money			−0.82				0.47			−0.68	
23 Official discount rate		0.50	−0.69				0.73				
24 4-months certificates of security regulation fund	0.54		−0.76				0.94				
25 1-month interbank rate	0.48		−0.81				0.95				
26 3-month interbank rate	0.54		−0.75				0.92				
27 3-month Treasury paper	0.52		−0.76				0.94				
28 Prime rate	0.51	0.42	−0.72				0.73				
29 Cash certificates and bonds of public credit institutions		0.90							0.81		
30 Government loans: 2-5 years	0.42	0.61								0.78	
31 Government loans: over 5 years	0.40	0.65		0.49						0.77	
32 Investment loans: over 5 years		0.93		0.56					0.82		
33 Mortgage loans		0.88							0.73		
34 Shares	0.81										
35 Rate of inflation		0.63			0.74		0.41				−0.60
36 US long-term interest rate	0.72			0.51		0.76					
37 German long-term interest rate				0.87		0.58					0.62
$\phi_k(\%)$	76.40	8.10	5.40	3.40	1.50	38.50	15.20	8.40	7.50	5.10	3.30
$\sum \phi_k(\%)$	76.40	84.50	89.90	93.30	94.80	38.50	53.70	62.10	69.60	74.70	78.00

Note: Factor loadings smaller than 0.40 have been omitted.

Table 3.8: Contribution of the first five principal components to the total variation of the first differences at 14 interest rates and the rate of inflation in Belgium

Component	1	2	3	4	5
Contribution (%)	41.8	14.4	12.7	7.0	6.4
Cumulative contribution	41.8	56.2	68.9	75.9	82.3

Table 3.9: Contribution of the first five principal components to the total variation of the first differences at 20 interest rates and the rate of inflation in The Netherlands

Component	1	2	3	4	5
Contribution (%)	56.9	14.8	7.8	4.0	3.8
Cumulative contribution	56.9	71.7	79.5	83.5	87.3

3.5 Summary and Conclusions

A major problem with the sort of analysis reported in this chapter is that it does not test a particular economic hypothesis or put forward well-defined estimation results, as economists prefer to do. The present chapter has been written with an entirely different approach in mind. It is an attempt to explore the field of interest rates without any a priori hypothesis. Consequently, we wish to speculate about our findings in economic terms. This may provide further researchers with rough but new material to formulate alternative economic hypotheses on interest rates. In spite of the fact that this is not common in economics or econometrics, we believe this to be as legitimate as the more conventional approach.

In this chapter, we presented a sequel to earlier principal components analyses of interest rates in Belgium and The Netherlands. To summarise, the analysis for Belgium shows a clear distinction between the money and the capital market but compared with the study of Vercruysse *et al.* a substantial decline of the explanatory power of the first principal component at about 15 percentage points. This indicates an increase of the maturity aspect. The Dutch data also show some market segmentation but with a different pattern, while the explanatory power of the first component hardly changed over time.

As to the interpretation of the other empirical findings, peculiar differences between the countries are observed. In Belgium, the second principal component reflects maturity of debt. For The Netherlands, this component is mainly correlated with the yield of shares while the third component is related to the maturity of loans. In Belgium, we identify the third component as reflecting risk. The fourth component could, in the Dutch case, be interpreted as the foreign influence on interest rates. For Belgium, we could not find this. Pooling the data for Belgium and The Netherlands seems to support the observed differences between the two countries as far as the financial markets are concerned.

The interesting question is, how to explain in economic terms these findings of our exploratory analysis. This brings us back to the three questions all raised at the beginning of this chapter.

As to our *first* question, the results of our analysis support the earlier interpretation of the first principal component as the true rate of interest, the marginal productivity of capital or thrift. This holds for both Belgium and The Netherlands separately as well as pooled together.

As to our *second* question, the answer is less decisive. Over time, the results for The Netherlands are more stable than those for Belgium, and the contribution of the first two components to total interest rate variation differs substantially between the two countries. It is tempting to interpret this result in terms of financial innovations, particularly because this phenomenon dominates present financial markets. In view of this, our results indicating distinguishable aspects of financial instruments support the hypothesis that, unlike The Netherlands, in Belgium financial innovation on the capital market had already started in the early 1980s (see, for example, Akhtar (1983), Steel, Vleminckx, and Schreurs (1986), BIS (1986)). However, an entirely different explanation is that the differences reflect the fact that Belgium's external position in our sample period was considerably weaker than the Dutch position, and moreover, that public finance in Belgium started to deteriorate earlier than in The Netherlands. This, of course, has nothing to do with the financial innovation noted above. As to the differences in the results for the two countries, one may speculate further and assume that this is a mere reflection of the fact that the Belgian financial market is still more separated than the Dutch. This may be due to the fact that the Belgian money market is less mature than the Dutch, as Advokaat (1987) has suggested.

As to the dominance of foreign interest rates over domestic interest rates, which is our *third* question, our analysis shows an obvious influence of foreign rates on Dutch interest rates, but this is less clear for Belgium. However, unlike The Netherlands during the period 1980–1984, Belgium has accumulated foreign debt, meaning that domestic capital market rates were set by the international capital market. Therefore, it would be wrong to conclude from our analysis that exposure to the international financial markets in Belgium does differ from that in The Netherlands, as the two are both small open economies dominated by the international scene. Moreover, the increased diversity of financial instruments such as RUF's, FRN's and (S)NIF's would encourage further financial integration and thus lead to increased international interdependence of domestic interest rates. As both countries are now on the eve of these new developments (see Duisenberg (1985)), one would not expect them to be reflected in our results yet. However, they will certainly show up in an analysis like ours for the second half of the 1980s. This is an issue for future researchers.

4. International Convergence of Capital Market Interest Rates

4.1 Introduction

Interest rate convergence, defined as the tendency to synchronization of interest rates across countries, is a theme recurring regularly in both scientific literature and discussions of monetary policy, as is shown in, for example, Mishkin (1984), Cumby and Mishkin (1986), Pigott (1993), OECD (1996) and Christiansen and Pigott (1997). From an economic point of view, international interest rate convergence is important, as greater sensitivity to worldwide economic developments may make domestic interest rates less sensitive to domestic economic conditions and monetary policy. Especially after the worldwide capital market interest rate rise in 1994, this was seen as a major problem, as declining inflation rates and rising unemployment in Europe seemed not to warrant higher interest rates.

The theory behind the increased convergence is that, as a result of increasing deregulation, international capital mobility has greatly increased both the speed and volume of international capital movements. As capital flows are highly sensitive to differences in expected returns on highly substitutable financial assets, theory predicts that interest rates in the major industrialized countries will be brought closely into line. This predicted development is analogous to that which took place at a much earlier date in many individual countries where, as a result of removing the strict segregation of money and capital markets, short and long-term interest rates increasingly converged (Fase 1973).

This chapter explores the extent to which there has, in fact, been convergence of interest rates in a number of important countries, and the reasons behind this convergence. To this end, we begin by examining the theory behind interest rate convergence. Subsequently, the extent of convergence will be examined for both interest rate changes —

Reprinted from *De Economist*, **146**(2) (1998), M.M.G. Fase and P.J.G. Vlaar, 'International convergence of capital market interest rates', 257–269, ©1998 with kind permission from Kluwer Academic Publishers.

using the statistical technique of principal components analysis[1] — and nominal and real interest rate levels — using multivariate cointegration techniques as a statistical method. Since the extent of convergence may differ with the exchange rate regime, separate analyses will be made for EU countries on the one hand, and countries with freely floating exchange rates on the other. Convergence of money market interest rate changes and exchange rate volatility will also be analysed, as they might offer an explanation for the capital market interest rate convergence. The presumed decoupling of European interest rates from domestic circumstances was one of the main motivations for examining interest rate convergence. As a result, and in order to deepen our understanding of the explanatory factors behind this convergence, the relationship between German and American interest rates will be examined in greater detail. A brief summary of the main results and conclusions rounds off this chapter.

4.2 Theoretical Background

The driving force behind international interest rate convergence is the tendency of capital flows to seek the highest possible risk-adjusted return. With the gradual abolition of capital controls (Gruijters 1995), financial assets of different countries have become better substitutes. As a consequence, portfolios have become more and more internationally diversified (Tesar and Werner 1992) and both the speed and volume of international capital flows have greatly increased (Frankel 1992). The potential effects of these developments on interest rates can be described by the interest parity condition, stating that the difference between any two countries' nominal interest rates is equal to the expected depreciation (over the lifetime of the instrument) of the one country's currency against the other's, plus a risk premium. This risk premium can be subdivided into two parts: the exchange rate risk premium on the one hand, and the difference between the country-specific risk premia — attributable to, for instance, lack of liquidity, term premia, or default risk — on the other. The interest parity condition reflects the fact that for each maturity, the risk-adjusted expected return has to be equal across countries.

Portfolio managers diversify funds not only over currencies, however, but also over instruments with different maturities. In order to assure equal expected returns on financial assets of different maturities denomi-

[1] For applications of this method to money market interest rates, share prices, and capital market interest rates, see Fase (1973, 1976, 1981b) and Fase and Steel (1987).

nated in the same currency, the expectations theory of the term structure states that long-term interest rates should be equal to an average of current and expected future short-term interest rates, possibly augmented by a country-specific risk premium. The expected future short-term interest rates are in turn determined by, among other features, domestic inflation, real income and monetary policy actions.

The extent to which long-term interest rates are dominated by either foreign interest rates or by domestic current and expected future short-term interest rates, probably depends on exchange rate volatility. The higher the exchange rate volatility, the greater will be the changes in expected depreciations and exchange rate risk premia. The latter is particularly important, as the fulfilment of the interest parity condition depends crucially on the assumption that this premium can indeed be identified. However, a major problem with this identification is the two-sidedness of the foreign exchange market. As agents in two countries have objectives measured in different currencies, it is not clear which of the two will be willing to pay the exchange rate risk premium and whether this will be the same party all the time. If the exchange rate risk is high, neither of the countries will be willing to lend large amounts of capital to the other, unless the difference in expected return is considerable. Therefore, interest rates among countries can still behave relatively independently, even in a fully liberalized world, as long as the exchange rate risk is substantial.

If, on the other hand, the exchange rate risk is negligible, as is the case in a credible target zone or under fixed exchange rates, interest rates in a small country are completely dominated by the anchor country. Since this holds for short as well as long-term interest rates, the expectation theory of the term structure can still be maintained in both countries. In that case, the short-term interest rates in the small country no longer reflect domestic economic circumstances, however, but primarily the conditions in the anchor country.

4.3 Historical Evidence for Convergence

4.3.1 Interest Rate Changes

By using principal components analysis, a system of correlated series can be transformed into a system of uncorrelated series, each describing a common factor of the original series (for a detailed description of this method, see for example, Lawley and Maxwell (1967), or Malinvaud (1964, pp. 39 et seq.)). These new series are construed as a linear combination of the original series. The first principal component represents the best possible one-dimensional image of the multidimensional world of the original series, in the sense that it gives the maximum percentage of the total variation in the different series, which can be explained by just one common factor or principal component. This explanatory power will be the greater, the closer the correlations between the different series, or the more strongly they reflect the same feature. The second and subsequent principal components then summarize the residual variation in the original series. The principal components can be based on both the correlation matrix and the covariance matrix. In our analysis, the former will be applied, as all series are weighted equally. An important condition for the use of this technique is that the original series are statistically stationary. As this is the case only for interest rate changes rather than interest rate levels — especially within the relatively short sample period of 60 months used in this study — we apply our analysis to differentials. We discuss the results using graphs.

Figure 4.1 shows the explanatory power of the first four principal components of changes in capital market interest rates over time in twelve countries (including six EU countries), *viz.* The Netherlands, Germany, Belgium, France, the United Kingdom, Italy, Switzerland, the United States, Japan, Canada, Australia and New Zealand, calculated for a moving period of 60 months from 1972 onwards. The first principal component can be considered to be the most representative of interest rates. The explanatory power of this component has strengthened over

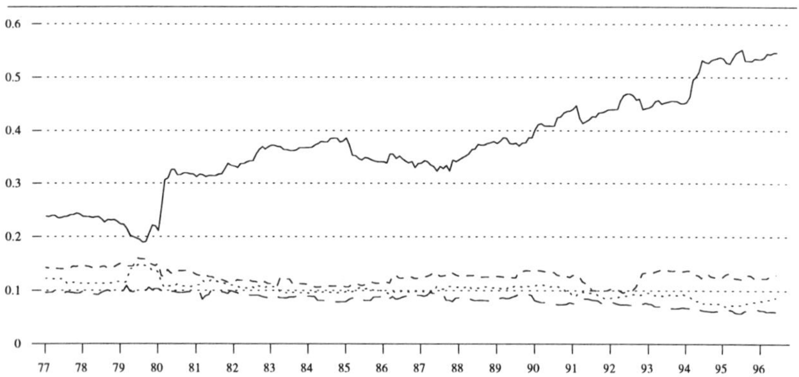

Figure 4.1: The first four principal components of the long interest rate changes for twelve countries, calculated over a moving period of 60 months

most of the sample period, explaining approximately 55% of the total variation over the period 1992–1996. This means that the correlations between interest rate changes have increased over time, indicating increased convergence. The second to fourth principal components with an explanatory power of approximately 13%, 8% and 7%, respectively, during the 1990s are small and relatively stable over time, and therefore have not been included in the economic analysis.

Apart from the ever greater liberalization of international capital movements, the increased interest rate convergence might also reflect reduced exchange rate volatility. This seems to be particularly true within the European Union, because the exchange rate mechanism of the EMS had gained credibility over time. Another possible cause of the increased interest rate convergence could be the greater degree of consensus on, or coordination of, monetary policy among the countries considered. Again, this argument is particularly valid for the countries within the European Union.

To verify these hypotheses, a separate principal components analysis was made for the six old EU countries and the four major countries with floating exchange rates, *viz.* Germany, USA, Japan and Switzerland. Again, we present the results graphically (Figure 4.2).

The two panels in Figure 4.2 show the results, focusing on the explanatory power of the first principal component (FPC), regarding changes in long and short-term interest rates, respectively, and the average exchange rate volatility vis-à-vis the Deutsche Mark. The volatilities are calculated here by using five years of daily percentage changes in the exchange rates relative to the Deutsche Mark (the volatilities are not annualized). The panel on the left depicts the results for the six EU countries; the panel on

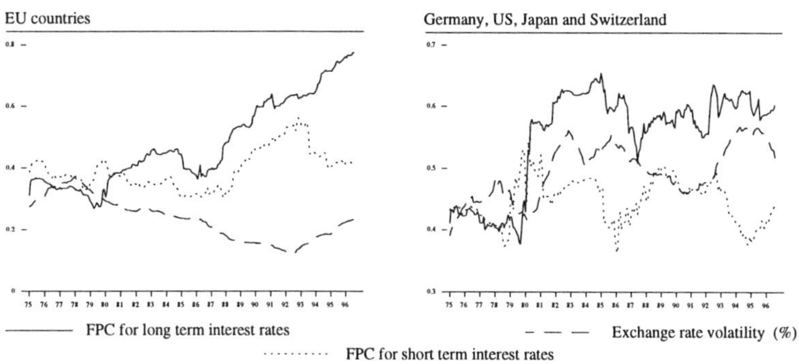

Figure 4.2: Principal components analysis of interest rate changes, calculated over a moving period of 60 months

the right shows the four countries with floating exchange rates, specified above. The left-hand graph suggests a gradual convergence of capital market interest rates in the EU, which appears to be still continuing. Prior to the ERM crisis of September 1992, this process was helped by the reduction in exchange rate volatility. Further examination of the graph also indicates that the degree of money market interest rate convergence — especially between August 1987, when the Basle-Nyborg accord was reached, and the summer of 1993, when the fluctuation margins were widened — was of some significance.[2] The gradual abolishment of capital restrictions probably also played a significant role in this process. The fact that capital market interest rate convergence has not stopped after the ERM crisis of 1992 presumably has to be seen in the light of the current EMU process.

The picture for the countries with floating exchange rates, shown in the panel on the right of Figure 4.2, is totally different. As the graph indicates, convergence of capital market interest rates shows a sudden increase around 1980. Since then, however, there has been no evidence of any further increase. The explanation for this pattern of capital market interest rate convergence presumably lies in the sharp reduction of capital restrictions around 1980; Japan in particular eased capital restrictions considerably during that year (see Gruijters (1995)). This view is supported by the fact that exchange rate volatility has been significantly greater in the 1980s and 1990s than in the preceding period, without any increase in convergence of short interest rates. This means that the sudden increase in the convergence of capital market interest rates cannot simply be attributed to developments in money market interest rates or exchange rates alone.

4.3.2 Interest Rate Levels

As far as domestic economic development is concerned, the important thing is the extent to which the influence of international interest rates on domestic interest rates is a permanent feature. The greater the extent to which international interest rates affect the level of domestic capital market interest rates, the less sensitive that level will be to domestic fiscal and monetary policy and the domestic economic circumstances.[3]

---

[2] In the Basle-Nyborg Accord, the countries participating in the Exchange Rate Mechanism agreed to make more active use of interest rates to support exchange rate stability.

[3] In the MORKMON policy model, for instance, the level of long-term interest rates in The Netherlands depends on long-term interest rates in Germany and the money market interest rate, the rate of inflation and the size of the public sector borrowing requirement in The Netherlands. See Els and Vlaar (1996).

In the absence of any restrictions on international capital movements, according to the uncovered interest rate parity theory, the size of the interest rate differential between two countries should correspond to the expected change in the exchange rate between their two currencies. If the expected exchange rate change is negligible, which in theory is the case for two currencies within a credible exchange rate mechanism, the domestic nominal interest rate of a small country is dominated by international influences. However, given floating exchange rates, with uncovered interest rate parity, an expected depreciation of exactly zero is unlikely. If, on the other hand, the expected depreciation were equal to the difference in the rate of inflation between the two countries, as the purchasing power parity theory predicts, the real interest rates on government bonds in these countries would have to be equal. Real interest rates, in addition to the nominal interest rates, will accordingly be taken into consideration.

We examined the relationship between different national interest rate levels using the cointegration trace test procedure (see Johansen (1991)). This statistic tests for the existence of stationary linear relations between several non-stationary series. These stationary combinations — called cointegrating relations — can be interpreted as long-term equilibrium relationships.

Figure 4.3 shows the results of the above-mentioned trace test for both nominal and real capital market interest rates in the two groups of countries considered in this study. As a meaningful interpretation of this cointegration requires a long sample period, the test statistic was calculated for a moving sample of 120 months. A value for the test variable in excess of the 5% significance level means that the assumption of no cointegrating relationship has to be rejected, indicating that at least one of the interest rates considered is entirely dominated in the long-run by those of the other countries.

Looking at the graph on the left-hand panel of Figure 4.3, no clear patterns are discernible in the test statistic for the EU countries considered. Therefore, it is impossible to establish any equilibrium relationship between real capital market interest rates in general terms. Moreover, the test statistic exhibits a clearly downward trend during the 1990s. There is no convincing evidence either for the existence of cointegration between the nominal capital market interest rates. We may therefore conclude that, despite the increased convergence of interest rate changes within the EU, the German interest rate does not persistently dominate long-term interest rate levels in other countries. A possible explanation for this could be the fact that a varying exchange rate risk over time leads to a variable risk premium in the capital market interest rates of

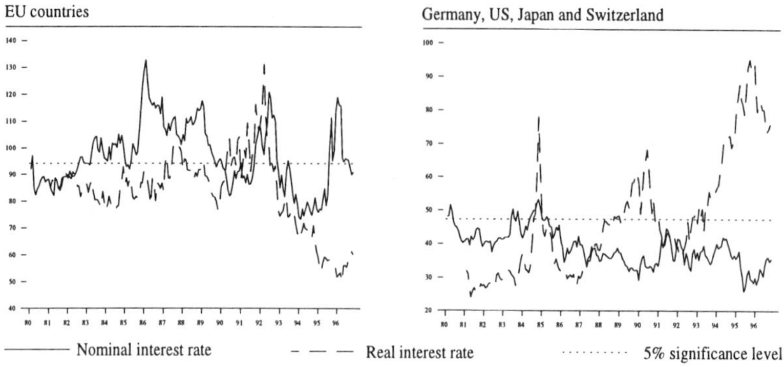

Figure 4.3: Trace test on capital market interest rates, calculated over a moving period of 120 months

other countries.

For the countries with floating exchange rates, the graph on the right-hand panel of Figure 4.3 reveals a totally different pattern. The test statistic for the nominal interest rates of this group of countries is almost consistently below the significance level, indicating the absence of cointegration between the long-term interest rates of these countries. This result is hardly surprising, as the expected exchange rate changes for floating exchange rates will be greater and more variable. However, for real long-term interest rates, the hypothesis of no cointegration has to be rejected from 1993 onwards. The cointegrating relationship is significant only for the Japanese real interest rate, whose level seems to depend in the long-run on an average of the real long-term interest rates in Germany and the US. A possible explanation for the dominance of foreign influences on the Japanese real interest rate might be that investment opportunities in Japan, apart from bonds, have not been favourable in the 1990s. Following the collapse of the stock market, the official central bank interest rates have declined drastically. As a consequence, both stock market and money market investments have lost popularity, whereas expected returns on foreign bonds outperformed those on domestic bonds. Therefore, the interest parity condition contrasted favourably to the expectations hypothesis of the term structure.[4]

Although the German interest rate turned out to be weakly exogenous for the cointegrating relation between real interest rates only, we cannot rule out the hypothesis that the abolition of capital controls has

[4] For the 1990s, a significant statistical influence of domestic money market interest rates on Japanese capital market interest rates was found. However, Japanese inflation or GDP growth rates turned out to be insignificant.

led to greater influence of US interest rates on German rates as well. If the equilibrium level of German interest rates depends on foreign as well as domestic influences, cointegration analysis between interest rates alone will not reveal this. To explore this hypothesis further, the influence of US interest rates on the level of interest rates in Germany will, by way of illustration, be examined in greater detail below with the help of regression technique.

4.4 Relationship Between the US and Germany

The presumed decoupling of European interest rates from domestic circumstances was one of the main motivations for examining interest rate convergence. To deepen our understanding of the rationale (that is, the explanatory factors) behind the convergence, the relationship between interest rates in the US and Germany — being illustrative of Europe — is examined in greater detail. Figure 4.4 describes the developments in the convergence of interest rate changes between the US and Germany. The results correspond to those for the group of four countries with floating exchange rates (see right-hand panel in Figure 4.2). Around 1980, the correlation between changes in capital market interest rates in Germany and the US showed a sharp increase, and has since fluctuated around this higher level. Exchange rate volatility over the same period has in fact increased, and correlations between short-term interest rate changes have declined.

In order to quantify the impact of long-term interest rates in the US on the interest rates in Germany, the following regression equation was estimated:[5] [6]

$$\underset{}{\Delta r_l^{ge}} = \underset{(3.1)}{0.22} + \underset{(5.9)}{0.26}\Delta r_{l_{-1}}^{ge} + \underset{(6.9)}{0.13}\Delta r_s^{ge} + \underset{(5.2)}{0.27}\Delta r_l^{us} + \underset{(2.2)}{0.08}\Delta r_{l_{-1}}^{us}$$

$$- \underset{(3.9)}{0.05}\Big(r_{l_{-1}}^{ge} - \underset{(3.1)}{0.26}r_{s_{-1}}^{ge} - \underset{(2.5)}{0.28}\dot{p}_{c_{-1}}^{ge} - \underset{(1.7)}{0.05}\dot{y}_{i_{-1}}^{ge} - \underset{(1.3)}{0.09}r_{l_{-1}}^{us}\Big)$$

$$\bar{R}^2 = 0.45 \qquad DW = 1.90 \qquad Q(1) = 1.07 \qquad Q(12) = 13.47$$

The change in long-term interest rates in Germany (Δr_l^{ge}) was found to depend mainly on the change in German money market interest rates

[5] The influence of German interest rates on long-term interest rates in the US was also examined, but was found to be insignificant in both the short and the long-run.

[6] Estimated for the sample period August 1963–November 1996, using instrumental variables, taking the changes in short-term interest rates in the US as instruments for the non-lagged changes in the long-term US interest rates.

Figure 4.4: Correlations of interest rate changes and exchange rate volatility between Germany and the US, calculated over a moving period of 60 months

(Δr_s^{ge}) and on changes in long-term interest rates in the US (Δr_l^{us}). Both explanatory variables probably reflect sensitivity of highly liquid financial capital flows to differences in expected returns, in the short-run. However, in the long-run, the US interest rates were found not to play any significant role. The same was true for real interest rates in the US. The level of German long-term interest rates is, in the long-run, mainly determined by domestic factors — in accordance with the expectations theory of the term structure — *viz.* the short-term interest rate (r_s^{ge}), German inflation ($\dot{p}_c^{ge}$) and the annual growth in industrial output in Germany ($\dot{y}_i^{ge}$). This variable measures the state of the German economy, and perhaps signals future short-term interest rate changes. The influence of the public sector borrowing requirement, or the national debt, turns out to be insignificant.

A possible increase in the importance of US interest rates for long-term interest rates in Germany, was examined by means of the method of recursive regression. This involves the estimation of coefficients for moving sampling periods as new data become available.

Figure 4.5 shows the estimation results of this recursive procedure for the coefficients of the US long-term interest rates, together with a confidence interval of approximately twice the standard deviation. After the collapse of the Bretton-Woods system in 1973, Figure 4.5 (A) shows a sharp drop in the instantaneous effect on interest rate changes. Although this is readily explained by the increased exchange rate volatility, the empirical evidence is not provided by the analysis of correlation

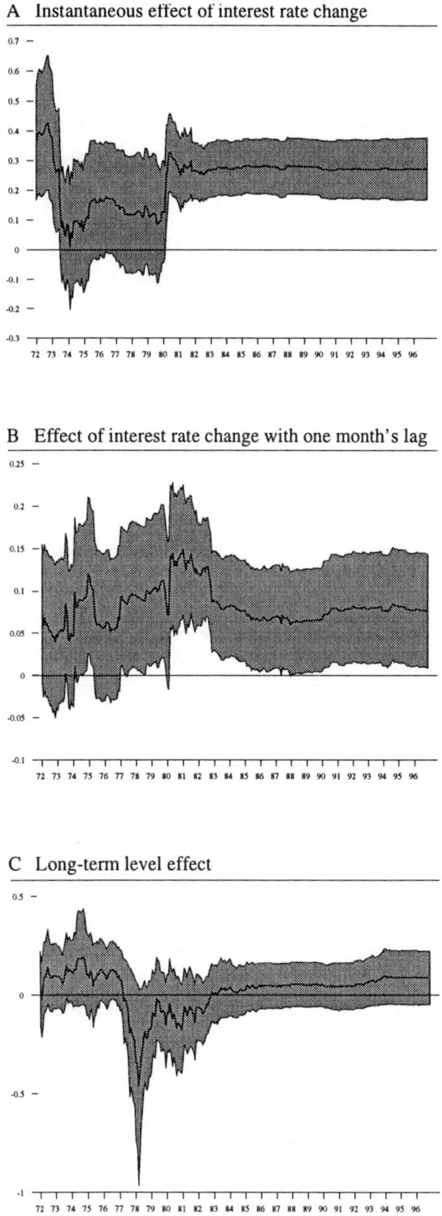

Figure 4.5: Recursive coefficients for the influence of capital market interest rates in the US on those in Germany

coefficients shown in Figure 4.4. Around 1980, another sharp increase occurred in the instantaneous effect of interest rate changes. Since then, however, the coefficient has stabilized. This picture supports the previously established pattern of correlation between interest rate changes on the capital markets of the US and Germany from 1980 onwards. Figure 4.5 (B) shows a volatile pattern for the coefficient for lagged interest rate changes prior to 1983, but a much more stabilized pattern since then. Figure 4.5 (C) shows the estimates of the recursive coefficient for the level of long-term interest rates in the US: a slight upward trend through the 1980s and into the 1990s is obvious. However, the estimate remains relatively small and is never statistically significant. Thus, the conclusion is that neither the increase in the international capital flows, nor the introduction of new financial instruments, has increased the impact of long-term interest rates in the US on interest rate levels in Germany.

4.5 Conclusion

This chapter offers a statistical analysis of the extent of interest rate convergence in Europe and a number of other countries. This analysis was made on the basis of three different statistical methods. The results are the following.

The degree of correlation between changes in capital market interest rates has increased gradually within the EU since the early 1980s. In the period up to 1993, this increased correlation was accompanied by a gradual reduction in exchange rate volatility, a relaxation of capital restrictions, and increased convergence of money market interest rates. Since 1993 the convergence has continued, probably because of the upcoming EMU. In spite of this, no evidence was found for complete dominance of the German interest rates.

Within the group of countries with floating exchange rates, the increase in the correlation between changes in capital market interest rates occurred abruptly around 1980. Since then, however, this greater degree of correlation has remained roughly constant. The cause of this sudden increase probably lies in the lifting of capital controls around 1980 rather than in the exchange rate volatility or money market interest rates. Moreover, since the 1990s, the level of real long-term interest rates in Japan seems to have been influenced by real interest rates in Germany and the US. The presumed greater influence of US long-term interest rates on the level of interest rates in Germany could not be detected.

We may conclude that the liberalization of capital flows has indeed increased correlations between capital market interest rate changes and thus, interest rate convergence. However, the ever greater volume of international capital movements and the introduction of new financial instruments has not so far affected the degree of correlation between long-term interest rates among countries with floating exchange rates. Moreover, in these countries, with the possible exception of Japan, the increased convergence has not changed the impact of domestic monetary policy actions on long-term interest rates.

5. Bond Yields and Expected Inflation: A History of Dutch Experience

During the sixties, the economic aspect of our society was characterized by increasing inflation. Simultaneously, interest rates rose to, in those days, almost unprecedented heights. In a ten-year period, the interest level roughly doubled. The present essay is an attempt to unravel the factual connection between these two phenomena in The Netherlands, both from a theoretical and an empirical viewpoint. Briefly, our topic is the Gibson paradox applied to The Netherlands.

5.1 The Gibson Paradox

Some 40 years ago, when Keynes published his *Treatise on Money*, he also enriched economic literature by introducing the Gibson paradox. Keynes gave this somewhat peculiar name to the phenomenon, paradoxical in his view, that fluctuations in the value of money are almost invariably accompanied by reciprocal fluctuations in interest rates. In this, he referred to a series of articles in *Bankers' Magazine* of the day, in which A.H. Gibson showed that there had been a positive correlation between inflation and bond yields in Britain for more than a hundred years. In periods of rising prices, bond yields invariably climbed, while they fell in years of falling prices. The surprising thing was mainly that the received economic doctrine of the time could not account for it. Consequently, the empirical correlation was largely ignored by professional economists. Keynes himself did not succeed in producing a convincing explanation of the paradox, either; he largely attributed it to the banking system's actions, which could produce a discrepancy between the natural

'Bond yields and expected inflation: A quantitative analysis of the Dutch experience' by M.M.G. Fase, *Amsterdam-Rotterdam Bank Economic Quarterly Review*, **30** (September 1972), 5–10, is reprinted by permission.

rate of interest and the money or market rate.

Interest in the Gibson paradox ebbed away at the time, since the economic circumstances of the thirties, and the welter of theoretical and practical problems they created, demanded all attention. Revival of interest in the Gibson paradox, in recent years especially noticeable in the US, is no doubt largely inspired by the conditions of the sixties and seventies with their almost unprecedented high rates of interest.

The following section describes the connection in The Netherlands between bond yields and price levels during the first 70 years of this century. Subsequently, some possible explanations of the Gibson paradox, which have been advanced, are discussed. Finally, an attempt is made to use the most promising elements from these explanations, inspired in particular by Irving Fisher (1930), in quantifying the relation between interest rates and prices in The Netherlands for the sixties. The main conclusion from this research is that high levels of interest rates can quite satisfactorily be explained by inflation. However, the statistical results are preliminary and should only be regarded as a first examination of the field.

5.2 Interest Rate Levels in Historical Perspective: 1901–1971

The beginning of the twentieth century is a useful starting point for a historical review of price and bond yield movement patterns. In the first place, there are indications that Dutch industrial capitalism started to play a part on the capital market about the turn of the century, partly induced by Western Europe's recovery from the depression of 1895, with the result that economic activity began to affect interest rate levels. Moreover, there are hardly any data on price developments for earlier years.[1] Figure 5.1 shows the development of consumer prices and of the yield on perpetual government bonds for the first 70 years of this century. It shows some well-known aspects of Dutch economic history: comparatively stable prices up to World War I as well as in the golden years preceding the depression of the thirties; rising prices during the war and in the immediate post-war years. The pattern is repeated after World War II. The marked parallelism between price and yield movements is quite surprising: up to 1936, high prices and

[1] Our data have been derived from Centraal Bureau voor de Statistiek (1970). Longer series are available for yields on government loans; see *e.g.* Verrijn Stuart (1917, pp. 398–400). General price data are much sparser; see Spek (1971, pp. 418–426). For specific price series see *e.g.* Vries (1971, pp. 203 ff.).

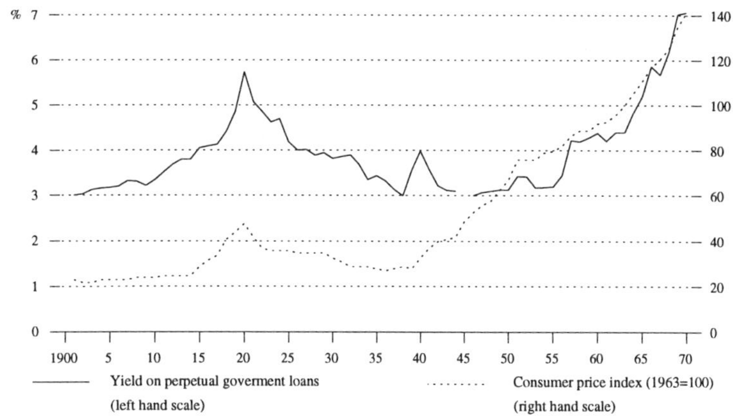

Figure 5.1: Interest rates and prices in The Netherlands, 1901–1971

yields alternate with a degree of regularity with low prices and interest rates. From 1936, when the golden standard era was definitely over and substantial intervention in the economic process started, up to the early fifties, there is no such relationship. Prices rose slowly though steadily; bond yields fluctuated only mildly after a sharp movement just before the outbreak of World War II. After 1950, when the Dutch economy had recovered to some extent, both prices and bond yields rose virtually without interruption, though the yield series show minor fluctuations not found in the price series. Finally, it is quite striking that in 1970 bond yields reached an unprecedented height, exceeding the previous 1920 record by more than 1.25 percentage points.

Calculation of a number of correlation coefficients presents a somewhat different approach than the above graphical analysis. These results are reported in Table 5.1. The calculations confirm the outlines sketched previously. For the whole period, the correlation coefficient between bond yields and consumer prices is 0.68. Subdividing it into three subperiods, we find that, in the years around World War II, the correlation is negative and moreover, exceptionally low. This supports the conjecture that the Gibson paradox does not appear in a strictly planned economy. This seems acceptable on theoretical grounds. In the other two subperiods, however, the correlation coefficients are positive and very high.

This picture hardly changes if wholesale prices, instead of consumer prices, are correlated with bond yields (column 2 of Table 5.1). The same applies if mortgage rates are considered in stead of bond yields, as shown in the last column of Table 5.1. It must be added, though, that

Table 5.1: Coefficients of correlation for yield and price levels, 1901–1971

Period	Government bonds and consumer prices	Government bonds and wholesale prices	Mortgage rates and consumer prices
1901–1971	0.68	0.61	0.45
1901–1936	0.93	0.80	0.81
1937–1951	−0.27	−0.20	−0.63
1952–1971	0.98	0.95	0.97

in this case the negative correlation in the 1937–1951 period is far more marked.

Summarizing we may conclude that the Gibson paradox also appeared in The Netherlands during the first seventy years of this century.

5.3 Some Theoretical Reflections

Cagan (1965, pp. 249–259) remarks, in an interesting monograph on the 1875–1960 period in US monetary history, that the Gibson paradox has repeatedly been taken as criticism to classical monetary theory, in which the interest rate expresses the value of money. According to the quantity theory, a change in money supply influences the general price level in the same direction and the interest level in the reverse direction. An increase in money supply was supposed, eventually, to result in a price rise while at the same time lowering the interest level. The negative correlation between interest and price level in the classical monetary view follows from this argument.

As we have shown above, the historical evidence for The Netherlands presented in the preceding section provides little support for this view. The experience of the US and the UK, during many years, likewise contradicts it. An interesting aspect of these reflections on the quantity theory is that they clearly show that a relationship between fluctuations in prices and interest rates — leaving aside the sign of the correlation for the time being — does not necessarily imply any causality. In the argument outlined, both phenomena are symptoms of a variety of macroeconomic relationships, some of which are implicitly assumed. In contrast to this interdependent model is the consecutive or causal view of the Gibson paradox, in which high rates of interest are caused by inflation expectations. In the following, some attention will be paid to both arguments.

We already mentioned that Keynes, in discussing the Gibson paradox, could offer no satisfactory explanation. Wholly in Wicksell's spirit, Keynes in his *Treatise* sought to explain it by the possible divergence between the natural interest rate on one hand and the market rate on the other. The *natural rate* is the rate that will bring planned savings into equilibrium with *ex ante* investment, and equals the marginal productivity of capital. The *market rate* is the rate resulting in the capital market; it is regularly reported in financial press. In Wicksell's argument, equality of the two rates is a condition for price stability. Disruption in equality leads to price changes. If the natural rate is below the market rate, prices will decline, with the reverse situation resulting in price rises. The essential point in Keynes' argument is that market rates only follow changes in the natural rate very slowly and imperfectly. As a result, the banking system will not readily recognize, for example, a decline of the natural rate, and the actual decline of market rates will then be less than needed to avoid a price fall. A similar argument applies to rises in the natural rate.

The economic relationships appear more clearly than in the Wicksellian model, if one starts with a condensed macroeconomic model in the form of the well-known IS-LM paradigm. In this, the IS-curve represents the set of equilibrium points for the economy's real sector at various interest rates and levels of expenditure. The LM-curve describes the set of equilibrium points in the monetary sector, also at all conceivable levels of interest and expenditure.[2] Assuming that the two curves are neither horizontal nor vertical near the intersection point, an increased propensity to invest, for example, under full utilization of production capacity, will in the first instance produce a rise in interest rates which will be accompanied by price rises. Evidently, full utilization of production capacity is an essential assumption in this argument, as well

[2] This may be illustrated by the chart below: Increased propensity to invest will shift the IS-curve to the right: additional money creation will similarly shift the LM-curve to the right.

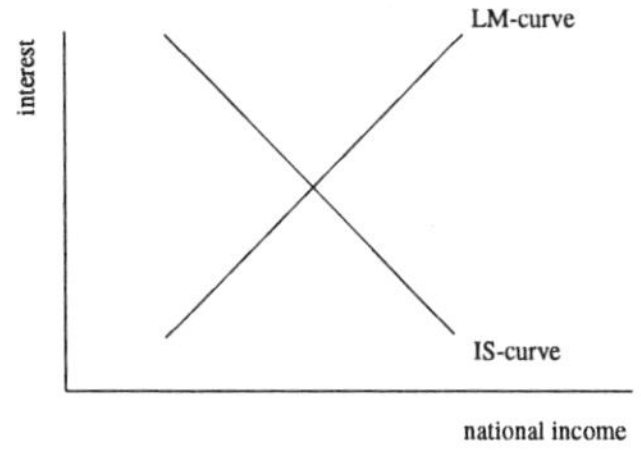

as the existence of price flexibility. On the other hand, the framework outlined also permits construction of cases in which price rises are not accompanied by rising interest rates.

The IS-LM framework indicated above was not primarily evolved for a dynamic world in which expectations play any role. The theory requires amplification, especially on the point of expectations. After all, the interest rate gives the exchange rate between the value of money at present and that of money in the nearer or farther future. It is obvious, therefore, that expectations concerning future price developments must play a substantial role in explaining interest rates. That has again been pointed out very recently by Hicks in an essay on inflation and interest in thirty countries.[3] A particularly important author in this respect is Fisher, who did a great deal of research that was finally laid down in his *Theory of Interest* (especially Fisher (1930, Chapters II and XIX)) which appeared in 1930. Fisher's work is an example of what has above been called the consecutive or causal approach.

The central idea in Fisher's reasoning is that the interest rate represents the exchange rate between present and future goods. At steady prices, there will be no difference between real and nominal interest rates. However, if a lender or an investor in bonds expects substantial price rises, he will require compensation for the depreciation of his money, over and above the real interest rate in keeping with the loss of future purchasing power of his loan or investment. If the future were completely transparent and price changes could be perfectly forecast, the difference between nominal and real rates would exactly equal the anticipated inflation during the lifetime of the loan or investment. This may be illustrated by a simple example. Assuming a real interest rate of 5 per cent and an anticipated inflation of 4 per cent during the period of investment, as well as perfect foresight, the nominal rate will come to 9 per cent. Under the same assumptions, if a price decline of 1 per cent is anticipated, the nominal rate would be 4 per cent.[4]

Similar to the ideas of Wicksell, Fisher distinguishes real and nominal interest. The real or natural rate of interest, or if one prefers it, the marginal productivity of capital goods, is not directly observable, as the nominal market rate is. The latter equals the yield on bonds or other loans. Its level no doubt depends partly on the productivity of investment, but is likewise affected by conditions on the capital market, the propensity to invest, and in the long-run, by inflation expectations. It is this last aspect that has been examined thoroughly by Fisher. Re-

[3] Hicks (1970, pp. 261–275); see also his *Capital and Growth* (Hicks 1965); Muiswinkel (1971, pp. 165–181).

[4] Since interest revenue is also affected by changes in the value of money, these nominal interest percentages, to be precise, are 9.2 and 3.95.

markably, Fisher has made attempts to verify his theoretical arguments statistically. His main finding was that nominal interest can in fact be quite well explained by historical percentage price changes, though there is a considerable lag in the adjustment, which takes place only partially anyway. According to Fisher, this suggests imperfect foresight of future price changes. Fisher's argument may be supplemented by adding that complete adjustment is unlikely on account of real cash effects due to price rises, which influence savings by way of wealth adjustment.[5]

Recently, Fisher's statistical research inspired various economists to renewed research into the relationship between interest rates and inflation.[6] Some have based themselves on the more comprehensive IS-LM approach, though without going as far as to formulate a simultaneous econometric model in this context. Others start from the less ambitious causal approach Fisher used, and sometimes achieved remarkable results. This last approach has the advantage of avoiding the trap of a kind of reduced form equations that disguise the economic mechanism, while it moreover permits the use of improved estimation techniques for distributed lags developed since Irving Fisher's days.

5.4 Quantification of the Gibson Paradox

Fisher's approach has the attraction of simplicity, and has moreover been given in a form amenable to statistical verification. As has been outlined previously, this approach is connected with the idea of a real rate of interest that can diverge form the market rate due to inflation expectations. The market rate r_t equals the real rate r_N plus the expected inflation in the period under consideration, say $\dot{p}^E$. This is expressed in the equation:

$$r_t = r_N + \dot{p}^E. \tag{5.1}$$

Unfortunately, price expectations cannot be directly observed, making a further assumption necessary. The obvious procedure is to look at the past. We will assume that the expected percentage price change is the weighted sum of percentage price changes in the past, $\dot{p}_t, \dot{p}_{t-1}, \ldots, \dot{p}_{t-n}$.

5 Mundell (1971).

6 Some of the important articles include: Meiselman (1963, pp. 112–133), Sargent (1969, pp. 127–140), Yohe and Karnosky (1969, pp. 18–38), Feldstein and Eckstein (1970, pp. 363–375), Feldstein (1970, pp. 1325–1339), Hamburger (1971, pp. 354–371) and Fand (1972, pp. 23–64). Of historical interest is Centraal Bureau voor de Statistiek (1943, pp. 61–68).

These are observable, by which we may postulate in regard to p^E:

$$\dot{p}^E = \sum_{i=0}^{n} w_i \dot{p}_{t-i}, \tag{5.2}$$

where w_i represents the weights still to be set. Combining the two equations, the market interest rate is explained by:

$$r_t = r_N + \sum_{i=0}^{n} w_i \dot{p}_{t-i}. \tag{5.3}$$

Relationship (5.3) may be taken as a regression equation with the w_i-terms as regression coefficients and r_N as constant term. It may be useful to recall that it represents the real interest rate which is assumed to equal the marginal productivity of capital. Formulating (5.3) as a regression equation implies that this marginal productivity of capital is assumed to be constant. In the comparatively short period of say ten years, such an assumption does not appear overly bold. To determine the weights w_i — that is, the regression coefficients — an assumption concerning their pattern must be made. An attempt was made to do this through the *Koyck lag schema* (that is, the weights form a convergent geometric series, permitting computation of the w_i terms) and through the *Almon technique* (that is, the w_i lie on a certain curve).[7]

Regression equation (5.3) has been estimated with monthly data for the period 1961–1970 in which a substantial interest rise took place. The interest rate has been observed through the yield on the last three government loans. The figures are the effective yields on a set of three issues whose composition varies with each new issue of a loan with at least 20 years maturity. The yields are monthly averages. They are shown in Figure 5.2. It strikingly illustrates the great interest rate rise since the early sixties. We have shown elsewhere that this series does indeed describe 'the interest rate' quite satisfactorily.[8]

The price rise was measured by the consumer price index. After all, the public observes price inflation through this index, or rather through its components. Percentage changes have been calculated by comparing the index for a month in a given year with that of the same month of the preceding year.

---

[7] Almon (1965, pp. 178–196).
[8] See Fase (1973).

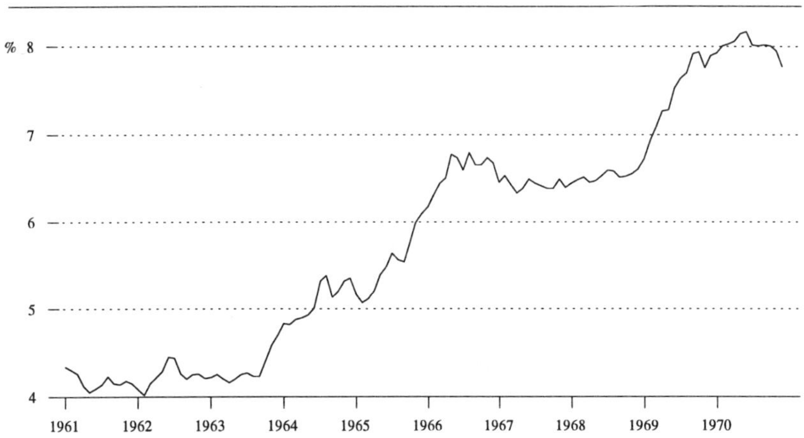

Figure 5.2: Yield on government loans in The Netherlands, 1961–1970

5.5 Results for 1961–1970

As stated above, equation (5.3) was estimated according to the Koyck method and to the Almon technique. The results of the Koyck estimates are hardly encouraging: the estimate of the constant is virtually zero while the average lag is some 5 years.[9] The Almon method produces rather more satisfactory results for both the constant and the average lag.

Determination of the optimum lag period n was less satisfactory. Since calculations, in which n varied between 6 and 60, gave no indication of the most suitable value n, we have opted for $n = 12$. This assumes *a priori* that the public does not look farther back than 12 months in forming its expectations. This introduces an extremely important assumption whose realism may be open to doubt. Moreover, the results of our analysis are affected by this assumption. For that reason, some alternative extimates are presented in Appendix 5.A.

The result of our regression analysis is:

$$r_t = 3.48 + \sum_{i=0}^{11} w_i \dot{p}_{t-i}.$$

[9] The estimated Koyck equation is:

$$\underset{(0.04)}{r_t = 0.03} \; + \underset{(0.008)}{0.984 r_{t-1}} + \underset{(0.005)}{0.022 p_t},$$

with the standard errors in parentheses.

Table 5.2: Estimated results of equation (5.3) with Almon lags

i	w_i	standard error (in per cent of w_i)
0	0.016	46.2
1	0.030	37.2
2	0.043	29.1
3	0.054	21.8
4	0.062	15.9
5	0.067	11.7
6	0.070	10.7
7	0.069	12.9
8	0.064	16.7
9	0.055	20.9
10	0.042	25.3
11	0.023	29.5

Note: $\sum_{i=0}^{11} w_i = 0.595(0.064)$, $r_N = 3.48(0.29)$, $R^2 = 0.45$.

The estimated weights as well as the standard errors and some other statistics, have been brought together in Table 5.2. We may point out that some of the standard errors of the weights are rather large.

The results show that an additional one percentage point anticipated inflation will eventually raise the market interest rate by about 0.6 per cent. This implies that adjustment takes place only partially; in other words, it indicates that the public is subject to money illusion. Along with money illusion, the individual investor may also be subject to a tax illusion if he does not realize that the compensation for inflation is taxable income. We will leave this microeconomic aspect aside here. We may point out, though, that the absence of a tax illusion will reinforce the impact of price rises on interest rates. Another result is our estimate of the natural rate of interest which is 3.5 per cent (with a standard error of 0.29). This presupposes, though, that one may indeed assume that the real rate was constant in the period under consideration. It finally appears that our extremely simple formula explains roughly 45 per cent of the interest rate variation of the sixties. It is perfectly possible that part of the unexplained residual may be accounted for by the other determinants of the interest rate indicated in section 5.3. For further analysis, Figure 5.3 splits the total interest rate variation into the part accounted for by expected inflation and the part attributed to the constant term and the residual together.

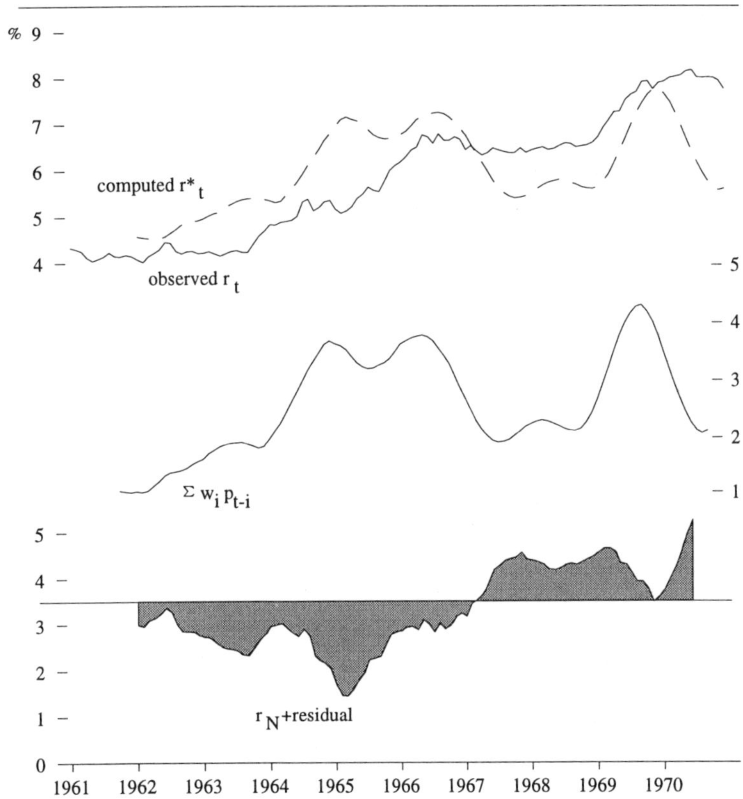

Figure 5.3: The interest equation $r_t = 3.48 + \sum_{i=0}^{11} w_i \dot{p}_{t-i}$

Figure 5.3 shows some remarkable features. In the first place, the price component in the market rate shows marked fluctuations that are not reflected in the observed interest rates. At the end of 1970, for example, the price component is substantially lower than it was in December 1969 or in early 1965. Moreover, there is a systematic pattern to the residual: up to about the middle of the sample period it is steadily negative, and after that, almost steadily positive. This indicates the presence of other determinants not considered in the present analysis.[10] As far as the latter is concerned, it may serve our purpose to confine ourselves to considering whether there could have been a trend rise of the natural interest rate. Examination of the curve for r_N + residual

[10] See for this Stevers (1963) and Bakhoven (1971, pp. 577–588). Neither author pays any attention to inflation expectations.

does suggest this, though it leaves unanswered the question to which factors such a trend rise must be attributed. To answer it, our causal approach should be supplemented by a simultaneous explantion of r_N. In any case, the third conclusion from this graphical analysis must be that there are reasons to suppose that the natural or real rate also rose in the period 1961–1970. This implies that our initial assumption of a constant real rate has indeed been too bold. This last is surprising in view of American studies on the same lines as the present essay, which do not cast doubt on the assumption of a constant natural rate of interest.[11]

5.6 Summary and Conclusion

The present chapter analyses the Gibson paradox for The Netherlands. A general review of interest and price series on the years 1901–1971 gave grounds to the assumption that there is a positive relationship between the two. Of the possible theoretical explanations for this estimation, Irving Fisher's was statistically verified by using monthly data of the sample period 1961–1970. This shows that the observed rise of the nominal rate can only partly be explained from inflation. Graphical examination of the (unexplained) residuals suggests the presence of other influences side-by-side with inflation. A trend rise of the real interest rate may be one of these influences. Both this hypothesis and the lag pattern of the impact of inflation require, however, further research.

[11] See the article by Yohe and Karnosky quoted in footnote 6 and Pyle (1972).

Appendix 5.A Some Alternative Estimates

As stated previously we have used the Almon technique with lags starting from $n = 6$ up to $n = 24$ with intervals of 3, and after that, with intervals of 6. For each experiment we have made the calculations for curves described by the polynominals of the second to the fifth degree. It became apparent in these calculations that for any given n, the degree of the curve hardly affected the results. On the other hand, variations in n do have a clear influence on the result. Unfortunately, our calculations provide no evidence concerning the statistically most acceptable value of n, though the relevant literature sometimes claims that. In keeping with the rule that the scientist needs to be objective, but the way he makes progress is through following up subjective insights, we have opted for $n = 12$. Since our results are to some extent determined by this choice, we have in Table 5.A.1 given the results of some alternative estimates on $r_N, \sum w_i$ and the coefficient of determination, R^2, for various values of n. The figures in parentheses are the standard errors for r_N.

This table demonstrates that our results, and consequently our conclusions, are indeed affected by the choice of the size of the lag. This property in particular requires further research. It should also be kept in mind when interpreting our findings.

Table 5.A.1: Some alternative estimates

n	r_N		$\sum_i w_i$	R^2
6	3.9	(0.3)	0.47	0.37
18	2.9	(0.3)	0.76	0.55
24	2.2	(0.3)	0.93	0.64
30	1.8	(0.4)	1.05	0.64
36	1.7	(0.4)	1.10	0.58
48	−0.4	(0.8)	1.59	0.52
60	0.6	(1.3)	1.41	0.27

Note: Standard errors between parentheses.

6. Anticipated Inflation and Interest Rates in an Open Economy: A Study of the Gibson Paradox for The Netherlands

6.1 THE GIBSON PARADOX

The view that inflation expectations have an impact on the level of interest rates is now widely accepted among economists and this issue would seem to be one of the newer growth industries in applied monetary economics. This does not mean that earlier writers have ignored the topic completely. Some fifty years ago, A.H. Gibson, a British banker, wrote about the positive correlation between interest rates and prices over a long period of time. Gibson prompted Keynes (1930, pp. 198–210) to name this relationship the "Gibson paradox" as it was believed to contradict the traditional monetary theory of the time.

The high and increasing rate of interest of today, together with the accelerating rate of inflation in almost all western countries, has undoubtedly stimulated the present revival of interest in the Gibson paradox. This in turn has brought about an abundance of empirical papers on the topic. Most of this research dates back to Irving Fisher's work on appreciation and interest (see Fisher (1930, pp. 399–451)). Fisher's theory is that the nominal rate of interest, r_t, is assumed to be the sum of the real or natural rate of return ρ_t and the anticipated rate of inflation π_t:

$$r_t = \rho_t + \pi_t. \tag{6.1}$$

In this equation, ρ_t should be seen as a long-run real rate of return, determined mainly by the marginal productivity of capital. It has been

Reprinted from 'Anticipated inflation and interest rates in an open economy: A study of the Gibson paradox for The Netherlands' by M.M.G. Fase and M. van Nieuwkerk, in *Econometric Research in European Central Banks*, F. Masera, A. Fazio and T. Padoa-Schioppa (eds) Rome 1975, pp. 297–321.

assumed that, from a statistical point of view, ρ_t could be treated as a constant, which implies that variations in the real rate of return are captured by the statistical error term of the regression equation. Combination of equation (6.1) with a hypothesis about the formation of the public's expectations of the rate of inflation, leads to an equation suitable to statistical verification. Fisher, and most of his followers, hypothesised π_t to be a weighted sum of observed past rates of inflation $\dot{p}_{t-i}$ *i.e.*:

$$\pi_t = \sum_{i=0}^{\infty} w_i \dot{p}_{t-i}. \tag{6.2}$$

Substitution of equation (6.1) into equation (6.2) with $\rho_t = \rho$, yields

$$r_t = \rho + \sum_{i=0}^{\infty} w_i \dot{p}_{t-i}. \tag{6.3}$$

Fisher estimated this equation and, as indicated above, his results inspired many others in their empirical work on the Gibson paradox.[1]

A major criticism of equation (6.3) is that it does not make clear whether it should be treated as a structural or as a reduced form equation. This is an important question, since only if it is a reduced form equation are we able to make the underlying economic structure explicit and to interpret the estimation results properly. Here we share Sargent's view, and presumably also that of Fisher himself, as reflected in his studies on interaction of inflation expectations and nominal rates of interest within the context of a structural model.[2]

This chapter is an attempt to analyse the apparent correlation between interest rates and inflation in The Netherlands in the period 1958–1972, illustrated with quarterly data in Figure 6.1.

To explain this correlation we develop, in section 6.2, a highly aggregative macroeconomic model in which expected inflation is the key variable. Section 6.3 sets forth how, in our view, the formation of expectations may be described and empirically estimated. To this end we show in the same section that the ARIMA model offers a proper statistical framework. In section 6.4, we use our results to describe the actual behaviour of long-term interest rates in The Netherlands. As will be demonstrated, our results offer an appropriate tool for understanding the widely divergent results obtained by other Dutch authors.[3] Their

---

[1] Extensive references to the literature may be found in *e.g.* Yohe and Karnosky (1969), Fase (1972a), Sargent (1972) Sargent (1973b) or Visco (1975).

[2] See Sargent(1972, 1973a 1973c 1973d).

[3] See Post (1973), Driehuis (1973) and Nieuwenburg and Leemreize (1974).

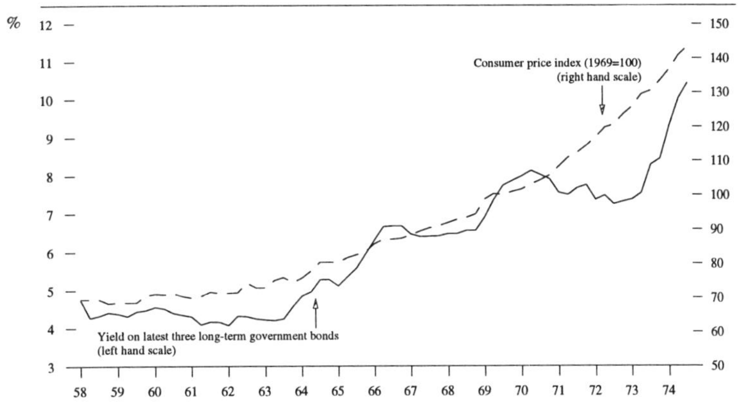

Figure 6.1: Interest rates and prices in The Netherlands, 1958–1974

studies have in common that they all take the Fisherian approach applied by one of the present authors to the Dutch case (see Fase (1972a)) as their main point of reference, focusing almost exclusively on the contribution of inflation expectations to the explanation of nominal interest rates. However, it should not be ignored that equation (6.3) may be seen as a reduced-form equation. This implies that the interpretation varies with the hypothesis on the underlying economic structure. Our conclusions are summarised in section 6.5, where we briefly indicate possible implications for monetary policy.

6.2 Inflation Expectations in a Simple Macroeconomic Framework

The main purpose of this section is to analyse the interactions between expected price changes and interest rates on the basis of a simple and highly aggregative structural model of an open economy. To begin with, we assume the aggregate demand function:

$$y_t = \alpha_0 + \alpha_1 y_{t-1} + \alpha_2(r_t - \pi_t) + \alpha'\mathbf{z}, \tag{6.4}$$

with y_t the logarithm of real national output in quarter t, r_t the nominal rate of long-term interest, π_t the expected rate of inflation and $\mathbf{z}$ a vector with exogenous variables affecting aggregate demand, to be discussed below. Similarly α is a vector with coefficients α_3 and α_4, where $\alpha_3 > 0$, and $\alpha_4 > 0$.

As to the monetary sector we assume the familiar demand for money equation:

$$m_t^D = \beta_0 + \beta_1 m_{t-1} + \beta_2 y_t + \beta_3 r_t + \beta_4 p_t + \beta_5 c_t, \qquad (6.5)$$

with m_t^D the logarithm of the demand for money, p_t the logarithm of the price level and c_t some exogenous trade cycle indicator. This functional form has been prompted by earlier work on the demand for money (see Fase and Kuné (1974b)). Furthermore we assume portfolio equilibrium, so that money demand m_t^D equals money supply m_t^S.

For an open economy there are three sources of money creation, namely the banking sector, the government sector and the foreign sector. Since, with fixed or almost fixed exchange rates, interest-rate differentials affect the money supply in an open economy, we assume the foreign component of domestic money supply to be endogenous. However, to keep the analysis simple we assume that the other sources of domestic money supply are exogenously determined.[4] With respect to foreign capital flows, we postulate, following an analysis for The Netherlands by Koning (1974), a stock-flow model summarised by

$$M_t^K = \kappa_0 + \kappa_1 \Delta(r_t - r_t^F) + \kappa_2(r_t - r_t^F), \qquad (6.6)$$

with M^K capital flows in period t and r_t^F the prevailing foreign interest rate on the bond market. The money supply identity is

$$m_t^S = m_{t-1} + \eta \Delta \underline{m} + \zeta M_t^K, \qquad (6.7)$$

with m^S the logarithm of total money supply M^S, $\underline{m}$ the logarithm of the exogenously given money supply component $\underline{M}$, while

$$\eta \equiv \frac{\underline{M}}{M_{-1}} \text{ and } \zeta \equiv \frac{1}{M_{-1}}.$$

To complete the model we introduce an equation to explain the change in prices:

$$p_t - p_{t-1} = \gamma_1 (y_t - \bar{y}_t) + \gamma' \mathbf{p}, \qquad (6.8)$$

where $\bar{y}$ is the logarithm of the exogenously determined full-employment level of real national output, and $\mathbf{p}$ the vector with variables representing autonomous influences on the rate of change in prices (see below) and γ a vector with coefficients.

[4] We assume this only for the sake of simplicity. An alternative route is offered by the work of Brunner and Meltzer and their followers see *e.g.* Brunner and Meltzer (1972) and, for the Dutch case, Korteweg (1973).

We note that equation (6.4) summarizes the real side of the economy in one equation. The monetary sector is a little more elaborated and described by equations (6.5)–(6.7) together with the equilibrium condition mentioned above, while equation (6.8) resembles a Phillips curve. Equation (6.4) posits that aggregate demand depends on the expected real rate of interest in the current period. We shall demonstrate that this assumption is crucial to our problem. The most appropriate way to introduce the real rate of interest is by incorporating it into the investment-decision process. We have assumed that this process is a trade-off between marginal rates of return on capital and the cost of investment, which equals the real rate of interest. As to the vector $\mathbf{z}$, we assume that the most important exogenous variables are government expenditure g and the foreign impulse m_w (weighted world trade) which denotes the openness of the economy. Thus we have $\alpha'\mathbf{z} = \alpha_3 m_w + \alpha_4 g$. We recall that equation (6.4) is a sort of IS-curve for an open economy. This means that, from the viewpoint of a large econometric model builder, it is a semi-reduced form equation, still containing three endogenous variables: y_t, r_t and p_t.

Equation (6.5) is a simplified version of the demand for money equation, already studied by the author. The major idea of this specification is that adjustment of actual to desired or optimal money balances needs some response time, the speed of adjustment depending on β_1. An important feature of our demand for money equation is that the nominal interest rate r_t and the cyclical indicator are explanatory variables.

Equation (6.6) combines both the stock- and the flow-model commonly used to explain long- and short-term capital movements. It has been inspired by earlier work within the Bank (see Koning (1974)). In this view capital movements arise from two different sources. The first, named the stock-effect, is the result of a reshuffling of existing portfolios because of a change in the interest-rate differential. The second, named the flow-effect, is the result of an allocation of current savings caused by a differential between the domestic and foreign bond-rate. Koning has shown that, for The Netherlands, the stock-effect predominates.

The remaining components of total money supply are predetermined, as shown by identity (6.7). This defines the logarithm of total money supply as a linear combination of the logarithm of total money supply in the previous period, the rate of change in the money supply under control of the policymaker and the endogenous capital flow. The particular structure of this identity comes from the fact that some of the variables are measured as logarithms. Assuming portfolio equilibrium, appropriate substitution leads to the interest equation

$$r_t = \frac{1}{\beta_3 - \zeta(\kappa_1 + \kappa_2)} \Big\{ (\zeta\kappa_0 - \beta_0) + (1 - \beta_1)m_{t-1} + \eta\Delta\underline{m} - \beta_2 y_t - \beta_4 p_t - \beta_5 c_t - \zeta\kappa_1 r_{t-1} - \zeta(\kappa_1 + \kappa_2) r_t^F + \zeta\kappa_1 r_{t-1}^F \Big\}. \quad (6.9)$$

We notice that equation (6.9) summarises the monetary sector. Since it still contains three endogenous variables it may be viewed as a semi-reduced form too. We believe that this highlights an interesting feature, namely, that in a purely monetary framework, interest rates can be described while ignoring inflation expectations completely.

As indicated, equation (6.8) is a version of the Phillips curve. Since we do not believe that full-employment income should necessarily be consistent with stable prices, we have added the vector $\mathbf{p}$. [5]. The most relevant components of this vector are the rate of change of import prices, $\dot{p}_m$, and autonomous influences $\dot{p}_a$, such as a change of indirect taxes, EU measures and payment of social security. Thus we have $\gamma'\mathbf{p} = \gamma_2\dot{p}_m + \gamma_3\dot{p}_a$.

The equations (6.4), (6.8) and (6.9) describe the interactions between the sectors of our simplified economy. In this model π_t is the variable of major interest.

By solving our system of equations for r_t, we are able to derive the relationship between nominal interest rates and anticipated inflation. Appropriate substitution yields

$$\begin{aligned} r_t = & \frac{1}{\beta_3 + \alpha_2(\beta_2 + \gamma_1\beta_4) - \zeta(\kappa_1 + \kappa_2)} \Big[(1 - \beta_1)m_{t-1} + \eta\Delta\underline{m} - \beta_0 \\ & - \beta_5 c_t - \beta_4 p_{t-1} + \beta_4\gamma_1\bar{y}_t - \beta_4\gamma_2\dot{p}_m - \beta_4\gamma_3\dot{p}_a \\ & + \zeta[\kappa_0 - \kappa_1 r_{t-1} - (\kappa_1 + \kappa_2) r_t^F + \kappa_1 r_{t-1}^F] \\ & - (\beta_2 + \beta_4\gamma_1)(\alpha_0 + \alpha_1 y_{t-1} + \alpha_3 m_w + \alpha_4 g) \Big] \\ & + \frac{(\beta_2 + \beta_4\gamma_1)\alpha_2}{\beta_3 + \alpha_2(\beta_2 + \gamma_1\beta_4) - \zeta(\kappa_1 + \kappa_2)} \pi_t. \end{aligned} \quad (6.10)$$

This relation shows how inflation expectations may appear in an interest equation, which, in our case, is the reduced form of a system of structural equations. So far, the expected rate of inflation, π_t, has been treated as

[5] In view of Phelps (1970) and Sargent (1973d) one may wonder if inflation expectations should be included into equation (6.8). However, it can be derived that inclusion of a term $\delta\pi_t$ will, given the purpose of our analysis, make the model unnecessarily complicated.

a parameter of the system. Now we must devise a scheme describing the formation of price expectations.

6.3 The Formation of Price Expectations and Their Measurement

On the face of it, there are two different approaches to the empirical incorporation of expected inflation rates into our model. One way is to conduct sample surveys to obtain data on the public's inflation expectations. This direct approach has gained a certain importance in assessing the buying intentions of consumers. A few authors have used such data on anticipated price changes in studying the Fisher effect (see Pyle (1972), Gibson (1972) or Carlson and Parkin (1975)). However, this source of information seems to be less reliable when the interviewee has no necessity to act in accordance with his reported expectations. Since there are virtually no data on price expectations for The Netherlands, we need not concern ourselves with this approach here. The alternative, applied in the present analysis, uses extrapolations of current and past values to assess anticipated magnitudes. Fisher's work provides an early example of how anticipated price changes may be approximated. Nerlove (1972) has pointed out that the lag structure arising from expectations formation must be estimated independently of the particular application being investigated. This means that we must avoid simultaneous testing of the expectations hypothesis and the model containing the expectations variable.

Econometric literature gives many instances of expectations-generating mechanisms, some of which are optimal predictors in the sense of minimising the mean square error. A simple and well-known example is offered by the adaptive expectations mechanism:

$$\pi_t - \pi_{t-1} = \lambda(\dot{p}_{t-1} - \pi_{t-1}), \tag{6.11}$$

with $0 < \lambda < 1$. This mechanism can be viewed as a simple process of error-learning, where people revise their expectations π_t on the basis of their most recent error $(\dot{p}_{t-1} - \pi_{t-1})$ only. For a particular type of time series, Muth (1960) has shown that behaviour according to (6.11) generates optimal forecasts for all future values.

A general framework for generating expectations is offered by Box and Jenkins in their ARIMA (p,d,q) models — *i.e.* AutoRegressive Integrated Moving Average processes of order p, d and q — which are of the form

$$\phi_p(B)(1-B)^d z_t = \theta_q(B)a_t, \tag{6.12}$$

where z_t is a variable and a_t white noise. The autoregressive operator $\phi_p(B)$ and the moving average operator $\theta_q(B)$ are polynomials of order p and q respectively; $(1 - B)^d$ is the difference operator of order d and B is the backshift operator, *i.e.* $B^n z_t = z_{t-n}$. Assuming that the two polynomials satisfy stationarity and invertibility conditions it follows that equation (6.12) describes a stationary linear process in the dth difference of the variable z_t. For more details we refer to Box and Jenkins (1970) and to our summary in Appendix 6.A.

In an interesting paper, Rose (1972) has demonstrated that ARIMA processes may be viewed as generalised error-learning models of expectations formation. The adoption of equation (6.12) means that expectations are revised taking *all* past errors into account. This approach has an intuitive appeal and, moreover, encompasses a large class of specific expectations-generating schemes often used in economic and econometric analysis.

We now turn to the empirical estimation of the anticipation parameter π_t. As indicated in Appendix 6.A, equation (6.12) hypothesises that anticipated inflation is linearly dependent on past rates of inflation and on forecasting-errors computed from an appropriate ARIMA process. Our first objective is to choose this appropriate model empirically by identifying the dimensions (p,d,q). This is accomplished by computing sample autocorrelations of the relevant series $\dot{p}_t$, *i.e.* percentage change in consumer prices. Since we require the process to be stationary in the series $\dot{p}_t$, it may be necessary to difference the series if the autocorrelations do not tail off, until the series $(1 - B)^d \dot{p}_t$ may be assumed to be stationary. The sample autocorrelations of the series $(1 - B)^d \dot{p}_t$ are then used to identify the specific ARIMA process (see Box and Jenkins (1970, p. 176, Table 6)).

We have estimated the most appropriate ARIMA model, with both monthly and quarterly data on percentage changes in consumer prices between one period and the corresponding period in the previous year. Estimates of ϕ and θ which minimise the sum of squared residuals $\sum_{t=1}^{n} a_t^2$, were obtained by an iterative procedure, as described by Box and Jenkins. Moreover, we made some diagnostic checks to test the adequacy of the fitted model, such as testing the residuals for randomness and testing the model for overparameterisation.

Results for Monthly Figures

The ARIMA process applied to monthly observations for 1958–1972 for the identified p,d,q, yields a modified MA(1) process in $\dot{p}_t - \dot{p}_{t-1}$ of the form

$$(1-B)\dot{p}_t = \underset{(0.07)}{(1-0.19B)}\underset{(0.06)}{(1-0.61B^{12})}a_t \tag{6.13}$$

$$\hat{\sigma}_a = 1.17.$$

Estimated standard errors are given in parentheses, $\hat{\sigma}_a$ is the estimated standard deviation of the error term. We note that this representation of the model slightly differs from formulation (6.12) by the factor $(1 - 0.61B^{12})$.[6] In error-learning form, this model implies that three errors are necessary to revise inflation expectations, namely a monthly error e_t, a yearly error e_{t-11} and the error e_{t-12} associated with the two preceding errors. Therefore we rewrite (6.13) as

$$\pi_t(1) - \pi_{t-1}(1) = 0.81e_t - 0.61e_{t-11} + 0.11e_{t-12}. \tag{6.14}$$

This result shows that if actual inflation in the last month exceeds expected inflation in that month, the expectation is revised with the error e_t but is less than proportional. On the other hand, the error e_{t-11} may be caused by the way we measured the rate of inflation, that is by comparing the price-index for a certain month in a given year with that of the same month in the preceding year. Therefore, in the reference period, a relatively high price level in a certain month of year $(t-1)$ was followed by a relatively low price level in the corresponding month of year t.

Another interesting point is that the residuals of equation (6.13) are substantially larger in the first half of the period than in the second half. This may be due to the higher rate of inflation in the latter period. For this reason we have re-estimated the model for two sub-periods. The results are:

1958–1965

$$(1-B)\dot{p}_t = \underset{(0.10)}{(1-0.25B)}\underset{(0.08)}{(1-0.63B^{12})}a_t \qquad \hat{\sigma}_a = 1.50 \tag{6.15}$$

or, in error-learning form:

$$\pi_t(1) - \pi_{t-1}(1) = 0.75e_t - 0.63e_{t-11} + 0.16e_{t-12} \tag{6.16}$$

1966–1972

$$(1-B)\dot{p}_t = \underset{(0.11)}{(1+0.14B)}\underset{(0.09)}{(1-0.76B^{12})}a_t \qquad \hat{\sigma}_a = 0.48 \tag{6.17}$$

6 This point is elaborated somewhat in Appendix 6.A.

Table 6.1: Estimation results for quarterly models

Period	$\hat{\theta}_1$	$\hat{\Theta}$	$\hat{\sigma}_a$
1958–1972	−0.06	0.65	1.54
	(0.13)	(0.10)	
1958–1965	−0.02	0.72	1.83
	(0.19)	(0.14)	
1966–1972	−0.22	0.97	0.90
	(0.21)	(0.14)	

or, in error-learning form:

$$\pi_t(1) - \pi_{t-1}(1) = 1.14e_t - 0.76e_{t-11} - 0.11e_{t-12}. \tag{6.18}$$

Note that in (6.17) the sign of θ_1 has changed. The meaning of this is understandable if the error-learning forms of the estimated equations are considered. In (6.14) and (6.16), the revision of inflation expectations is less than proportional to last month's error; in (6.18) the revision is more than proportional. So, for the period 1966–1972, our model predicts an acceleration of anticipated inflation, which is in accordance with actual price behaviour.

Results for quarterly figures

The general form of our quarterly model is chosen analogous to the model for monthly observations.[7] It is

$$(1 - B)\dot{p}_t = (1 - \theta_1 B)(1 - \Theta_4 B^4)a_t. \tag{6.19}$$

Fitting this model to quarterly observations for the whole sample period and two sub-periods, we obtain estimates for the parameters θ_1, Θ_4 and σ_a, which are reported in Table 6.1. Estimated standard errors are given in parentheses.

We note that the standard error of $\hat{\theta}_1$ is invariably rather large. This may be due to the fact that the number of observations decreased considerably, and is rather small by the standards suggested by Box and Jenkins.

The error-learning form of the model for the whole period may be written as:

$$\pi_t(1) - \pi_{t-1}(1) = 1.06e_t - 0.65e_{t-3} - 0.04e_{t-4}.$$

[7] We have also estimated the additive version. The results are shown in Appendix 6.B.

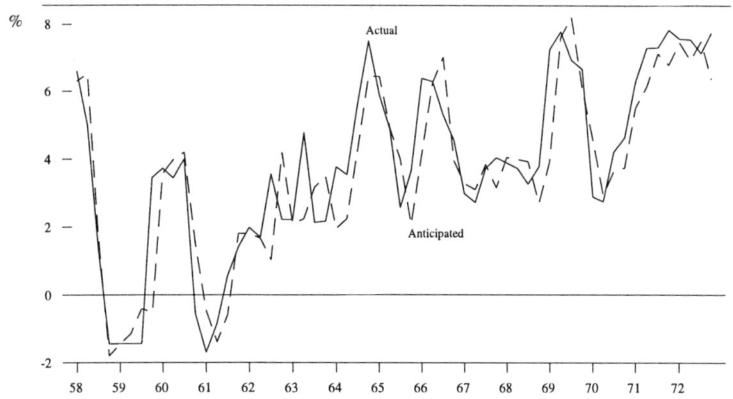

Figure 6.2: Actual and anticipated rates of inflation, 1958–1972

The expected rate of inflation computed with this model is plotted in Figure 6.2, together with the actual rate of inflation. As the model already suggests, the expected rate of inflation is — by approximation — nothing but the actual rate of inflation lagged one quarter.

6.4 Response of Interest Rates to Expected Rates of Inflation

In this chapter, we are primarily interested in the economic hypothesis that seeks to explain the observed relationship between interest rates and inflation in The Netherlands, rather than in estimating this relationship econometrically. Therefore, to use our structural model empirically we took parameter values from existing literature and combined them with estimates based on our own judgement. For this purpose we were fortunate enough to be able to draw upon the large quantity of serious econometric work available for The Netherlands. For the parameter π_t — the expected rate of inflation — we have used the estimation results for quarterly figures reported in the preceding section. The parameter values for the equations (6.4), (6.5), (6.6) and (6.8), as well as the parameter values for the definitional equation (6.7) and the formation of expectations, are displayed in Table 6.2.

Appropriate interpretation of the model up on which the equation for capital flows is based, shows that the parameters κ vary with the size of the portfolio (see Koning (1974)). For the sake of simplicity, however, we have taken fixed parameter values, which are fairly close to reality in

Table 6.2: Parameter values of the model

Aggregate demand					
α_0=6.30	α_1=0.30	α_2=−0.03	α_3=0.40	α_4=0.10	
Money demand					
β_0=−1.0	β_1=0.60	β_2=0.40	β_3=−0.02	β_4=0.40	β_5=0.04
Capital flows					
κ_0=300	κ_1=1000	κ_2=20			
Phillips curve					
γ_1=0.10	γ_2=0.40	γ_3=0			
Money supply					
η =0.77	ζ =variable				
Expectations					
θ_1=−0.06	Θ_4=0.65				

the latter part of the period only. Similarly, the parameters η and ζ of the money supply identity vary with the quarter considered. However, to facilitate the computations, we have fixed $\eta = 0.77$; the value of ζ declines monotonically over time from 752×10^{-7} in 1957 to 176×10^{-7} in 1973. This means that the reduced-form coefficients of our model also vary over time.

We recall that $\pi_t \equiv \pi_{t-1}(1) \equiv \hat{\dot{p}}_t$ where

$$\hat{\dot{p}}_t = \dot{p}_{t-1} + 0.06e_{t-1} - 0.65e_{t-4} - 0.04e_{t-5},$$

with e_{t-j} the residual at $t - j$ for $j = 1$, 4 and 5.

Plugging the parameter values of Table 6.2 into our reduced-form interest equation (6.10) together with our expectations estimates yields for 1972-IV (with $\zeta = 212 \times 10^{-7}$):

$$\begin{aligned} r_t = {} & 32.21 - 7.30m_{t-1} - 14.04\Delta\underline{m} + 0.73c_t + 7.29p_{t-1} - 0.73\bar{y}_t \\ & + 2.92\dot{p}_m + 2.41y_{t-1} + 3.21m_w + 0.809 + 0.24\pi_t + 0.39r_{t-1} \\ & + 0.39r_t^F - 0.39r_{t-1}^F. \end{aligned} \tag{6.20}$$

Similarly, we obtained for M_t^K, p_t, y_t and m_t

$$\begin{aligned} M_t^K = {} & 33\,154.20 - 7\,466.00m_{t-1} - 14\,320.80\Delta\underline{m} + 744.60c_t \\ & + 7\,435.80p_{t-1} - 744.60\bar{y}_t + 2\,978.40\dot{p}_m + 2\,458.20y_{t-1} \\ & + 3\,274.20m_w + 816.00g + 244.80\pi_t - 602.20r_{t-1} - 622.20r_t^F \\ & + 602.20r_{t-1}^F \end{aligned} \tag{6.21}$$

$$\begin{aligned} p_t =& 0.53 + 0.02m_{t-1} + 0.04\Delta\underline{m} + 0.98p_{t-1} - 0.10\bar{y}_t + 0.39\dot{p}_m \\ & + 0.02y_{t-1} + 0.03m_w + 0.01g \end{aligned} \quad (6.22)$$

$$\begin{aligned} y_t =& 5.33 + 0.22m_{t-1} + 0.42\Delta\underline{m} - 0.02c_t - 0.22p_{t-1} + 0.22\bar{y}_t \\ & - 0.09\dot{p}_m + 0.23y_{t-1} + 0.30m_w + 0.08g + 0.02\pi_t - 0.01r_{t-1} \\ & - 0.01r_t^F + 0.01r_{t-1}^F \end{aligned} \quad (6.23)$$

$$\begin{aligned} m_t =& 0.70 + 0.84m_{t-1} + 0.74\Delta\underline{m} + 0.02c_t + 0.16p_{t-1} - 0.02\bar{y}_t \\ & + 0.06\dot{p}_m + 0.05y_{t-1} + 0.07m_w + 0.02g + 0.01\pi_t - 0.01r_{t-1} \\ & - 0.01r_t^F + 0.01r_{t-1}^F. \end{aligned} \quad (6.24)$$

Equation (6.20) shows that inflation expectations are only partially translated into higher interest rates. However, we notice that the lagged consumer price p_{t-1} and changes in import prices $\dot{p}_m$ have also a direct impact on interest rates. More important is that our reduced form shows that the domestic interest rate also depends on movements in the foreign bond rate. Our structural equations show that inflation expectations are transmitted through the system via the real sector represented by equation (6.4). This means that the parameter α_2 is of critical importance in evaluating the response of interest rates to inflation expectations. Unfortunately, empirical evidence on α_2 is hardly available for The Netherlands. Therefore, we have done a sensitivity analysis of the impact multiplier of π_t with respect to α_2. Some of the numerical results are reported in Table 6.3.

Table 6.3: Impact multiplier of π_t for different values of α_2

α_2	−0.02	−0.03	−0.04	−0.05	−0.06	−0.07	−0.08	−0.09	−0.10
impact multiplier π_t	0.17	0.24	0.30	0.35	0.39	0.43	0.46	0.49	0.51

Of course, variation of α_2 also affects other impact multipliers but these are of minor importance for our case (see Appendix 6.C.1). The results of Table 6.3 confirm our conjecture about the importance of α_2. Since no reliable evidence on α_2 could be produced we have selected $\alpha_2 = -0.03$. In this case, the simulated long-term interest rates, within and outside the sample period 1958–1972, fitted rather well with the actual long-term interest rate, indicated by the rather low value of the inequality coefficient of 0.077.[8] This is also illustrated in Figure 6.3 which

[8] The inequality coefficient is defined by $\left(\frac{\sum_t (A_t - F_t)^2}{\sum_t A_t^2}\right)$ with A_t the actual and F_t the simulated value of the variable considered. With respect to the variables p_t, y_t, m_t and M_t^K we found respectively: 0.022, 0.030, 0.002, 1.681.

indicates that the reduced form of r_t underestimates actual interest-rate behaviour slightly. Moreover, also the reduced-form equations for p_t and y_t show a good fit to actual data in the sample period. As for the reduced-form equation of M_t^K and m_t the fit improves with time. This is due to the fact that, in order to keep the model as simple as possible, we ignored the relationship between the κ and the size of the portfolio.

From equation (6.10) it follows that the impact multiplier of π_t equals

$$\frac{\alpha_2(\beta_2 + \gamma_1\beta_4)}{\beta_3 + \alpha_2(\beta_2 + \gamma_1\beta_4) - \zeta(\kappa_1 + \kappa_2)}.$$

It is interesting to observe that the importance of α_2 disappears if we restrict ourselves to a closed economy with a zero interest elasticity of the demand for money, *i.e.* $\kappa_1 = \kappa_2 = 0$ and $\beta_3 = 0$. In this case, which Fisher had in mind, the impact multiplier of π_t equals 1. However, in the present case the value of $\beta_3 - \zeta(\kappa_1 + \kappa_2)$ becomes crucial too. This conclusion holds only for the short-run or impact multiplier. However, Visco (1975) has pointed out that the results might be different if, for example, real money balances are incorporated into the aggregate demand equation.

Our analysis enables us to solve the joint hypothesis problem by breaking down the overall effect of price changes into the impact of π_t on r_t and the impact of consumer price changes in the past on π_t. The relationship can be derived from equation (6.19) by rewriting it to yield

$$\pi_t = (1 - \theta_1 B - \Theta_4 B^4 + \theta_1\Theta_4 B^5)^{-1}(1 - \theta_1 - \Theta_4 B^3 + \theta_1\Theta_4 B^4)\dot{p}_{t-1}.$$

Unfortunately, this expression does not have a finite number of terms, which renders simplification elaborate. However, it is easily established that the mean lag is

$$\frac{\Theta_4 - \theta_1\Theta_4 + \theta_1}{(1 - \theta_1)(1 - \Theta_4)},$$

which is 2.0 quarters for the relevant parameters of Table 6.2.[9] If we look at the two sub-periods reported in Table 6.1, we obtain mean lags of 2.5 quarters for 1958–1965 and of 26 quarters in 1966–1972. This latter result cannot be taken seriously since, as indicated before, the underlying estimates are rather unreliable.

[9] The mean lag has been obtained using the well-known notion of the lag-generating function. See, for example, Griliches (1967, p. 19).

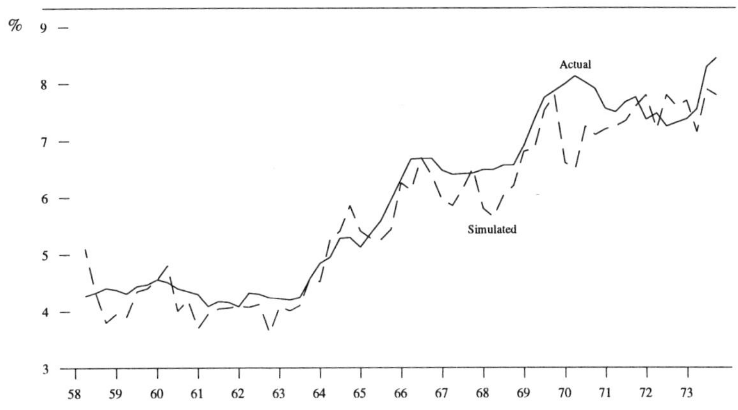

Figure 6.3: Actual and simulated rates of interest for The Netherlands, 1958–1973

6.5 Conclusions and Policy Implications

In their stimulating paper on interest rates and price level changes, which is largely responsible for the current Fisherian renaissance, Yohe and Karnosky (1969) concluded:

'Most significant is the finding that price level changes, rather than real rates, account for nearly all the variation in nominal interest rates since 1961. Furthermore, the addition of variables to the regressions to account explicitly for the real rate components of nominal rates does not appreciably alter these findings.'

The results of the present study seem to modify this finding largely, in our view, because of the way in which the problem is stated. In contrast to the unicausal approach implied by Fisher's theory, we achieved our results by starting from a simple structural model of the economy, allowing for interaction between nominal and real forces and foreign influences. Our main finding is that changes in nominal interest rates in The Netherlands are accounted for by several factors to which the expected rate of inflation and the foreign bond rate belong. This reduces the impact multiplier of expected inflation considerably.

A second result of our investigation is to separate the twin hypothesis of how inflation expectations are formed from past prices and how these expectations affect nominal interest rates. As to the first hypothesis, we found a fairly short lag. As to the second one, we found an impact multiplier of 0.24, which, however, increases with the interest rate elasticity of real expenditure. Since other studies failed to identify the two hypotheses, it is difficult to compare our results with findings obtained by anyone else.

The finding that nominal interest rate movements are not dominated exclusively by price level changes, has an important implication for monetary policy. Disregarding controversy over the appropriate indicator for monetary policy, it is obvious that any preference for interest rates — or rather interest-rate changes as Kessler (1974) has emphasised — requires some adjustment for expected inflation. Our results indicate that the short-run elasticity of expectations is below 1. This seems to confirm Kessler's conjecture.

Appendix 6.A Brief Introduction to ARIMA Processes

AutoRegressive Integrated Moving Average, or ARIMA, models are a class of linear stochastic models to describe stationary and non-stationary time series. Like others (see, for example, Nelson (1972)) we have employed ARIMA models to generate optimal forecasts. What follows is a brief introduction to the relevant concepts; for details we refer to Box and Jenkins (1970) upon which we rely heavily.

Basically a discrete time series (z_t) may be represented as an autoregressive or as a moving average process. An autoregressive or AR model is defined by

$$z_t = a_t + \sum_{j=1}^{\infty} \pi_j z_{t-j}, \tag{6.A.1}$$

with z_t the deviation of the process from its origin or from its mean if it is stationary, and a_t a random shock with zero mean and constant variance σ_a^2. Relationship (6.A.1) may economically be written as

$$\pi(B) z_t = a_t, \tag{6.A.1$'$}$$

where $\pi(B) = 1 - \pi_1 B - \pi_2 B^2 - \pi_3 B^3 - \ldots$ and B is a lag operator, *i.e.* $B^i z_t = z_{t-i}$. Alternatively, the moving average or MA model is defined by

$$z_t = a_t + \sum_{j=1}^{\infty} \Psi_j \, a_{t-j},$$

which, in general, may be written as

$$z_t = \Psi(B) a_t, \tag{6.A.2}$$

where $\Psi(B) = 1 + \Psi_1 B + \Psi_2 B^2 + \Psi_3 B^3 + \ldots$. From (6.A.1$'$) and (6.A.2) it follows that

$$\Psi(B)\pi(B) z_t = \Psi(B) a_t = z_t.$$

Hence

$$\Psi(B)\pi(B) = 1$$

or

$$\Psi(B) = \pi^{-1}(B). \tag{6.A.3}$$

If (6.A.2) represents a stationary process, the sequence Ψ_1, Ψ_2, Ψ_3, ... must be either finite or infinite and convergent. On the other hand, process (6.A.1′) is always stationary because of (6.A.3). Process (6.A.1′) is called invertible if the π weights form a convergent series.

In practice, we are mainly interested in AR an MA models with a finite number of parameters. A useful special case of (6.A.1′) in which only the first p parameters π_j are non-zero, is

$$\phi_p(B)z_t = a_t, \tag{6.A.4}$$

where

$$\phi_p(B) = 1 - \phi_1 B - \phi_2 B^2 - \ldots - \phi_p B^p.$$

The process (6.A.4) is called an AR(p) process.

Similarly, a moving average process MA(q), when only the first q weights Ψ_j are non-zero, is

$$z_t = \theta_q(B)a_t \tag{6.A.5}$$

where

$$\theta_q(B) = 1 + \theta_1 B + \theta_2 B^2 + \ldots + \theta_q B^q.$$

Combining processes (6.A.4) and (6.A.5) we obtain the mixed autoregressive-moving average of ARMA (p,q) process

$$\phi_p(B)z_t = \theta_q(B)a_t, \tag{6.A.6}$$

where $\phi_p(B)$ and $\theta_q(B)$ are again polynomials of degree p and q in B. We note that $\phi_p^{-1}(B)\theta_q(B) = \Psi(B)$ and $\theta^{-1}(B)\phi_p(B) = \pi(B)$.

In order to satisfy invertibility and stationarity conditions, the roots of $\phi_p(B)$ and $\theta_q(B)$ must lie outside the unit circle in the complex plane. From these conditions restrictions on the ϕ and θ are easily established. For instance, stationarity for a AR(1) process requires $|\phi_1| < 1$; invertibility for a MA(1) process requires $|\theta_1| <1$.

Stationarity is sometimes obtained by differencing a process z_t d times. These models are called AutoRegressive Integrated Moving Average processes of order p, d, q, or simply ARIMA (p,d,q) processes, written as

$$\phi_p(B)(1 - B)^d z_t = \theta_q(B)a_t, \tag{6.A.7}$$

with $(1 - B)^d$ the dth difference operator, such that *e.g.* $(1 - B)z_t = z_t - z_{t-1}$.

For some representations of time series, it appears useful to supplement ARIMA processes with a special operator, similar to the difference operator $(1 - B)$, to capture special movements like seasonality or variability connected with the measurement of the series. The resulting modified ARIMA(p, d, q) process is written as

$$\phi_p(B)(1 - B)^d z_t = \theta_q(B)(1 - \Theta_A B^A)a_t, \tag{6.A.8}$$

with $(1 - \Theta_A B^A)$ a special operator to capture periodic components. A particular example is $A = 12$ to capture the annual components in monthly data, or $A = 4$ to capture them in quarterly data. Note that (6.A.8) is a special representation of a more general model discussed in Box and Jenkins (1970, Ch. 9).

ARIMA processes may be viewed as generalised error-learning models of expectations formation (see Box and Jenkins (1970) and Rose (1972)).

Let $\hat{z}_t(\ell)$ be a forecast of z_t at lead time ℓ. Suppose the best forecast is

$$\hat{z}_t(\ell) = \Psi^*_\ell a_t + \Psi^*_{\ell+1} a_{t-1} + \Psi^*_{\ell+2} a_{t-2} + \ldots \qquad (6.A.9)$$

while the actual value is

$$z_{t+\ell} = \Psi(B) a_{t+\ell}.$$

Then the mean square error of the forecast is minimised by setting $\Psi^*_{\ell+j} = \Psi_{\ell+j}$. Hence $z_{t+\ell}$ may be written

$$\begin{aligned} z_{t+\ell} &= \Psi(B) a_{t+\ell} \\ &= (a_{t+\ell} + \Psi_1 a_{t+\ell-1} + \ldots + \Psi_{\ell-1} a_{t+1}) \\ &\quad + (\Psi_\ell a_t + \Psi_{\ell+1} a_{t-1} + \ldots) \\ &= e_t(\ell) + \hat{z}_t(\ell), \end{aligned}$$

with $e_t(\ell)$ the error of the forecast $\hat{z}_t(\ell)$ at lead time ℓ. We note that for $\ell = 1$, we obtain

$$e_t(1) = z_{t+1} - \hat{z}_t(1) = a_{t+1}.$$

Hence, for minimum mean square error forecasts, the random disturbance turns out to be the one-step-ahead forecast error. This result enables us to establish an error-learning interpretation. Because of $a_t = e_{t-1}(1) \equiv e_t$ and (6.A.9) we can easily derive

$$\begin{aligned} \hat{z}_t(\ell) &= \sum_{j=\ell}^{\infty} \Psi_j e_{t+\ell-j} \\ &= \sum_{j=\ell}^{\infty} \Psi_j (z_{t+\ell-j} - z_{t+\ell-j-1}(1)). \end{aligned} \qquad (6.A.10)$$

Following Rose, equation (6.A.10) can be written as

$$\hat{z}_t(\ell) - \hat{z}_{t-1}(\ell) = \Psi_\ell e_t + \sum_{j=0}^{\infty} (\Psi_{\ell+j} - \Psi_{\ell+j-1}) e_{t-j-1}$$

or

$$\hat{z}_t(\ell) - \hat{z}_{t-1}(\ell) = \Psi_\ell\big(z_t - \hat{z}_{t-1}(1)\big) + \sum_{j=0}^{\infty}(\Psi_{\ell+j} - \Psi_{\ell+j-1}) \times \big(z_{t-j-1} - \hat{z}_{t-j-2}(1)\big).$$

We note that for $\Psi_1 = \Psi_2 = \Psi_3 = \ldots \Psi$ we obtain Cagan's well known adaptive expectations or error-learning mechanism:

$$\hat{z}_t(1) - \hat{z}_{t-1}(1) = \Psi(z_t - \hat{z}_{t-1}(1))$$

which is in fact the ARIMA (0, 1, 1) model with $\Psi = 1-\theta$. However, the adaptive expectations model is more restrictive than the ARIMA$(0,1,1)$ process because the first model requires $0 < \theta < 1$ and the second $|\theta| < 1$.

Appendix 6.B Alternative Estimates: Additive Version of the Estimated Models

In the main text we presented and used the estimation results for a multiplicatively modified ARIMA process. In order to test the adequacy of the fitted model we have also estimated an additive version of the process, the results of which are summarised in this Appendix. The general form of the model for monthly and quarterly figures, respectively, is

$$(1 - B)\dot{p}_t = (1 - \theta_1 B - \theta_{12} B^{12})a_t$$

and

$$(1 - B)\dot{p}_t = (1 - \theta_1 B - \theta_4 B^4)a_t.$$

The estimation results are presented in Table 6.B.1.

Table 6.B.1: Estimation results for monthly and quarterly models

	Monthly models			Quarterly models		
Period	$\hat{\theta}_1$	$\hat{\theta}_{12}$	$\hat{\sigma}_a$	$\hat{\theta}_1$	$\hat{\theta}_4$	$\hat{\sigma}_a$
1958–1972	0.08	0.60	1.18	−0.01	0.64	1.54
	(0.06)	(0.06)		(0.10)	(0.11)	
1958–1965	0.12	0.62	1.53	0.01	0.72	1.83
	(0.08)	(0.08)		(0.14)	(0.14)	
1966–1972	−0.09	0.75	0.48	0.00	1.00	0.92
	(0.08)	(0.09)		(0.12)	(0.13)	

Table 6.B.2: Reduced-form interest equation for alternative values of α_2 (with $\zeta = 212 \times 10^{-7}$)

α_2	Const.	m_{t-1}	$\Delta \underline{m}$	c_t	p_{t-1}	$\bar{y}_t$	$\dot{p}_m$	$\bar{y}_{t-1}$	m_w	g	π_t	r_{t-1}	r_t^F	r_{t-1}^F
−0.10	20.62	−4.67	−8.99	0.47	4.67	−0.47	1.87	1.54	2.06	0.51	0.51	0.25	0.25	−0.25
−0.09	21.74	−4.92	−9.48	0.49	4.92	−0.49	1.97	1.63	2.17	0.54	0.49	0.26	0.27	−0.26
−0.08	22.98	−5.21	−10.02	0.52	5.21	−0.52	2.08	1.72	2.29	0.57	0.46	0.28	0.28	−0.28
−0.07	24.38	−5.52	−10.63	0.55	5.52	−0.55	2.21	1.82	2.43	0.61	0.43	0.29	0.30	−0.29
−0.06	25.96	−5.88	−11.32	0.59	5.88	−0.59	2.35	1.94	2.59	0.65	0.39	0.31	0.32	−0.31
−0.05	27.75	−6.29	−12.10	0.63	6.29	−0.63	2.51	2.07	2.77	0.69	0.35	0.33	0.34	−0.33
−0.04	29.81	−6.75	−13.00	0.68	6.75	−0.68	2.70	2.23	2.97	0.74	0.30	0.36	0.37	−0.36
−0.03	32.21	−7.30	−14.04	0.73	7.29	−0.73	2.92	2.41	3.21	0.80	0.24	0.39	0.39	−0.39
−0.02	35.02	−7.93	−15.27	0.79	7.93	−0.79	3.17	2.62	3.49	0.87	0.17	0.42	0.43	−0.42

Appendix 6.C List of Symbols

r	long-term rate of interest as a percentage (domestic bond rate)
r^F	long-term foreign interest rate as a percentage (yield on long-term US government bonds)
ρ	real or natural rate of return
p	logarithm of consumer price index
$\dot{p}$	percentage change in consumer price index with respect to corresponding period in the previous year
π	expected rate of inflation, measured in the same way as $\dot{p}$
p_m	logarithm of import price-index
$\dot{p}_m$	percentage change in import price-index
p_a	logarithm of autonomous price-index
$\dot{p}_a$	percentage change in autonomous price-index
M^K	capital flows (including leads and lags)
M	total money stock, broadly defined
m	logarithm of money stock
$\underline{M}$	exogenous component of M
$\underline{m}$	logarithm of $\underline{M}$
y	logarithm of real national output
$\bar{y}$	logarithm of full employment level of real national output
g	logarithm of autonomous expenditure (government expenditure, investment of government enterprises and construction of dwellings)
m_w	logarithm of weighted world trade
c	trade cycle indicator (logarithm of the male labour reserve expressed as a percentage of the male labour force excluding self-employed)

7. The Fisher Hypothesis and Exchange Rates in EMU

7.1 Introduction

Many empirical studies on the Fisher hypothesis have shown that interest rates adjust at some delay and only partially to the anticipated rate of inflation. This chapter considers the extent to which this delayed and partial adjustment is due to the openness of an economy, to international influences and to the prevailing exchange rate system. It also considers the effect on these findings of ignoring the determinants of real interest rates. To study these two topics, an equation is estimated for the long-term or capital-market interest rates in the core group of EMU countries (The Netherlands, Belgium, France and Germany) using quarterly data for the period 1973–1994. This was repeated for the sub-periods 1973–1979 and 1979–1991, whereby the latter ends before the sample period as a whole so that the predictive power of the estimated interest rate equation can be examined. The countries studied are in the leading group of EMU but differ with regard to their size and degree of openness. The two sub-periods roughly coincide with the two exchange rate systems used in Europe following the collapse of Bretton Woods. The consideration of the entire period and the two sub-periods is interesting for a number of reasons. According to the theory of nearly rational behaviour — which in essence postulates that newly available market information is not immediately discounted in prices — it might be expected that the influence of inflation on interest rates in the first sub-period would be less rapid and complete than in the second sub-period, when the exchange rates of the countries in question were more or less linked together by means of the exchange rate mechanism of the EMS. Furthermore, any differences that arise in the interest rate equation between the two periods may be indicative of changes in economic structure or policy.

Translation of 'De Fisher-hypothese en wisselkoersen in de kopgroep van de EMU' by M.M.G. Fase and L.A. van Geijlswijk, *Maandschrift Economie*, **59**(6) (December 1995), 482–493,

The interest rate equation for the entire period and the two sub-periods also provides an indication of the influence of the determinants of real interest rates on nominal interest rates.

7.2 The Fisher Hypothesis

The parallelism between inflation and bond yields observed for more than a century in the UK, was named by Keynes the "Gibson paradox" after the London banker and publicist who studied it in the 1920s. Keynes noted that this paradox ' ... is one of the most completely established empirical facts within the whole field of quantitative economics, though theoretical economists have mostly ignored it'.[1] The Fisher hypothesis is the best known explanation of this paradox. It states that changes in the anticipated rate of inflation lead to equally large changes in the nominal interest rate, because investors seek compensation for the loss of purchasing power that would have occurred without the change in the interest rate during the term of a loan. There is consequently an *ex ante* constant real interest rate. The Fisher hypothesis ranks as the most influential explanation of the parallel movement of nominal interest rates and inflation.[2]

The Fisher hypothesis that the real interest rate is constant *ex ante* is often misinterpreted as an assumption that the *ex post* real interest rate is also constant. This is only the case, however, if expectations are perfect. Fisher recognized, though, that expectations were not perfect and came to the conclusion that 'It requires the cumulative effect of a long rise, or of a marked rise in prices, to produce a definite advance in the interest rate'.[3] Since inflation expectations adjust to actual inflation at a delay, inflation only has a discernible effect on the nominal interest rate when both show a trend.

In the short-term, therefore, a change in inflation has an impact only on the real interest rate. If the higher rate of inflation persists, however, inflation expectations will be affected and consequently, so will the nominal interest rate. It therefore takes some time before the real interest rate returns to equilibrium. This new equilibrium need not necessarily be the same as the old one, since the real interest rate is also influenced by such determinants as the national debt ratio and the

---

[1] Keynes (1930, p. 198).

[2] The hypothesis was worked out around 1900 by Wicksell, while Owen and Visser referred to the 19th century writer on economics, Thornton, in this context. See Fase (1992) and Visser (1980, pp. 151–153) and Shiller and Siegel (1977). See also, Owen (1993). Both Owen and Visser refer to Thornton (1802).

[3] Fisher (1930, p. 416). See also Mishkin (1992).

profitability of capital.[4] In the longer term, therefore, the real interest rate is not constant.

The negative short-term relationship between the real interest rate and inflation was particularly apparent in the period from the end of World War II to the beginning of the 1970s. This apparent reputation of the Fisher hypothesis prompted several authors to reject the hypothesis. In 1983, for example, Carmichael and Stebbing (1983) launched what they called the 'Inverse Fisher Hypothesis'. This hypothesis presupposes a long-run inversely proportionate relationship between the real interest rate and inflation, so that the nominal interest rate is also constant in the long-run.

7.3 Exchange Rates and the Relationship Between Long-term Interest Rates and Inflation

So far, we have considered only the direct influence of domestic inflation expectations on interest rates. If the Fisher hypothesis is considered in an open economy, however, interest rates are also influenced by the effect that inflation has on anticipated exchange rates. The theoretical background to this lies in the theory of covered interest parity. According to this exchange rate theory, investors are not risk neutral, and expected returns on investments in differing currencies may diverge so as to create risk premiums. As a result, a difference may arise between the forward exchange rate and the expected rate. It is then interesting to know what influence the exchange rate system has on the transmission of inflation to interest rates via the exchange rate expectation, and what consequences this has for the validity of the Fisher hypothesis in an open economy.

From a theoretical point of view, the exchange rate system has an influence on the relationship between inflation and interest rates, especially in the shorter term. This influence is felt both through the market and through the policy of the monetary authorities, whereby the former is particularly important for long-term interest rates. Short-term interest rates, by contrast, are influenced chiefly by the monetary authorities and are therefore determined mainly by their policies. The exchange rate system influences the market forces mainly through the creation of expectations in the various exchange rate systems.

A well-known theory in this respect is that of nearly rational behaviour.[5] According to this theory, a system of flexible exchange rates is

[4] For a consideration of the determinants of the real interest rate, see, inter alia, Howe and Pigott (1991).

[5] Cf., for example, Grauwe (1989).

characterized not only by the market participants' uncertainty about future macroeconomic and monetary policies, but also by the effect that those policies will have on exchange rates. As a result, exchange rates are determined by nearly rational behaviour, whereby expectations of future exchange rates are based on historical trends, in so far as the rates remain within a given margin. As a result, new information is not immediately discounted in the exchange rate, which may consequently diverge from its real equilibrium value for some time before the market participants react. The assumed partial effect of the fundamental determinants of exchange rate expectations on the market participants' behaviour, means that an expected change in exchange rates leads to only a partial change in the forward rate, and therefore in the forward premium. Changes in the forward premium, according to the theory of covered interest parity, have an immediate influence on the interest rate differential. A partial change in the forward premium, according to this theory, would immediately lead to a partial adjustment in interest rates when there is a change in the fundamental determinants of the exchange rate. As a result, there is a negative relationship between expected exchange rate movements and the risk premium, as demonstrated earlier by Fama (1984). The volatility of the risk premium is thus proportionate to that of the exchange rate expectations while the forward premium is relatively stable.

Sufficient empirical data have been produced to corroborate the relative inflexibility of forward premiums in flexible exchange rate systems. Between 1978 and 1986, for example, forward premiums for EMS exchange rates fluctuated more than, for instance, the DM/dollar and the yen/dollar exchange rates.[6] It can be inferred from this that in a system of more or less fixed exchange rates, forward premiums are a better reflection of expected exchange rate movements. This also means that exchange rate expectations are better expressed in the interest rate differential.

It follows from the above, that the relative certainty regarding policy and its effects in a system of fixed or nearly fixed, exchange rates, influences the market effect of inflation on interest rates. As a result, market participants can form their expectations with more certainty and, according to the theory of covered interest parity, fluctuations in forward premiums correspond more closely to exchange rate expectations. Furthermore, each change in forward premiums is expressed in interest rates, since the monetary authority adjusts short-term interest rates to achieve its exchange rate targets. A system of fixed, or nearly fixed exchange rates might thus lead to a faster adjustment of, and a higher correlation between, inflation and interest rates than would be the case under a

[6] See Grauwe (1989, p. 175).

flexible exchange rate system, or in a closed economy where exchange rates are not of importance.

The nominal anchor of the EMS is the Bundesbank's monetary policy. Both the short and long-term interest rates in the other EMS countries are determined largely by the monetary policy of the Bundesbank.[7] This system produces asymmetric effects when there are differences in the level of inflation among the countries concerned. A positive inflation differential with Germany will be reflected in a positive interest rate differential. Lower inflation than in Germany, by contrast, is less likely to lead to a negative interest rate differential. As a result, there may be an increase in the real interest rate in countries that have lower inflation than Germany. The same reasoning is applicable to the other domestic factors that influence the German interest rate. Since these have little influence on the Deutsche Mark exchange rate expectations, they lead, via an increase in German interest rates, to a change in interest rates in the other EMS countries.

This German dominance should be expressed through the inclusion of the nominal German interest rate in the interest rate equation for the other countries, in addition to inflation and the determinants of the real interest rate. An increase in the nominal German interest rate would then have a direct positive effect on the interest rate in other counties.

7.4 Considerations About a Test of the Fisher Hypothesis

To test the Fisher hypothesis, a standard has to be set for the expected inflation since it cannot be observed directly. If such a standard is not set or if it is thought desirable to overcome the problems of indirect measurement, the Fisher hypothesis can be tested by means of a long-term comparison in which the nominal interest rate and inflation are specified in levels. It is then assumed that anticipated long-term inflation is equal to actual inflation, which obviates the need to estimate anticipated inflation. By working in this way, however, a significant relationship can only be found in so far as the specification is estimated for a period in which both inflation and interest rates show a trend. It is generally known, and can be regularly observed, that a specification of the relationship between interest rates and inflation into levels produces

---

[7] The Basel-Nyborg agreement concluded in September 1987 by the EC Member States further increased this influence. The priority it gives to exchange rate targets and the removal of capital restrictions are leading to the Member States closely following the autonomous policy of the Bundesbank.

three problems. These help justify our choice for an error correction approach in our empirical estimation. The three problems just indicated are as follows:

First, there is a danger of trend correlation without an actual causal relationship. Statistically, this problem can be resolved by testing for cointegration. Since this test lacks rigour, however, it would seem sound, in principle, to base conclusions on the cointegration of interest rates and inflation on the significance of the coefficient of the error correction term. Second, on the basis of a specification in levels, it cannot be said with certainty that inflation affects interest rates owing to the expectations or owing to another mechanism. To form an opinion on this, it is necessary to consider changes in inflation expectations in one way or another. Third, our analysis assumes that the real interest rate can also change in the long-term. It is therefore impossible to draw conclusions on the validity of the Fisher hypothesis on the basis of a regression equation of the nominal interest rate with inflation alone; the determinants of real interest rates must also be considered.

Real interest rates are influenced in the short-run, at least in theory, by such determinants as the government's budgetary policy and the balance on current account. As a result of this and under the influence of inflation, real interest rates in the EMS countries have continued to fluctuate against each other even after 1979, albeit less so than before 1979. In the exchange rate mechanism of the EMS, the determinants of real interest rates, and inflation, influence the nominal interest rate through exchange rate expectations and risk premiums. The decline in fluctuations between real interest rates is due chiefly to the decline in the volatility of inflation differentials in comparison with the variability of interest rate differentials. This stability of real interest rates has also occurred at a structurally higher level. This international increase in interest rates, which has been a puzzle for some time, is currently attributed to a combination of non-adjusting inflation expectations and the increased influence of the long-term determinants of real interest rates. In particular, the gross profit rate and the national debt ratio have increased in nearly all countries. The international convergence of domestic real interest rates, moreover, has probably been strengthened by the liberalization of the capital markets.

In this present study, the gross profit rate and the national debt ratio are included in the interest rate equation as long-run determinants of real interest rates. Short-run determinants also include the balance on current account, the public sector net lending/borrowing ratio, an indicator of the business cycle and the short-term interest rate (as an indicator of monetary policy) in order to explain deviations from equilibrium. Both the short and long-run considerations can be verified both empirically and simultaneously by the error correction specification.

7.5 Empirical Testing

The influence of the exchange rate system on the relationship between inflation and interest rates in The Netherlands, Belgium, France and Germany was tested by estimating an error correction equation for long-term interest rates during a period with flexible and during a period with more or less fixed exchange rates. As part of the test, the sample period from 1973:II to usually 1994:I was divided into two sub-periods. In the period 1973:II to 1979:I there were, at least for France and Germany, flexible exchange rates and in 1979:II to 1991:IV exchange rates were linked to each other in the ERM. This second period lasts in the present analysis to 1991:IV instead of 1994:I, in order to obtain eight quarters to test the predictive power of the four estimated interest rate equations.

7.5.1 The Interest Rate Equation

Based on the above considerations, apart from a number of dummy variables used for the actual estimation, the assumed interest rate equation is as follows:

$$\begin{aligned}\Delta r_l^i = {} & \alpha_0 - \beta_1 \left(r_{l,-1}^i - \beta_2 infl_{-1}^i - \beta_3 ror_{-1}^i - \beta_4 deb_{-1}^i - \beta_5 r_{l,-1}^D\right) \\ & + \alpha_1 \Delta bud^i + \alpha_2 \Delta ca^i + \alpha_3 \Delta infl^i + \alpha_4 \Delta r_k^i + \alpha_5 \Delta r_l^D \\ & + \alpha_6 \Delta conj^i + \alpha_7 \Delta r_{l,-1}^i\end{aligned}$$

where:

r_l^i and r_k^i	long and short-term interest rate in country i, where $i = NL$, B, F and D
infl	inflation (annual)
ror	rate of return on capital, defined as the ratio of corporate profits before depreciation to the gross stock of capital goods
deb	total national debt (of non-financial institutions) as a percentage of GDP, for Belgium: public sector debt as a percentage of GDP
r_l^D	long-term interest rate in Germany; in case of Germany, replaced with the long-term interest rate in the US
bud	net public sector lending/borrowing as a percentage of GDP

ca net current account balance as a percentage of GDP

conj indicator of the economic cycle

In the above equation, the term with parameter β_1 represents the equilibrium relationship — or the fundamental relationship — for the long-term interest rate. The other terms, together with the error correction coefficient β_1, represent the short-term influences. This means that in the fundamental interest rate equation, the long-term interest rate depends on inflation, relative profitability, the total national debt position and the long-term interest rate in Germany. In the short-term, however, net lending/borrowing, the current account balance and the economic cycle, as well as the length of the return to equilibrium, that is the reciprocal of β_1 — the degree of error correction — play a role.

7.5.2 Estimation Results

The estimation results of our regression equation are summarized in Table 7.1 and are highly divergent among the countries considered. For all countries, however, the estimated equations in the two sub-periods are not identical with regard to the variables included and the lag structure. As a result, and contrary to intuitive expectations, the value of a coefficient in the interest rate equation on the basis of the entire sample period is not equal to the average of the values found in the two sub-periods. Coefficients that assumed the opposite sign or were not significant were subsequently set at zero, but then accepted for practical reasons. As a consequence of this method, as shown in Table 7.1, a relatively large number of non-significant estimated coefficients remained. The coefficient of the error correction term — EC in Table 7.1 — is significant throughout the entire sample period in all countries and occasionally not so for the sub-periods. This means in any event that the nominal interest rate and inflation are cointegrated and that there is therefore no trend correlation. The coefficients of EC are considerably lower in all countries throughout the entire sample period than in the two sub-periods and, with the exception of France, they are reasonably close to each other in the various countries. According to the estimated interest rate equation this means that equilibria in Belgium, Germany and The Netherlands are restored at a comparable speed. The entirely different pattern of estimated coefficients in the equilibrium equations for the other explanatory variables for the sub-periods is also interesting. France is an exception in this. With regard to the adjustment path of interest rates to inflation, there are notable differences between the countries that seem to be related to the size of the country and the openness of the

Table 7.1: Estimation results, The Netherlands, Belgium, France and Germany

	Period	EC	$infl_{-1}$	deb_{-1}	$r^D_{l,-1}$	Δbud	Δca	$conj$	$\Delta infl$	Δr^D_l	$\Delta r_{l,-1}$	Δr_k	$\bar{R}^2$	Q(12)	SE	Sample period
NL	I	0.31	0.58[c]	0.32	0.82		−0.04[c]	0.06	0.17[b]	0.39		0.11	0.71	8.90	0.29	1973:II –1979:I
		(1.40)	(2.07)	(2.22)	(2.57)		(1.26)	(1.14)	(2.22)	(2.13)		(2.75)		(0.71)		
	II	0.47	0.32		0.75	0.01	−0.04[b]		0.08	0.79		0.09	0.85	19.25	0.18	1979:II –1991:IV
		(4.36)	(6.91)		(9.50)	(1.28)	(2.28)		(2.79)	(10.53)		(2.32)		(0.08)		
	Entire	0.08	0.50	0.03	0.63[b]	0.02[d]	−0.03[b]		0.04[b]	0.72		0.10	0.80	10.35	0.22	1973:II –1994:III
		(2.48)	(1.80)	(1.07)	(1.89)	(2.23)	(1.95)		(1.89)	(11.81)		(5.29)		(0.59)		
B	I	0.36	0.16	0.90[b,e]		0.25[a]			0.08	0.27[a]			0.61	15.31	0.20	1973:IV–1979:I
		(3.11)	(1.65)	(1.95)		(1.07)			(1.11)	(1.66)				(0.22)		
	II	0.22	0.44	0.44[d,e]	0.69		−0.03[a]		0.22	0.49	0.16	0.08	0.75	7.84	0.24	1979:II –1991:IV
		(2.52)	(3.01)	(1.99)	(2.90)		(1.79)		(3.14)	(5.06)	(1.75)	(2.36)		(0.80)		
	Entire	0.07	0.45	1.30[e]	0.54	0.08[a]	−0.02[a]		0.11	0.45		0.08	0.54	12.75	0.29	1973:III–1994:I
		(2.10)	(1.57)	(2.98)	(1.08)	(0.98)	(1.64)		(2.17)	(5.12)		(2.77)		(0.39)		
F	I	0.11	0.75[c]			0.31[d]			0.15			0.28	0.82	23.39	0.16	1973:II –1979:I
		(1.87)	(1.88)			(3.64)			(3.57)			(6.35)		(0.02)		
	II	0.08[d]	0.75[d]						0.16[b]	0.53		0.29	0.79	10.12	0.28	1979:II –1991:IV
		(2.44)	(4.84)						(2.33)	(5.15)		(6.50)		(0.61)		
	Entire	0.05	1.00			0.15[d]	−0.11[c]		0.04[d]	0.45		0.25	0.68	8.97	0.31	1973:II –1994:I
		(1.98)	(2.93)			(1.47)	(2.59)		(0.86)	(5.41)		(7.22)		(0.71)		
D	I	0.51	0.96				−0.12[a]	0.13	0.24	0.51[f]	0.50		0.65	12.34	0.31	1973:II –1979:I
		(3.54)	(12.53)				(1.53)	(2.08)	(1.30)	(1.77)	(3.08)			(0.42)		
	II	0.30	0.45[d]				−0.07[b]	0.40[h]	0.27[d]	0.24[f]	0.33[g]		0.75	4.11	0.23	1979:II –1991:IV
		(6.08)	(7.73)				(2.30)	(3.25)	(3.70)	(4.74)	(6.19)			(0.98)		
	Entire	0.09[b]	0.50[c]	0.05			−0.03[b]			0.25[f]	0.16[g]	0.24	0.62	16.40	0.29	1973:II –1994:I
		(2.20)	(2.21)	(1.32)			(1.04)			(4.10)	(2.67)	(6.61)		(0.17)		

Notes: t-values in brackets. Estimates of seasonal dummies, the 1983 realignment and 1990 German reunification are not stated. EC is the error correction term, the lags in this column relate to the long-term interest rate of the country in question. Q(12) is the Ljung-Box test statistic for auto-correlation, SE denotes the standard error of the residuals. [a], [b], [c], [d] 1, 2, 3 respectively 4 lags have been included in the estimation; [e] second difference Δ^2; [f] Δr_l^{US} instead of Δr_l^D; [g] $\Delta r_{l,-1}^{US}$ instead of $\Delta r_{l,-1}^D$; [h] $\Delta conj$ instead of $conj$.

economy. In The Netherlands and Belgium, the adjustment coefficient of inflation throughout the entire sample period is virtually equal and, in the sub-periods, often surprisingly different from that in France and Germany. The interesting question, and part of the problem considered in this chapter, is what economic significance lies behind this pattern of estimation results, and to what extent can the degree of openness and the exchange rate system provide an explanation.

It would therefore be appropriate to focus on the long-term effects, that is to consider the influence of the variables in the equilibrium formula on long-term or capital-market interest rates in the four countries studied. This has been done in Table 7.2. The information in this table again shows that the explanatory variables in the equilibrium equation for the small countries in the leading group, The Netherlands and Belgium, are national debt (as a percentage of gross domestic product) and the long-term interest rate in Germany, as well as inflation. In France, the only explanatory variable, given the estimation results, is inflation, while in Germany — where the national interest rate is obviously excluded and that of the US used instead, is of no statistical significance — long-term interest rates are influenced by public sector debt, along with inflation, only over the entire sample period. The effect of inflation is greatest in France. Over the entire sample period it is even 100% in the equilibrium situation (the fact that this is lower in both sub-periods is related to the differences between the regression equations). In Germany the effect is nearly 100% in only the first sub-period. In the second sub-period and in the entire sample period, the effect is about 50%, which is generally the case in Belgium and The Netherlands. With regard to these small countries, however, the long-run effect of inflation is greater, owing to the significant influence of German interest rates on the domestic interest rates. Finally, long-term interest rate elasticities for inflation have also been calculated from Table 7.2 — based on averages over the entire sample period — and these show a surprising pattern. For The Netherlands, Belgium and Germany, these key figures are consistently close to 0.25, while the figure for France is more than twice as high at 0.60. For the sub-periods, however, the picture is not as clear-cut. The same is true of the two other variables in the equilibrium formula.

Summarizing the above in the light of the general theoretical considerations set out in section 7.4, we can comment as follows. With regard to the theory of nearly rational behaviour, the results in Tables 7.1 and 7.2 show an interesting division between the small dependent countries and the two large countries with more autonomous policies. For The Netherlands and Belgium the faster (evidenced by the short-term effect

Table 7.2: Long-term effects of the variables on capital market interest rates

		Inflation	National debt as % of GDP	Long-term interest rate in Germany
The Netherlands	I	0.58	0.32	0.82
	II	0.32		0.75
	Entire	0.50	0.03	0.63
Belgium	I	0.16	0.90	
	II	0.44	0.44	0.69
	Entire	0.45	1.30	0.54
France	I	0.75		
	II	0.75		
	Entire	1.00		
Germany	I	0.96		
	II	0.45		
	Entire	0.50	0.50	

of a change in inflation), and in the case of Belgium more complete, adjustment of interest rates to changes in inflation in the period after 1979 supports the view that there are differences in adjustment in different exchange rate systems. This is not the case, however, for France and Germany. The fact that there is no difference in the inflation coefficient in France between the two sub-periods is probably related to the complete removal of restrictions on the movement of international capital at the end of the 1980s, so that during the sample period there is in effect no structural change in this phenomenon. For Germany, this is probably due to the fact that it lost little if any of its policy autonomy following the arrival of the EMS. In addition, the Bundesbank's policy even before 1979 was aimed at stabilizing the value of the Deutsche Mark. In this respect, the reduced flexibility of exchange rates after 1979 provided little additional certainty for the market participants. The slower effect of inflation on interest rates seen in The Netherlands and Belgium confirms, as already noted, the theory of nearly rational behaviour.

A second point of consideration is the consequence of this result for the Fisher hypothesis. An opinion on this can be based on the long-term coefficient of inflation. Since inflation did not feed through into interest rates in Germany and France in either of the two sub-periods, it follows that our conclusion on the applicability of the Fisher hypothesis is not influenced by the prevailing exchange rate system.

For the entire sample period, the Fisher hypothesis is supported by the estimation results for France. In this country, inflation fed through into interest rates in full, and capital market restrictions were in place during a large part of the sample period.[8] As expected, the influence of foreign interest rates is of great importance. This finding confirms the view that the value of the inflation coefficient in an open economy reflects the actual influence of inflation on interest rates to only a limited extent.[9] This is illustrated by the regression result (not presented here) that the inflation coefficient for The Netherlands throughout the entire sample period assumes the value 1 if the German interest rate were — erroneously — omitted from the interest rate equation. This does not undermine the fact, however, that this result is a striking one. For Belgium, contrary to expectations, this is not the case. It could be concluded from this that Belgium suffers from money illusion in comparison with The Netherlands. A possible explanation of this may lie in the nature of Belgian monetary policy, which for a long period hampered the consistent formation of expectations. In Germany, too, the influence of inflation on interest rates was incomplete. The reason for this is as yet uncertain, although it is conceivable that in the short-term, inflation may reduce the coefficient through US interest rates. The incomplete short-term effect of a change in inflation on interest rates is not surprising. It supports the presumption that inflation expectations adjust at a delay to actual inflation. On the basis of the complete sample period, the short-term effect of a change in inflation on interest rates reaches a peak of 0.11 in Belgium and is not even visible in Germany.

7.5.3 Predictive Power and Comparison with Earlier Studies

In order to test the predictive power of the estimated interest rate equations, the last eight quarters of the second sub-period were not used in the estimation of the regression equation. With an average quadratic prediction error of 0.30 for The Netherlands and Belgium, and nearly 0.80 for the two other countries, it proved surprisingly good.

The estimates obtained here provide some support for the Fisher hypothesis, producing a higher value of the long-term inflation coefficient for all countries than in previous studies. In four earlier studies of The Netherlands performed for slightly different sample periods, for example, the influence of inflation on long-term interest rates was, in most cases, considerably lower, with the total correlation coefficient lying between

[8] Cf. Fase and Nieuwkerk (1975).

[9] Cf. Fase and Nieuwkerk (1975).

0.24 and 0.39.[10] This may be because the particular studies considered use few, if any, other explanatory variables for long-term interest rates apart from inflation, and often implicitly assume that long-term interest rates are stable. Each of the determinants of real interest rates used in the present study in addition to inflation, appears to be significant, with the exception of profitability. The earlier studies may therefore suffer from a misspecification and accordingly produce biased estimates with low predictive power. In this respect, too, the results of the present analysis are to be preferred and they shed some new light on the Fisher equation issue.

7.6 Conclusion

Testing the theory of nearly rational behaviour with regard to the process of exchange rate formation, reveals a division between small dependent countries and large countries that have greater power for conducting an autonomous monetary policy. This view is confirmed by the results for The Netherlands and Belgium, in which countries inflation has a faster effect during the period after 1979, when exchange rates were in any event more or less fixed. The anomalous results for France and Germany in this respect, however, contrast with those for The Netherlands and Belgium. In the case of France, this may be due to the international capital restrictions in force until the end of the 1980s. The results for Germany confirm that the transition to another exchange rate system after 1979 had little effect on that country's monetary policy and the formation of expectations. For The Netherlands and Belgium, in neither of the two sub-periods does inflation feed through fully into interest rates. It can be concluded from this, that the exchange rate system did not influence this result. Our study also reveals that, contrary to earlier studies, there is empirical support for the Fisher hypothesis throughout the entire sample period in France and in the first sub-period in Germany. This is presumably related to the structure of those two economies. The long-term inflation coefficient estimated here is higher for all countries than in previous studies. This suggests that the earlier studies might have suffered from misspecification. Finally, the predictive power of the interest rate equations estimated for the second sub-period, is remarkable, although The Netherlands and Belgium score surprisingly better than the two other countries studied, where the predictions are still very satisfactory by current standards.

[10] See Fase (1972a), Fase and Nieuwkerk (1975), Mourik and Winder (1989) and Rietveld (1993).

8. The Demand for Mortgage Credit and the Mortgage Rate in The Netherlands

8.1 Introduction and Purpose

In The Netherlands mortgages account for about 20 per cent of the total supply of funds on the domestic capital market. The net supply of mortgage credit amounted to over *ƒ* 4.5 billions in 1974. Despite its considerable size, hardly any statistical investigations of mortgage lending have been made in The Netherlands. At first sight this is surprising, particularly since in the US and Canada much attention has been paid to this subject and various econometric models for the mortgage market have been developed. However, in those countries mortgage credit is, to a much greater extend than in The Netherlands, the principal means of financing residential construction. Hence the mortgage rate has a considerable political importance, which has evidently stimulated research in this field.

This chapter examines The Netherlands' mortgage market using a macroeconometric model. The following section outlines the mortgage loan as a financing instrument and its importance for the financing of residential construction. It is also describes trends in the supply of mortgage credit. In the third section, a model for the mortgage market is formulated; it comprises two demand equations and an interest equation. Sections 8.4 and 8.5 describe and examine the data used and the estimation results. Section 8.6 deals further with the market's supply side. Section 8.7 compares our findings with the results of several earlier econometric studies in the US and Canada. The final section contains the principal conclusions which may be drawn from this study.

Translation of *De Economist*, **125**(1) (1977), F.A.G. den Butter, A.M. Dongelmans and M.M.G. Fase 'De vraag naar hypothecair krediet en de rentevorming op de hypotheekmarkt: Een econometrische analyse voor Nederland', 43–74, ©1977 with kind permission from Kluwer Academic Publishers. The present version has been presented at the Econometric Society Meeting in Helsinki, 1976.

8.2 The Mortgage Loan as a Financing Instrument

A mortgage loan is one way in which owners of real estate can borrow money by mortgaging their property in favour of the lender, thus providing security for the money borrowed. This arrangement gives the mortgage loan a high degree of security in monetary terms.

Mortgage loans are most frequently related to the purchase of dwellings, but they are also granted for a number of other reasons. Table 8.1 shows the nature of the property pledged. We estimate the share in the finance of residential construction at 30 per cent.

The supply of mortgage credit comes from private financial institutions among others. The latter mainly consist of individuals and private enterprises; they accounted in 1974 for more than 25 per cent of the total new loans registered. In this study, we confine ourselves to mortgage loans granted by financial institutions.

Figure 8.1 shows the relative shares of the different categories of these institutions in the total of new mortgage loans granted. It is clear that this proportion fluctuates appreciably, but nevertheless a pattern can be discerned if one looks only at moving averages, as in the graph. Because there were considerable structural changes on the supply side during the period under investigation, we have compiled the information from the graph in Table 8.2, which gives the average proportion and the standard deviation for the whole period as well as the average for three sub-periods.

8.3 A Model for the Mortgage Market

8.3.1 The Demand Equations

The demand for credit is a derived demand in the sense that the determinants are the same as those for the transaction to be financed. The expenditure decisions which underlie the demand for credit are treated in this study as exogenous. The extent to which mortgages are used as a means of finance depends not only on the amount needed for the expenditure, but also on the relative cost of financing in this form, and on the availability of alternative sources of funds. For these reasons, it appears appropriate to distinguish residential mortgages from non-residential mortgages (mainly mortgages on buildings for trade and industry).

With regard to dwellings, the purchase will often coincide with the demand for mortgage credit. This means that the size of the housing

Table 8.1: Percentage distribution of newly registered ordinary mortgage loans according to nature of property pledged, 1965–1974 (per cent of total amount)

Nature of property pledged	1965	1966	1967	1968	1969	1970	1971	1972	1973	1974
Rural properties	10	8	9	7	6	8	4	4	3	3
Dwellings[a]	64	62	56	67	60	60	65	73	73	70
Business premises	18	23	24	17	23	17	19	11	14	15
Building sites	8	7	11	9	11	15	12	12	10	12
Total	100	100	100	100	100	100	100	100	100	100

Note: [a] includes dwellings combined with business premises.

transactions will largely determine the demand for such credit. This demand will, in principle, further depend on the level of the mortgage rate, and the cost of alternatives. Other borrowing conditions, such as the loan-to-value ratio and the terms of the contract, may also influence demand. Time-series data on these points are not available for The Netherlands. Accordingly they have not been taken into account. American studies of the mortgage market (see, for example, Dhrymes and Taubman (1969), and Jaffee (1972)) show that there is a close connection between the interest rate and these other conditions. For this reason their omission from the demand relation is presumable not so serious.

Finally the cyclical situation is a possible explanatory factor. At least

Table 8.2: Average percentage share of total mortgage lending done by financial institutions, and the standard deviation

Lending institutions	1960:II–1974:I Mean	SD [a]	1960:II –1965	1966 –1969	1970 –1974:I
Savings banks	10.2	2.9	10.8	8.4	11.1
Pension funds and life insurance companies	24.6	9.9	33.3	25.3	12.3
Mortgage banks	14.3	9.0	19.3	3.9	17.4
Banks	50.8	14.3	36.7	62.5	59.2
Commercial banks	11.1	10.2	2.6	15.3	18.6

Note: [a] Standard deviation.

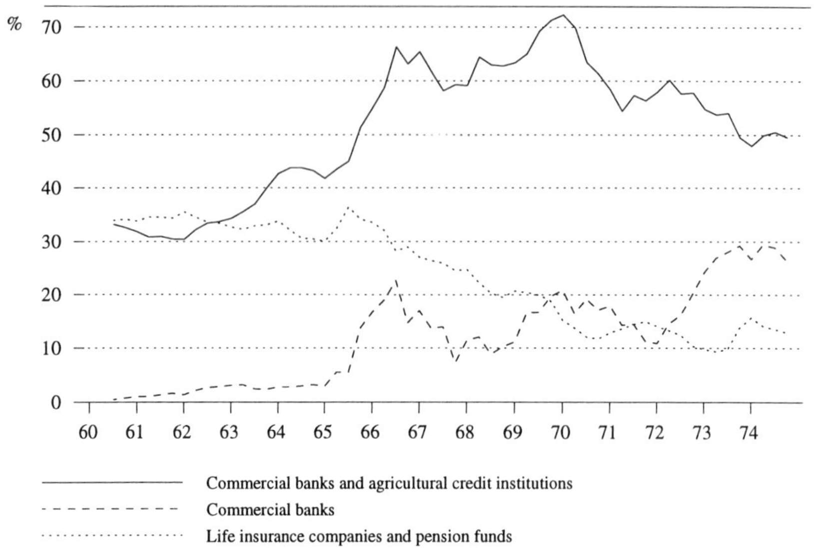

Figure 8.1: Relative shares in the total supply of new mortgage-credits by financial institutions

two reasons for this view can be given. First, it seems plausible that liquidity preference will tend to increase in a recession. This reasoning, which has been held in theory by Kessler (1958) and supported empirically by Fase and Kuné (1974a), may also apply to the capital market, because at a time of less favourable economic activity, the proportion borne by mortgage financing of total housing transactions will increase. On the other hand, a decline in activity may cause a decreased demand for mortgage credit, since the public will show some reluctance to incur debt. Clearly it is not easy to say which of these considerations will tip the scale. Therefore, we postulate the following relation for the demand for residential mortgage credit, BHW:

$$BHW = \alpha_0 + \alpha_1 BW + \alpha_2 (rh - r) BW + \alpha_3 rh\, BW + \alpha_4 c, \qquad (8.1)$$

where BW measures the turnover on the housing market, rh the mortgage rate, r the cost of alternative funds, and c a business-cycle indicator. The unscaled constant has been added for reasons of estimation.

By way of analogy to equation (8.1) the following relation has been assumed as regards demand for non-residential mortgage credit, BHO:

$$BHO = \beta_0 + \beta_1 BWT + \beta_2 (rh - r) BWT + \beta_3 rh\, BWT + \beta_4 c. \qquad (8.2)$$

In equation (8.2) BWT measures the transactions, outside the housing market, where mortgage financing is important. Mortgagors of buildings for trade, industry and other non-residential uses generally differ from those of dwellings where, as a rule, the latter seldom have important alternative possibilities of financing. The home mortgage loan is, by its nature, a semi-consumer's credit.

For a firm, the position is clearly different, since in most cases it will have access to alternative forms of finance, so that the substitution-effect may perhaps be of greater importance. It is important to point out these differences, because the formal analogy, taken by itself, between equations (8.1) and (8.2), does insufficient justice to the essential differences between the two categories of borrowers. We shall return to this when discussing the estimation results.

8.3.2 The Interest Rate Equation

When separate demand and supply equations are formulated, the price will result implicitly from the market equilibrium condition and hence no equation needs to be set up for it. If on the other hand, it is assumed, as we have done, that the amount of mortgage credit granted is demand-determined, then the interest rate — in this case the interest rate differential $(rh - r)$ — is an endogenous variable, which must be explicitly described by a separate structural equation. This interest rate equation is related to the supply equation (omitted here) in as much as the explanatory variables indicate the margin available for price-determination by the supplier. An important element in this is the rate of interest on the capital market, r, indicating the price at which the supplier of mortgage credit can, at that moment, attract resources at the capital market.

The starting-point for specifying the interest rate equation is that the *desired* interest rate differential $(rh - r)^*$ is determined by the ratio of total net mortgage loans granted to total new deposits plus borrowed funds, $NHT/\Delta D$, the rate of interest on the capital market, r, and the cyclical situation, c.

The insertion of $NHT/\Delta D$ is based on the conjecture that, on the one hand, the rate of interest serves to adjust the supply of mortgage credit to the demand, while on the other hand the suppliers, aiming at a balanced composition of their investment portfolio, will require a greater differential to increase the proportion of mortgages in their investment portfolios.

Insertion of the general interest rate on the capital market is chiefly prompted by the consideration that, when this rate alters, maturing debt components are replaced by others bearing also a different rate of interest, for example through issue of mortgage bonds. Therefore, it is reasonable to assume that a higher rate of interest on the capital market increases the required differential.

The addition of a cyclical indicator, c, to the interest rate equation is not unusual (see for example Stevers (1963)). Our reasoning is that in a depression, suppliers of mortgage credit are content with a smaller margin in order to achieve a degree of stabilisation of their investments. In a boom, on the other hand, they will strive to obtain a somewhat wider margin, as a reaction against the narrower margin they had to accept during the depression. We therefore suppose that a positive relationship may be expected between the course of economic activity and the interest rate differential.

By way of more precise definition, we postulate the following link between desired interest rate differential and explanatory variables:

$$(rh - r)_t^* = \gamma_0 + \gamma_1 NHT/\Delta D_{t-1} + \gamma_2 r_{t-1} + \gamma_3 c_t. \qquad (8.3)$$

It is further assumed that the actual interest rate differential follows the desired margin, with some time-lag corresponding to the modified partial adjustment mechanism:

$$(rh - r)_t = (rh - r)_{t-1} + \lambda \left((rh - r)_t^* - (rh - r)_{t-1} \right) + \gamma_4 \Delta r_t. \quad (8.4)$$

Addition of the term Δr to the usual partial adjustment formula is promoted by the idea that changes in the rate of interest on the capital market are not immediately reflected in the mortgage rate, and consequently affect the actual differential.

The interest equation follows from substitution of equation (8.3) into equation (8.4), and is:

$$\begin{aligned}(rh - r)_t =& \lambda\gamma_0 + (1 - \lambda)(rh - r)_{t-1} + \lambda\gamma_1\, NHT/\Delta D_{t-1} \\ &+ \lambda\gamma_2 r_{t-1} + \lambda\gamma_3 c_t + \gamma_4 \Delta r_t. \end{aligned} \tag{8.5}$$

8.4 The Data

The demand equations (8.1) and (8.2) have been estimated using quarterly data for the sample period 1965:II–1974:I. For the interest equation it was possible to use data covering the longer sample period 1960:II–1974:I. The data used have not been seasonally adjusted.

The new registrations of mortgage loans published by the CBS are used as the gross amount of mortgage loans granted, BHW and BHO. Difficulty arises when measuring the turnover variables BW and BWT, in as much as no data are available for the volume of transactions in existing dwellings and buildings. With regard to dwellings it has been assumed that the total expenditure on buildings licensed for residential construction in the private sector — hence BW in equation (8.1) — affords a reasonable yardstick to measure the transactions. On the same grounds, for granting of non-residential mortgages, equation (8.2), the volume of the transactions BWT has been approximated by taking the total expenditure on buildings entertained by the private sector.

The mortgage rate rh has been measured, as a quarterly average, from the rate of interest on a standard mortgage loan as reported monthly by mortgage banks to De Nederlandsche Bank.

Figure 8.2 shows the mortgage rate alongside the yield on the latest three long-term Government loans. We regard this yield as representative for r, the rate of interest in the capital market. As was to be expected, (see Fase (1973)), the graph reveals close connection between the two rates of interest, albeit with changing differentials.

Following Fase and Kuné (1974a) we have taken as cyclical indicator, c_t, the quarterly average of the male labour reserve as a percentage of the wage-earning male labour force. Although recent experience has somewhat impaired the significance of this indicator, we have refrained in this study from experimenting with other indicators because it is reasonable for the greater part of the reference period.

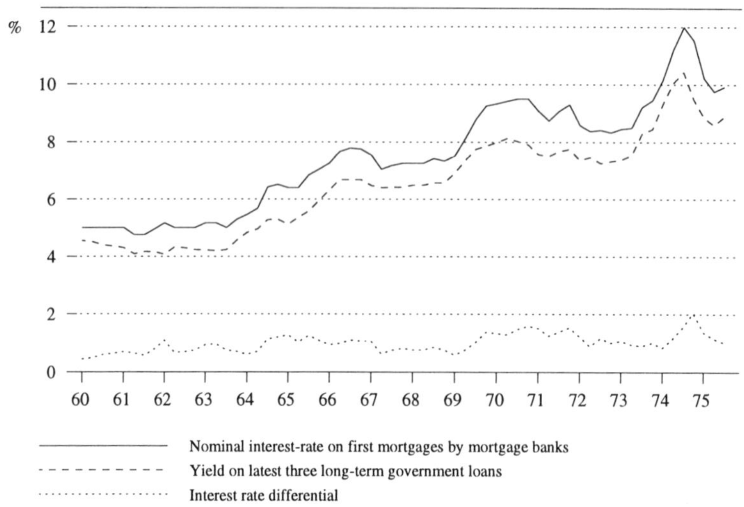

Figure 8.2: The interest rates on mortgages and government bonds

8.5 The Estimation Results

To begin with, the demand and interest rate equations postulated in section 8.4 have been estimated by ordinary least-squares using quarterly figures. On presenting the results of estimation, R^2 is the squared correlation coefficient adjusted for degrees of freedom, DW the Durbin-Watson statistic, and SE the standard deviation of the residuals. The t-value is shown in parentheses.

8.5.1 The Demand Equations 1965:II–1974:I

In practice, when mortgage loans are granted, some time elapses between the date of the contract and the actual payment. Furthermore, there is a time-lag between housing starts and housing purchases, because in most cases, building is not started on orders from the future occupant. With buildings for trade and industry this is less so. Therefore the demand equation postulated for housing mortgage loans has to be dynamised by a time-lag structure. As a second point, building activity, and therefore mortgage lending, is subject to seasonal fluctuations. To allow for this we have introduced seasonal dummies S_i. Finally it has been assumed that, for both kinds of mortgage loans, the dependent variable is not immediately adjusted to its equilibrium value.

After these modifications we have, for equation (8.1):

$$\begin{aligned} BHW_t = & -\underset{(0.07)}{0.005} + \underset{(3.53)}{0.517} BHW_{t-1} + \underset{(3.52)}{1.380} BW_{t-1} \\ & + \underset{(0.70)}{0.087} (rh - r)_{t-1} BW_{t-1} - \underset{(1.95)}{0.086}\, rh_{t-1} BW_{t-1} - \underset{(0.81)}{0.027} c_t \\ & - \underset{(6.39)}{0.330}\, S_1 + \underset{(0.74)}{0.035}\, S_2 - \underset{(2.92)}{0.129}\, S_3 \qquad (8.1') \end{aligned}$$

$$R^2 = 0.98 \qquad DW = 2.42 \qquad SE = 0.091.$$

For equation (8.2) we obtained:

$$\begin{aligned} BHO_t = & \underset{(3.50)}{0.485} + \underset{(0.74)}{0.150} BHO_{t-1} - \underset{(1.54)}{0.552} BWT_t \\ & - \underset{(3.24)}{0.240} (rh - r)_{t-1} + \underset{(2.48)}{0.105}\, rh_{t-1} BWT_t - \underset{(1.41)}{0.043}\, c_t \\ & - \underset{(3.04)}{0.158}\, S_1 - \underset{(2.85)}{0.127}\, S_2 - \underset{(3.07)}{0.140}\, S_3 \qquad (8.2') \end{aligned}$$

$$R^2 = 0.72 \qquad DW = 1.62 \qquad SE = 0.093.$$

The inclusion of both rh and $(rh - r)$ in equation (8.1′) and (8.2′) gives unsatisfactory results. This to some extent supports our surmise that the substitution-effects are not important for residential mortgages, but that they are important for non-residential mortgages. To verify this more closely, we re-estimated equation (8.1′) without the interest rate differential and equation (8.2′) without the interest rate level. The results are:

$$\begin{aligned} BHW_t = & \underset{(0.42)}{0.025} + \underset{(3.76)}{0.462} BHW_{t-1} + \underset{(3.53)}{1.367} BW_{t-1} - \underset{(1.96)}{0.067}\, rh_{t-1} BW_{t-1} \\ & - \underset{(1.21)}{0.037}\, c_t - \underset{(6.58)}{0.318}\, S_1 + \underset{(0.87)}{0.039}\, S_2 - \underset{(3.11)}{0.134}\, S_3 \qquad (8.1'') \end{aligned}$$

$$R^2 = 0.98 \qquad DW = 2.38 \qquad SE = 0.090.$$

and

$$\begin{aligned} BHO_t =& 0.182 + 0.519 BHO_{t-1} + 0.307 BWT_t \\ & (2.50) \quad (3.50) \qquad\qquad (3.18) \\ & - 0.104\,(rh - r)_{t-1} BWT_t - 0.061\, c_t - 0.177\, S_1 \\ & (1.92) \qquad\qquad\qquad\qquad (1.87) \qquad (3.16) \\ & - 0.141\, S_2 - 0.142\, S_3 \\ & (2.92) \qquad (2.85) \end{aligned} \tag{8.2''}$$

$$R^2 = 0.67 \qquad DW = 1.79 \qquad SE = 0.101.$$

We observe that in both equations the demand is positively correlated with economic activity. A shift in liquidity preference under influence of the business cycle is thus not apparent in our results. In so far as significance is to be assigned to the business cycle, our estimates do suggest that in a downswing, the demand for mortgage credit will, *ceteris paribus*, to some extent decrease. The foregoing results support the view that there is a clear difference between the financing behaviour of the two categories of borrowers. This is also evident from the short and long-term interest-elasticities calculated, at the sample mean, from equations (8.1″) and (8.2″). These are:

$$\frac{\partial\, BHW}{\partial\, rh}\;\frac{rh}{BHW} = -0.61 \quad (-1.14)$$

$$\frac{\partial\, BHO}{\partial\,(rh - r)}\;\frac{rh - r}{BHO} = -0.28 \quad (-0.58).$$

The short and long-term (partial) elasticity of *BHO*, as against the interest rate level *rh* from equation (8.2″), is on the other hand much greater, at −2.11 and −4.38 respectively. The great interest rate sensitivity of new registrations in the case of other mortgage loans is striking, but plausible.

The regression equations (8.1″) and (8.2″) have been depicted in Figure 8.3 and Figure 8.4 respectively. These graphs show, once again, that equations (8.1″) and (8.2″) satisfactorily explain the demand for mortgage credit in the period considered. In addition to this we have, for the quarters from 1974:II to 1975:II, investigated the predictive performance of equations (8.1″) and (8.2″). Calculation of the overall inequality coefficient for equations (8.1″) and (8.2″) yield 0.253 and 0.269 respectively. These values, measured according to the usual standards, are not unreasonable, indicating that the demand relations are fairly stable.

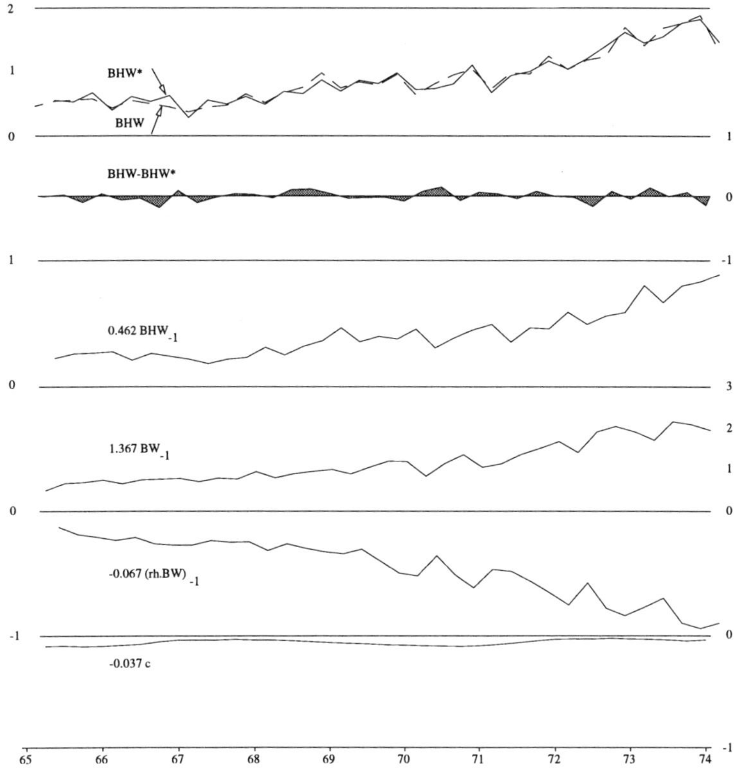

Figure 8.3: The demand for housing mortgages

8.5.2 The Interest Rate Equation 1960:II–1974:I

Estimation of the interest rate equation (8.5) results in:

$$
\begin{aligned}
(rh - r_t) = & -0.114 + 0.421(rh - r)_{t-1} + 0.464(NHT/\Delta D)_{t-1} \quad (8.5') \\
& \quad (1.03) \quad (4.55) \qquad\qquad\qquad (2.63) \\
& -0.143c_t + 0.139r_{t-1} - 0.231\Delta r_t \\
& \quad (4.23) \qquad (5.67) \qquad (2.78)
\end{aligned}
$$

$$R^2 = 0.77 \qquad DW = 1.75 \qquad SE = 0.133.$$

The fit is satisfactory. The minus sign of the coefficient for Δr_t confirms that the interest rate differential does not immediately follow the movement of the general interest rate, but in the first instance

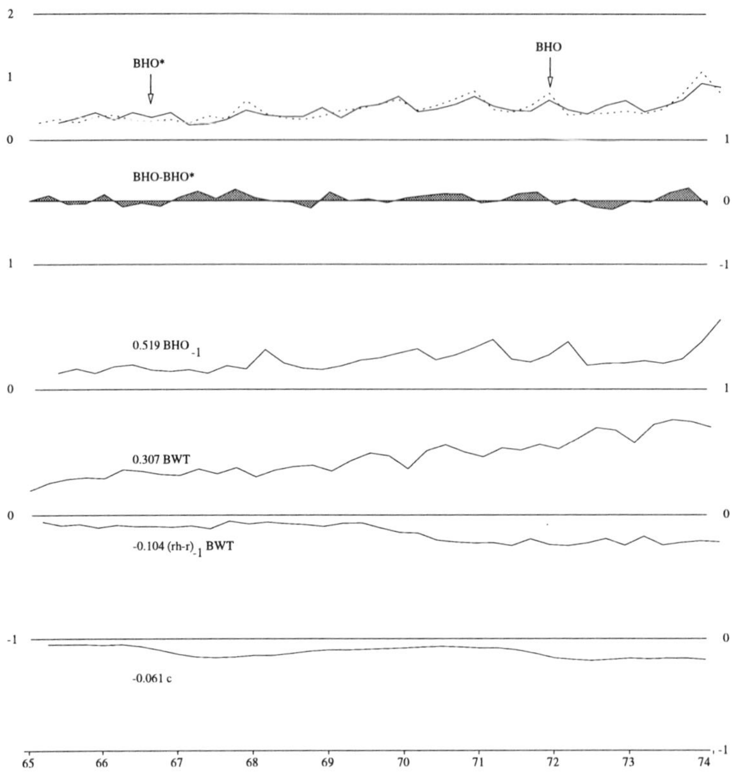

Figure 8.4: The demand for non-housing mortgages

actually affects that differential in the opposite direction. From the value of the $(rh - r)$ coefficient, it can be calculated that adjustment to the equilibrium differential takes place for nearly 60 per cent, within one quarter. The average time-lag is almost three-quarters of a quarter. It is interesting to note that a 1 per cent point increase — for example from 23 per cent to 24 per cent — in the ratio of new mortgage lending to the growth of new resources $(NHT/\Delta D)$ causes the interest rate differential to increase by only 0.005 per cent. The interest rate differential will ultimately rise, *ceteris paribus*, by nearly 0.008 per cent. Equation (8.5′) is reproduced in Figure 8.5.

The graph shows, once again, that the equation yields a good explanation of the interest rate differential. Finally the *ex post* predictive power of equation (8.5′) for the period 1974:II–1975:III, measured by the value 0.205 of the inequality coefficient, is found to be reasonable. The interest rate differential equation is thus reasonably stable.

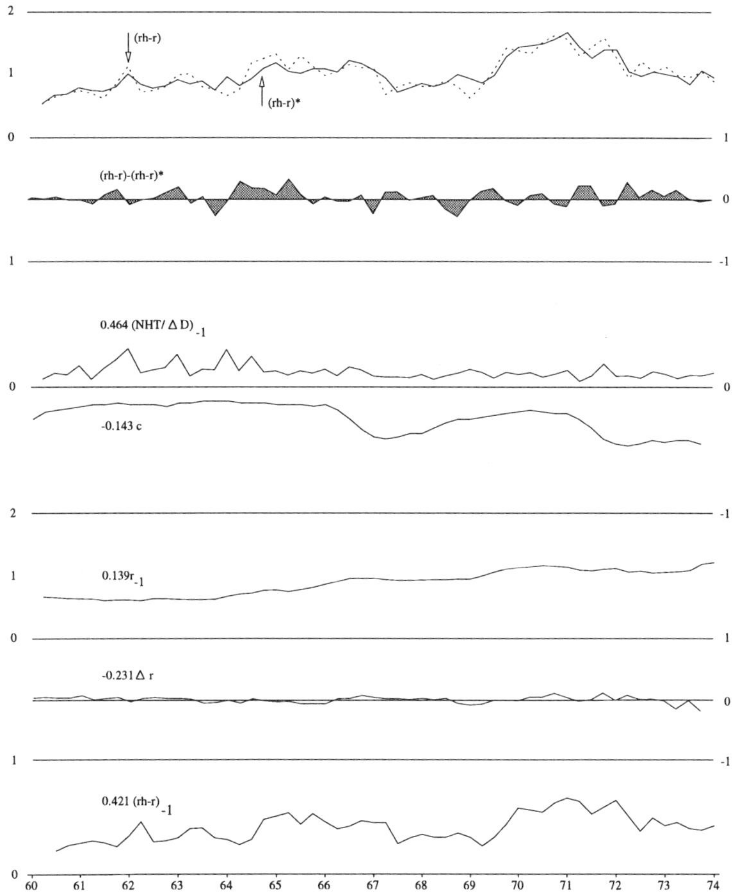

Figure 8.5: The interest rate differential between mortgages and government bonds

To facilitate the interpretation, we may rewrite equation (8.5′) as:

$$\begin{aligned} rh_t = & -0.114 + 0.421 rh_{t-1} + 0.464(NHT/\Delta D)_{t-1} \\ & -0.143 c_t + 0.718 r_{t-1} + 0.769 \Delta r_t. \end{aligned}$$

This formulation clearly shows that to predict the mortgage rate, knowledge of the lagged values of rh and r does not suffice. The explanation of the current r falls outside the scope of this investigation, but forms an important link with the other sections of the capital market as well as with the real sector of the economy. Explanation of NHT forms the topic of the next subsection.

8.5.3 The Relationship between Net Mortgage Lending and New Registrations, 1965:II–1974:I

Due to the fact that new registrations of mortgage are classified according to the collateral given, it was possible to estimate separate demand relations for residential and non-residential mortgage loans. The empirical evidence has confirmed the logic of this separation. As mentioned above, the net, rather than the gross, amount of mortgages is the relevant variable for analysing the supply of mortgages and the mortgage rate. In this connection no subdivision according to property pledged is available. For these reasons, we tried to find a link between the total amount of new registrations BHT_t and the net total mortgage lending NHT_t, where

$$BHT_t = BHW_t + BHO_t. \tag{8.6}$$

The difference between new registrations and net mortgage lending results from four causes:

1. repayments on existing mortgage loans; these do not affect BHT, but do affect NHT;
2. revision of the conditions of existing mortgage contracts; this affects BHT, but not NHT;
3. time-lag between registration and payment; the shorter the period considered, the more effect this will produce;
4. errors and omissions.[1]

As regards repayments, there is an obvious relation to the amount of outstanding mortgage loans, HB. Mortgage contract revisions will also partly depend on this. Furthermore, it may be supposed that the readiness to revise a mortgage contract will increase as the interest rate falls. An attempt was made to eliminate both sources of difference by assuming a constant ratio to new registrations, supplemented by an interest rate variable. Experiments with interest rate variables had no success.

We finally retained the following simple equation:

$$\underset{}{NHT_t} = \underset{(6.96)}{0.651BHT_t} - \underset{(1.31)}{0.008HB_{t-1}} \tag{8.7}$$

$$R^2 = 0.97 \qquad DW = 1.61 \qquad SE = 0.133.$$

[1] A point of special importance here is that the figures for BHT include building societies and saving associations, while those for NHT do not.

Although the coefficient *HB* for the amount of outstanding mortgage loans is not significant, we retain this variable because it is plausible. Particularly the value of 0.008, implies a total of about 30 years to final maturity. This period agrees reasonably well with the term of many mortgage loans.

Finally, we investigated the performance of equation (8.7) to reflect the actual movement for the period 1974:II–1975:II. We calculated an inequality coefficient of 0.286.

8.6 The Allocation Among Financial Institutions

In section 8.3 we found that, during the period from 1960 to 1974, the four categories of financial institutions considered accounted for widely varying proportions of total mortgage lending. Calculation of a four-quarter moving average made little difference to this. In this section we attempt a statistical analysis of the movement in these proportions, — that is a system analysis — and this completes our model of the mortgage market.

The starting point is the systemwide model:

$$NH^i/NHT = \alpha_{i0} + \sum_j \alpha_{ij} x_j^i, \tag{8.8}$$

where NH^i/NHT is the share taken by category i of the financial institutions in total mortgage lending. The fact that $\sum_i NH^i$ always $= NHT$ implies, that $\sum_i \alpha_{i0} = 1$ and $\sum_i \alpha_{ij} = 0$ for all j.

If the same explanatory variables occur in each equation of the system, ordinary least-squares estimates of the separate equations will, of themselves, suffice to comply with the restrictions mentioned. For convenience sake we therefore apply this method.[2]

The relative growth of the resources available for investment is regarded as a first determinant for the share of the mortgage market taken by each group of financial institutions. It may be assumed that, together with a relatively greater growth of their deposits and borrowed funds, their share of mortgage lending will also rise. Experiments with these variables showed the relative share of the banks in total new resources, $\Delta D^B/\Delta DT$, to be predominant.

[2] We disregard the fact that the disturbance term for the separate equations are not independent. See Kmenta (1971). For an alternative approach, see Sparks (1974).

An important change in the allocation occurred in about 1965. Various causes of this change can be indicated. First, the period from 1964 to 1966 was marked by a cyclical capital shortage, accompanied by a considerable rise in the capital market interest rate. Second, the demand for mortgage credit was slow to rise in this period, or even actually declined. Both these factors were highly unfavourable to the mortgage banks in particular, because they depend almost entirely on the capital market for obtaining funds to finance their business. As regards the rate of interest, they were therefore in a relatively unfavourable competitive position, particularly in relation to the commercial banks, which could offer mortgage credit on terms more favourable to the borrower because they depend less on the capital market. Therefore it is natural to include the competitive mortgage conditions in equation (8.8) as explanatory variables. Because data on this point are lacking, however, we have constructed the proxy *rhv*. This is defined as the difference between the interest rate *rh* and the interest rate, published by the CBS, on *all* registrations. This difference indicates, to what extent the interest rate terms of mortgage banks differ from those of the other suppliers. Graphical inspection showed, moreover, that the differential *rhv* is negatively correlated with the mortgage banks' share of the market, which supports our method of working.[3]

Finally we included (NH^i_{t-1}/NHT_t), with $i = SP, PL, HB$, as explanatory variables, as to allow for adjustment inertia. The inclusion of (NH^B_{t-1}/NHT_t) did not yield any useful result. For the same heuristic reason we ultimately excluded interest variables such as rh, $rh - r$ and the money market interest rate from our system. Evidently, these interest rate variables did not effect the allocation of net mortgage lending among the four categories of institutions considered.

The estimation results are shown in Table 8.3. It is easy to verify that the estimates meet the restrictions mentioned above. The t-values are in parentheses.

The relative growth of the new resources of the banks as compared with those of the other institutions $(\Delta D^B/\Delta DT)$ has been accompanied, as expected, by growth in the banks' share of the market. The relevant estimates make clear that this occurred mainly at the expense of the share taken by life insurance companies and pension funds.

The table further shows that the mortgage banks, and to a lesser degree, the pension funds and life insurance companies, have been sensitive to price competition. Both categories found their share of the market shrinking with a high *rhv*. The banks gained from this by increasing

[3] To be precise, we have taken $rhv_t = rh_{t-1} - rh_t^{CBS}$; the reason lies in the method of registering the rates of interest.

Table 8.3: Estimation results for the allocation model, 1960:II–1974:I

Financial institution	Dependent variable	Explanatory variables								
	$\frac{NH^i}{NHT}$	constant	$\frac{NH^{SP}_{t-1}}{NHT_t}$	$\frac{NH^{PL}_{t-1}}{NHT_t}$	$\frac{NH^{HB}_{t-1}}{NHT_t}$	rhv_t	$\frac{\Delta D^B_t}{\Delta DT_t}$	DW	R^2	SE
Saving banks	$\frac{NH^{SP}}{NHT}$	0.108 (4.14)	0.399 (3.31)	−0.107 (3.17)	0.094 (2.42)	−0.014 (1.20)	−0.042 (0.94)	2.20	0.520	0.020
Pension funds and life insurance companies	$\frac{NH^{PL}}{NHT}$	0.375 (5.83)	−0.237 (0.79)	0.466 (5.60)	−0.213 (2.23)	−0.069 (2.47)	−0.264 (2.40)	1.69	0.749	0.049
Mortgage banks	$\frac{NH^{HB}}{NHT}$	0.338 (4.77)	−0.433 (1.32)	−0.390 (4.25)	0.588 (5.58)	−0.077 (2.50)	−0.162 (1.34)	2.15	0.631	0.054
Commercial banks and agricultural credit institutions	$\frac{NH^{B}}{NHT}$	0.178 (1.78)	0.270 (0.58)	0.030 (0.23)	−0.469 (3.15)	0.161 (3.67)	0.467 (2.73)	1.76	0.709	0.077

their share of the market. It may again be pointed out that *rhv* was particularly large when the commercial banks tried to penetrate the mortgage market.

The coefficients for the other variables all have the highest positive value, and the greatest significance, on their own explanatory variable. From the value of the estimated coefficients in Table 8.3 it can be seen that, as soon as the mortgage banks' share diverges from the normal level, this results in an opposite change in the share of banks and to a lesser degree, in the share pension funds and life insurance companies, while fluctuations in the share of this last group are most clearly reflected at the mortgage banks. The savings banks, on the other hand, have no obvious opposite number among any of the other institutions.

Finally we calculated, for each of the categories considered, the predictive performance of the relevant equation over the sample period 1974:II to 1975:II. The results are shown in Table 8.4. These results are less satisfactory than those for the corresponding single equations, indicating that the estimated allocation model is less stable.

8.7 Earlier Investigation and Policy Implications

At the beginning of this chapter, we mentioned that econometric studies of the mortgage market often relate to the US and Canada. In this section we shall look at a number of these investigations in order to put our own investigation, and its possible policy implications, into a broad perspective.

An important contribution is the broadly drawn, but principally descriptive and inventorial study by Klaman (1961) of residential mortgage lending in the US. This theme recurs in the American as well as the Canadian studies, and that is undoubtedly due to the great importance of mortgage loans for residential construction, and hence for the stabilisation of building activity. For these reasons, the mortgage market forms an area for application of monetary policy. This is illustrated by the view of Gramlich and Jaffee (1972b, p. 3, Chapter 1), where they write:

> [...] the markets for savings deposits, mortgages and residential construction form a crucial link in the chain that connects the monetary sector with the real sector.

Nevertheless, the earlier econometric models contain no separate equations for the mortgage market. They confine themselves to including interest rates, and the availability of credit, as elements in the equation for housing investments. This approach is, for example, adopted by

Table 8.4: Predictive power allocation model (8.8)

Lending institutions	Inequality coefficient
Savings banks	0.286
Pension funds and life insurance companies	0.446
Mortgage banks	0.304
Commercial banks and agricultural credit institutions	0.284

Brady (1967) in his attempt to describe the post-war building boom in the US. His investigation shows that both the availability of mortgage credit and interest ceilings in the mortgage market — with the result that resources flow out of it — have underlain the instability of the housing sector.

The investigators who present a sub-model for the mortgage market go further, although they display differences of emphasis which are worth pointing out on methodological grounds. The *first group* comprise the *demand and supply models* of Huang (1966) and of Ostas and Zahn (1975). In this approach, the demand for mortgage credit is derived from that for dwellings. The supply is determined by a number of interest rates, the increase of resources and the free reserve. Equilibrium is achieved through the downpayment ratio, and in the long-run by the interest rate. Both models explicitly admit a discrepancy between demand and supply, which is reflected in the equation for the mortgage rate. It is worth mentioning that Huang's analysis of the supply, classified according to institutions, is related to our supply formulation, although in Huang's case the quantity offered is positively correlated with conditions in the money market.

The *second group* could well be described as *supply-oriented* models. It includes the studies by Sparks (1967) and by Jaffee (1972) for the US, and the investigation by Smith and Sparks (1973) for Canada. The common feature of these studies is that they consist of supply and interest rate equations. This implies the assumption that the mortgage rate will ensure adjustment of demand, an approach also found in Vuchelen (1975) for Belgium. Just as we do, all these studies classify the supply of funds as between lending institutions. It is clear that our model is *demand-oriented.* The fact that this type is not found in the cited literature is, on closer consideration, not so surprising. The supply-oriented character of the models for the United States and Canada is a reflection of the practice, followed there, of using monetary means to stabilize building activity. That is why, following the studies mentioned above, a number of sub-models for the mortgage and building market have been set up. Examples include the models of Smith(1969, 1970) for Canada, and of Kalchbrenner (1971) and of Gramlich and Jaffee (1972a), for the US. In the case of Gramlich and Jaffee, whose model forms part of the FMP model (FMP is an abbreviation for Federal Reserve-MIT-PEN), a central feature is the interaction between savings and time deposits, mortgage lending and residential construction. This last sector includes the building of new houses as well as the letting and sale of existing houses. Prices are in this connection an important factor, while the various sectors are moreover influenced through capital costs, net-worth effects and credit rationing. The mortgage rate forms an important component of the capital costs incurred on investments in dwellings. The reaction of residential construction to the demand for mortgage credit forms the stabilising factor. Simulations show that the net-worth effect on residential construction, for instance through changes of share prices, are small in the long-run. Interest rate policy appears on the other hand to be more effective, at least according to Gramlich and Jaffee.

Meltzer (1974), in a critical study, has convincingly rejected the view that 'housing policy is mortgage policy'. After carefully analysing various monetary statistics in the US, as well as the results of several econometric models, Meltzer concludes that mortgage policy has hardly promoted residential construction at all. The chief result has been that such policy encouraged the public to substitute mortgage credit for other kinds of credit. In this connection, it is interesting to observe, as our investigation shows, that this substitution occurs only in the case of non-residential mortgage lending.

It is clear that the models discussed here, with their supply-oriented character and the related ability to regulate the availability of credit, reflect the situation in the US and Canada. In these countries — in contrast to the practice in The Netherlands — it is usual for builders to ensure at the start of a project that some financial institution is prepared to take over the long-term financing (advanced commitment). In The Netherlands, the mortgage loan is of less importance for the financing of house construction, while moreover, such construction is principally regulated by the authorities. A determining factor in this connection is the authorities' assessment of the need for housing, and of the desirable distribution between premium dwellings, unsubsidized dwellings and dwellings constructed under the Public Housing Act. Until now, the availability of credit has hardly been a serious limiting factor; nor is the mortgage rate used as an instrument in housing policy. That is why it is less easy in The Netherlands than in the US and Canada, with their market-oriented policy, to describe housebuilding and the mortgage market in a single submodel.

8.8 Summary and Conclusions

This chapter deals with The Netherlands mortgage market by means of an econometric model. Equations of the gross demand for residential and non-residential mortgage credit are estimated for the period from 1965:II–1974:I. Moreover, the model comprises a mortgage rate equation and a system of equations describing the allocation of mortgage credit over four categories of financial institutions, estimated for the period 1960:II–1974:I. We also established a link between new registrations and net mortgage lending, because the former is the dependent variable in the demand equations, whereas the latter is the relevant variable in the interest rate equation and the supply system.

We conclude the demand to be fairly interest-rate sensitive, provided that residential mortgage borrowing mainly responds to changes in the mortgage rate, while the demand for non-residential mortgage loans reacts, above all, to changes in the interest rate differential. The relevant long-term elasticities are -1.14 and -0.58, respectively. Extrapolation for five quarters indicates that both demand relations are reasonably stable.

The mortgage rate is closely connected with the general rate of interest on the capital market, and hence mortgage policy could be pursued on the bond market. The equation explaining the mortgage rate shows a good predictive performance.

Our results suggest that differences in the mortgage rate between suppliers significantly affect the allocation of the total amount of mortgage loans among the financial institutions. The most important determinant, however, is the relative growth of new resources at banks.

Finally, it appears that the mortgage market in The Netherlands is demand-oriented. In that respect it contrasts sharply with the supply-oriented market in the US and Canada. This is presumably due to the lending practice in The Netherlands, and to the fact that post-war housing policy has been pursued here through direct action, and not by influencing the supply of funds on the market for mortgage loans.

Appendix 8.A Explanation of Symbols Used, and Sources of Data

BHO The amount of ordinary mortgage loans, on security other than a dwelling or combination of dwelling and business premises, newly registered by mortgage banks, building societies, life insurance companies, saving associations, pension funds, general savings banks, the Postal Savings Bank, commercial banks and agricultural credit institutions, in billions of guilders, 1965:I–1974:II. Source: CBS, Monthly Statistics of Finance.

BHW The amount of ordinary mortgage loans, on security of a dwelling or combination of dwelling and business premises, newly registered by financial institutions mentioned under *BHO*, in billions of guilders, 1965:I–1974:II. Source: see *BHO*.

BHT $BHO + BHW$.

BW Total expenditure on dwellings (for individuals) for which a building permit has been granted, in billions of guilders, 1960:I–1974:I. Source: CBS, Monthly Statistics for the Building Industry.

BWB Total expenditure on building, for trade, industry and agriculture, for which a building permit has been granted, in billions of builders, 1960:I–1974:I. Source: see *BW*.

BWT $BW + BWB$.

c Quarterly average of the male labour reserve as a percentage of the wage-earning male labour force, seasonally adjusted, 1960:I–1974:I. Source: CBS, Monthly Review.

D^B Balance sheet total of commercial banks and agriculture credit institutions, in billions of guilders, 1960:I–1974:I. Source: De Nederlandsche Bank.

DT Combined balance sheet total for the following institutions, in billions of guilders: commerical banks, mortgage banks, agricultural credit institutions, life insurance companies, private pension funds and savings banks. In the case of pension funds, owing to the great size of the break affecting the series in the fourth quarter of 1960, the first three quarters have been proportionately adapted. As balance sheet total for the mortgage banks the long-term borrowings have been used; 1960:I–1974:I. Source: De Nederlandsche Bank.

$\Delta D^B/\Delta DT$	Moving four-quarter average change in the balance sheet total for commercial banks and agricultural credit institutions (D^B) as a fraction of the change in the balance sheet total for all financial institutions (DT).
NH^{SP}	Change in the savings banks' total mortgage lendings in billions of guilders, 1960:I–1974:I. Source: De Nederlandsche Bank.
NH^{PL}	Ditto for pension funds and life insurance companies.
NH^{HB}	Ditto for mortgage banks.
NH^B	Ditto for commercial banks and agricultural credit institutions.
NHT	Change in total mortgage lendings by all the financial institutions mentioned under DT, in billions of guilders. Source: De Nederlandsche Bank.
rh	Interest rate on first mortgage lendings by mortgage banks; nominal rate, as a percentage, 1960:I–1974:I. Source: De Nederlandsche Bank, Quarterly Report.
rhv	Average, for the last four quarters, of the difference between rh retarded by one quarter and the rate of interest on all newly registered ordinary mortgage loans secured by real properties, 1965:I–1974:I. Source: CBS, Monthly Statistics of Finance.
r	Yield on the latest three long-term Government loans, in per cent, 1960:I–1974:I. Source: De Nederlandsche Bank, Quarterly Bulletin.
S_i	Seasonal dummies, $i = 1, 2, 3$.

9. Seventy Years of Interest Rates: Theory and Empirical Evidence

9.1 INTRODUCTION

In 1922, Regout (1922) published *Het rentevraagstuk*, originally presented in Utrecht as a doctoral thesis. The most notable feature of this work is the way Regout approached his topic. *Het rentevraagstuk* took a predominantly normative line, consistent with the ethical thinking which held sway amongst economists at the time. This aspect was aptly highlighted by the young Leiden lawyer, Jole (1923), a self-confident critic of the thesis, who in 1923 considered Regout's book as an unsatisfactory attempt to use Böhm-Bawerk's theory of interest as a basis for reasserting the canonical prohibition of interest 'on very shaky economic grounds'. Bordewijk (1922), a professor at the University of Groningen, went even further when, in 1922, he referred to *Het rentevraagstuk* as an unsuccessful attempt to 'make a link between moral philosophy and independent science'. Another striking feature of Regout's book is the absence of any measurement of the rate of interest. In other words, while the treatise is interesting enough in its own right, not only is it predominantly normative, but it is also purely qualitative. As such, it is typical and illustrative of the way economics was practised in the early 1920s. Nevertheless, there were counterexamples to show that other approaches existed. The Rotterdam business economist Jongh (1921) is a splendid example to illustrate that others were engaged in scholarly work without any normative stance. Furthermore, his admirable treatise shows how close finance was to monetary economics in those days. This is also the case with the Ph.D-thesis by Polak (1950), which had a major influence in The Netherlands after the first of its numerous editions appeared in 1921.

This chapter is intended as a brief review of the way theory of interest

Translation of 'Zeventig jaar rente: De evolutie in theorie en empirie' by M.M.G. Fase in: M.M.G. Fase and I. van der Zijpp (eds), *Samenleving en Economie in de twintigste Eeuw*, Stenfert Kroese, Leiden/Antwerpen 1992, pp. 227–250. The translation is reprinted by permission.

has developed since that time, paying particular attention to the positive theory of interest: a comparatively low-profile and nowadays more or less fully completed area of monetary economics. The comparative lack of enthusiasm which modern monetary economists have for the theory of interest is, in part, a reflection of the fact that the field is now apparently a mature sub-discipline. Yet, in practice, interest rates play a dominant role and a great deal of attention is focused on the financial markets where the rates are actually determined. Accordingly, this chapter also pays particular attention to the actual development of interest rates since 1920, and endeavours to shed light on a number of significant features of this development. Finally, a summary is given of the way economists have sought to give empirical meaning to abstract interest rate theory in order to explain the interest rate changes that have taken place in the Dutch money and capital markets. Thus, this chapter is structured around these three topics.

9.2 Evolution in Theory of Interest

Roos and Wieringa (1953) pointed out that, around the turn of the century, Böhm-Bawerk's theory of interest enjoyed more or less general acceptance in The Netherlands. According to Roos and Wieringa, this was partly due to the theories put forward by Pierson (1912) in his *Leerboek der Staatshuishoudkunde*, the major Dutch textbook of its day. It is reasonable to assume that, around the twenties, Böhm-Bawerk's theory of interest still held sway, having been featured in numerous text books. As readers will know, the crux of his theory is the hypothesis that people value present goods more highly than future goods. According to Böhm-Bawerk, three considerations support this hypothesis. First, there is a difference between present and future needs. Second, and for several reasons, people tend to underestimate the future. Third, existing goods have the technical potential for use in production, thereby increasing future supply. This reflects their physical productivity as capital good. It is primarily the second psychological consideration, reflecting a positive time preference, which provides a convincing explanation for the phenomenon of interest. This was also one of the main pillars of Fisher's theory of interest(Fisher (1907, 1930)).

The theories put forward by Böhm-Bawerk and Fisher have much in common. Nevertheless, for various reasons, Fisher's theory does represent, perhaps, a more important development in the theory of interest than that of Böhm-Bawerk. It is not only that in Fisher's terminology 'time preference' and 'premium' were replaced with 'impatience'; he also expounded his theory in terms of marginal utility and productivity, which brought Fisher's theory into line with modern economic thinking. Furthermore, Fisher made a much clearer distinction between supply and demand factors than Böhm-Bawerk. Finally, Fisher took specific account of the fact that, in reality, the financial markets are not uniformly characterized by perfect competition. This was done by weakening the assumption of a homogeneous market and allowing various market sectors exhibiting imperfect competition.

While Böhm-Bawerk and Fisher belong to the main evolutionary line of the theory of interest, various divergent theoretical ideas have also been put forward along the way. Most, however, never became mainstream in economics. Like the theories of Böhm-Bawerk and Fisher, many of these ideas may be described as non-monetary (see, for example, Conard (1959)). The most notable and controversial digression was undoubtedly the one introduced by Schumpeter, who saw interest as derived from the profits enabling the entrepreneur to engage in economic activities. According to this theory, interest is identified with profit and should therefore disappear with profit. However, Schumpeter argued that this would not happen, so long as the economic dynamics continue to create new profit-making opportunities. Strikingly, the theory completely disregarded consumer credit, for which Schumpeter expressly accepts Böhm-Bawerk's principle of time preference. Another interesting theory, whose publication went largely unnoticed at the time and is now almost forgotten, was that developed by the Dutch economist Dorp (1937). She too saw the principle of interest as closely related to profit, suggesting that the rate of interest was determined mainly by the monetary authorities, and was thus a monetary phenomenon.

Much less controversial were the ideas of the American economists Lerner and Knight, who built upon Fisher's non-monetary theory of interest and made the link with monetary interest theories. Lerner emphasized the importance of the marginal productivity of capital, which for him was embodied in the marginal efficiency of investment, as a determinant of interest. For his part, Knight modified Fisher's approach by focusing on uncertainty and on the fact that, in the long-run, the distinction between capital goods and consumer goods is much less clear than many theories of interest had assumed. Being particularly concerned with entrepreneurial activity, Knight saw interest mainly as a consequence of uncertainty and of the marginal productivity of capital, rather than as a consequence of time preference.

Keynes' (1930) observation that classical interest theory was largely unrelated to the monetary concept of interest, is well known. Naturally, the monetary theories of interest — principally Wicksell's loanable funds theory and the liquidity preference theory advocated by Keynes — did not exhibit this shortcoming.

Wicksell described by Goedhart (1947) as a forerunner of the monetary interest theorists, is responsible for introducing the distinction between the natural or normal rate of interest and monetary or market rate of interest. The former is the rate of interest in an economy untroubled by monetary problems. According to Wicksell's theory, equality between the natural and monetary rates of interest or the equivalent equality between *ex ante* savings and investments or price stability is a yardstick for the neutrality of money. This situation was long regarded as the economic optimum by Dutch monetary theorists, such as Koopmans and Verrijn Stuart in the thirties and forties, who followed German-speaking economists such as Hayek. One of the problems with this approach was that the natural rate of interest is untangible and unobservable. The crux of the loanable funds theory, which is of Swedish origin, was that the rate of interest is the result of the supply of, and demand for, financial securities. Although advocates of the theory have developed this aspect in highly practical terms, not strictly adhering to the abstraction of a single rate of interest, it is clear that the acceptability of this abstraction depends entirely on the actual conditions. Certainly, however, there is always a confrontation between flows on the two sides of the market, with monetary forces dominant and reality somewhat obscured.

This 'flow' approach, used by advocates of the loanable funds theory, superbly summarized by Vermaat (1966), is the main point of contrast with Keynes' liquidity preference theory, which is based on the stock approach, and Hicks' (1939) general equilibrium approach, attempting to complete the liquidity preference theory. While Keynes saw interest rates as determined by the supply of, and demand for, liquidities in the sense of liquid securities as part of an investment portfolio, Hicks proved that in such a model, strictly speaking, interest rates cannot be determined without taking account of savings and investment. The result was the famous IS-LM framework, with its numerous amendments for exchange rates and balance of payments influences. According to the text books, this was the paradigm of modern theory of interest. Notably, this theory proves to contain elements of the old non-monetary approach, certainly if one examines the synthesis introduced by Hicks. As I shall illustrate, Hicks also expanded the theory of interest in a completely different direction, by looking specifically at maturity of loans. A second contrast between the liquidity preference theory and the loanable funds theory is that Keynes' focus was on the money market, while the loanable funds model focuses on the demand for and supply of bonds. As is well known, the assumption embodied in Walras' Law requires that, in a general equilibrium model, equilibrium in the money market implies equilibrium in the bond market as well.

In view of this, Hicks (1939) and Lutz (1940) introduced a framework that properly reflected financial reality. In this framework, financial securities are far from uniform in their maturity, risk or liquidity, while institutional circumstances are equally significant in the process of interest rate determination. This led to development of the doctrine of the term structure of interest rates, which was novel at the time.

The theory of term structure of interest rates involves a number of hypotheses which seek to explain differentials in interest rates associated with various terms of debt or maturities. The normal pattern is for interest to increase with maturity; when the reverse is the case (as it sometimes can be in practice), an inverted or abnormal interest rate structure is said to exist. Despite what such phraseology might suggest, the various theoretical schools of thought do not in all cases imply the existence of interest rates which increase with maturity.

The best known explanation is Hicks' liquidity or risk premium theory. This theory, which in a certain sense builds upon Fisher's 1896 expectation theory, assumes that investors prefer short-term loans, since they entail less sacrifice of liquidity and risk. In this view, the disadvantages of investment are, as it were, offset by a liquidity premium, which can also be regarded as payment for the intertemporal substitution. An alternative view is provided by the segmented market theory, which places the emphasis on institutional factors, so that the capital market is characterized by separate segments, and the term structure of interest rates is also determined by considerations other than liquidity and risk, like the size of the market. Another approach is the preferred habitat theory of Modigliani and Sutch (1966). Modigliani and Sutch (1967) is, in effect, a synthesis of the two schools of thought, based upon a generalization of the liquidity preference theory. The latter attaches considerable significance to supply and demand, in other words, investors' preferences, in addition to risk perceptions and expectations. Just as the general process of interest rate determination has been the focus of much empirical research, so a great deal of work has been done on interest term structures since the publication of Hicks' theory. Nelson (1972) and Roll (1970) serve as good early examples of the studies carried out in this field, which have been summarized by Dodds and Ford (1974) and Stokman (1990).

Without question, the doctrine of interest term structure is one of the most important, if not the most important, development in the theory of interest since the twenties. Furthermore, this theory lends itself very well to empirical testing, as shown by the abundance of studies.

Nevertheless, lack of uniformity has meant that the results obtained have not always been equally satisfactory. Since the seventies, monetary economists have perceived a greater need for the empirical verification of economic theories, and it should be noted that the monetary theory of interest supported by Keynes is no exception. I shall return to this point later. Another topic which deserves attention, primarily because of its practical significance, is the so-called Gibson paradox or Fisher hypothesis. Keynes coined the phrase 'Gibson paradox' in his Treatise to describe the apparently paradoxical phenomenon, observed by the London publicist Gibson, of inflation and interest frequently following a parallel course. Fisher (1925) drew attention to the same phenomenon in the US; his assumption was that the real interest rate was constant and that variations in nominal interest rates reflects inflation expectations. Gootzeit (1991) recently pointed out that Wicksell had already developed this idea around the turn of the century.

9.3 Interest Rate Movements in The Netherlands 1920–1990

In 1922, capital market interest, taken as the yield on perpetual government bonds, was less than 5%, while money market interest rates were, as usual, more than one percentage point lower. By 1991, the capital market rate being the yield on the five longest-term government loans was about 9%, while the money market rate, being the rate for three-month cash loans to local authorities, barely differed. In the meantime, interest rates had sometimes been higher and sometimes lower, with constant variations in the differential between capital and money market rates, influenced partly by cyclical factors and, in recent decades, partly by monetary policy. Figure 9.1, which shows variations in several interest rates, gives an impression of the extent to which the rates have fluctuated, both in absolute terms and relative to one another. The figure covers the period of 1920 to 1990 and shows movement in two short-term rates (the money market rate and De Nederlandsche Bank's discount rate) and in two long-term rates (the government state loan yield and the mortgage rate). The money market rate and De Nederlandsche Bank's discount rate have generally been quite similar, although the former was consistently around one percentage point lower, particularly between 1935 and 1955.

As the chart shows, De Nederlandsche Bank rarely manipulated interest rates for policy purposes during that period. The mortgage rate, which is set on the less competitive private sector of the capital market,

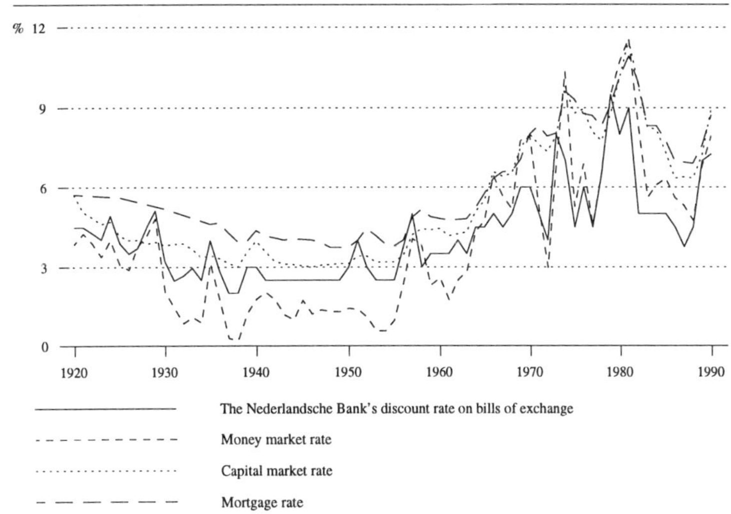

Figure 9.1: Movement in Dutch interest rates

has almost without exception been on average 0.75 percentage point higher than the loan yield. Thus, statistically speaking, the domestic interest rate pattern in The Netherlands has historically displayed remarkable stability. Nevertheless, there have been a number of fundamental interest rate shifts during the period considered. Since 1950, for example, the interest rate structure has been inverted on several occasions; competition on the mortgage market has become stiffer, while the public and financial institutions have become more pro-active on interest rates.

Table 9.1: Averages for, and standard deviations in, four Dutch interest rates (%)

	Average			Standard deviation		
	1920–59	1960–90	1920–90	1920–59	1960–90	1920–90
Discount rate	3.18	5.31	4.11	0.85	1.52	1.59
Money market rate	2.10	6.14	3.86	1.30	2.44	2.75
Government bond yield	3.71	7.39	5.31	0.66	1.86	2.26
Mortgage rate	4.65	7.60	5.94	0.72	1.68	1.91

If one summarizes the data on the four interest rates using the statistics as in Table 9.1, the picture presented in Figure 9.1 becomes clearer. First, it is immediately apparent that the averages also exhibit the structure discernible in the chart. More interestingly, the variability in mortgage rates and in the Bank's discount rates is not as great as that in government loan yields or in money market rates. The mortgage rate has gradually been edging closer to the government loan yield, while the money market figures have, perhaps, been influenced by more pro-active interest rate policies. Similar trends can be discerned in the sub-periods. Furthermore, it is apparent that in the first sub-period, not only was the average level of interest significantly lower than in the second sub-period, but also the variability in rates was not nearly as great.

This picture, with relatively low average rates and less variability prior to 1960, was not confined to The Netherlands, as Table 9.2 illustrates. The table shows data on long-term interest rates in The Netherlands and five other countries. Throughout the period, capital market rates in The Netherlands and the US were 1 to 1.5 percentage points lower than elsewhere, while German rates were similarly low between 1960 and 1990. The variability was greater in the UK than elsewhere, but there was little difference between the other five countries. When one considers the sub-periods separately, however, one finds marked differences from this general picture.

Everywhere, except in Germany, average capital market rates in the

Table 9.2: Averages for, and standard deviations in, capital market interest rates in six countries, together with inflation in the industrialized nations (%)

	Average			Standard deviation		
	1920–59	1960–90	1920–90	1920–59	1960–90	1920–90
US	3.11	7.62	5.08	0.80	2.80	2.96
UK	3.92	9.96	6.56	0.83	2.95	3.63
France	4.61	8.74	6.42	1.06	3.06	2.98
Germany	6.18	7.41	6.76	1.55	1.31	1.55
Belgium	4.65	8.40	6.28	0.59	2.33	2.46
The Netherlands	3.71	7.39	5.31	0.66	1.86	2.26
Inflation in industrialized nations	0.96	5.56	2.97	5.93	3.16	5.40

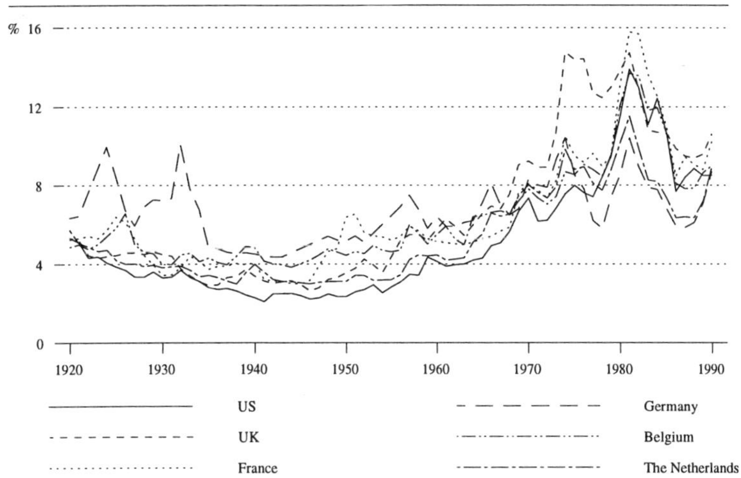

Notes:
Definitions of capital market interest rates: US: up to 1953, government bond yield, as from 1953, government long-term bond yield; UK and France: up to 1953, yield on perpetual state loans, as from 1963, government long-term bond yield; Germany, as from 1956, government bond yield. For earlier years, largely taken from Roos and Wieringa; no data is available for 1921, 1922 or the period 1944 to 1947; Belgium: average state loan yield; The Netherlands: up to 1957, perpetual state loans, 1958 to 1983, yield on the three most recent long-term state loans, as from 1984, yield on the five longest-term state loans. The consumer price index in the UK (taken from B.R. Mitchell's Historical Statistics) is used as the inflation figure for the period 1920 to 1951; for the period 1951 to 1990, the consumer price index for the main industrialized countries is used (taken from the IMF's International Financial Statistics).

Figure 9.2: Capital market interest rates in six countries

second sub-period were roughly twice as high as in the first sub-period. The standard deviation in the second sub-period was three times as great as in the first, with Germany again the sole exception. Graphical inspection of the data, as in Figure 9.2, offers a similar picture of increasing interest volatility and divergence over time. Germany's exceptional figures for the first sub-period are related to the hyperinflation of the twenties and post-war reconstruction.

From time to time, economists of both theoretical and practical persuasion have turned their attention not only to nominal interest, but also to real rates. The calculation of real interest rates is to some extent arbitrary, since real interest is an indefinite concept, being dependent upon the chosen time horizon. Reference was made to this fact by the Bank for International Settlements in its 1990 report (page 220), for instance. The real rate of interest is equal to the nominal rate, minus the expected rate of inflation during the term of the loan agreement. The strictly uncertain nature of the forecast rate of inflation is the main reason why it is difficult to arrive at a definitive figure for the real rate of interest.

Nevertheless, an attempt has been made to quantify real interest rates between 1920 and 1990 by deducting the four-year moving average of the actual inflation rate from the interest rate. The results are presented in Figure 9.3.

The most striking feature of the course traced by real interest rates in the seventy years considered here is that the interest rate was very high (3 to 7%) before World War II, and returned to similar levels in the period of 1980 to 1990. Such high rates would tend to indicate a shortage of capital. Also of interest is that real rates in the forties and early fifties appear to have been negative. This may have been due to the cheap money policy pursued in The Netherlands at the time with a view to encourage industrialization. Real interest rates were also negative in the late seventies, when inflation in The Netherlands, as elsewhere, was very high.

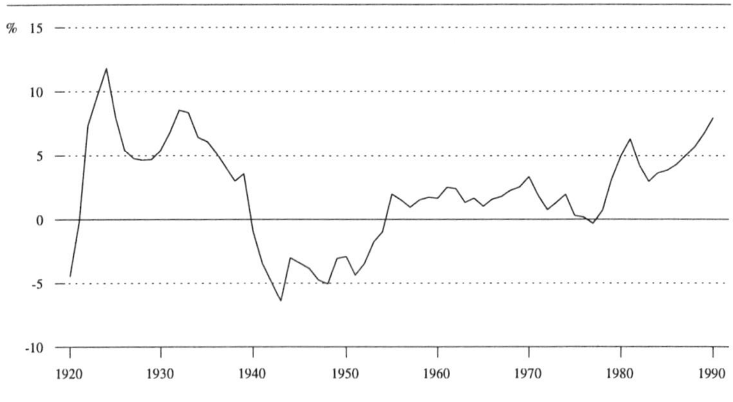

Note: Calculated as the yield on state loans, minus the four-year moving average inflation rate.

Figure 9.3: Real interest rates

9.4 A Survey of Empirical Interest Rate Equations for The Netherlands

In addition to the theoretical studies and the surveys of actual interest rates summarized in the preceding sections, a great deal of effort has been invested in recent decades in the estimation of interest rate equations for various countries, including The Netherlands. Elaborating in Tinbergen's work in the thirties, The Netherlands, as the centre of empirical econometrics, played a pioneering role in this field. Estimation of interest rate equation is one of the core businesses of what is known as monetary econometrics. The following sections present a brief survey of this field, to complete the picture presented so far with solid, empirically-slanted detail. For the sake of simplicity, I shall concentrate on the process of interest rate determination in The Netherlands. Interest rate equations, particularly those in empirical macroeconomic models, often involve a wide range of different types of interest. As a result, attention is not focused solely on capital market rates, but also on money market interest rates and on banks' deposit and lending rates. This broad focus is related to the fact that macroeconomic models often distinguish between several different financial markets and sectors. The empirical literature on Dutch interest rates considered here is concerned with five main markets:

1. the central bank credit market, or the money market in the narrow sense
2. the money market in the broad sense
3. the capital market
4. the market for bank loans
5. the market for bank deposits.

One important point which emerges from the empirical literature survey is that very different theoretical bases are used for the specification of interest rate equations. In the following section, therefore, the estimated equations are grouped into five broad categories on the basis of the type of model involved:

a implicit interest rate models, assuming interest rates are determined by the intersection of demand and supply;

b reduced form equations;

c interest rate setting models;

d central bank reaction equations;

e linked interest rate equations.

Type *a* models involve supply and demand equations, on the basis of which, assuming that market equilibrium exists, an interest rate equation results from the substitution of the equilibrium condition. In principle, this approach is valid, irrespective of the size of the structural model. Type *b* models describe the interest rate as a direct function of supply and demand factors. The thinking behind this approach effectively takes account implicitly of the interrelationships between such factors. Type *c* models are used for financial markets in which the supplier sets the rate of interest. In other words, the approach assumes the existence of a monopoly or oligopoly. In such a market, demand is determined by the pricing policy of the supplier of goods or services. The way banks set interest rates on savings, for example, is consistent with this model. Type *d* models reflect the situation in markets where a central bank sets interest rates. A particularly good example would be the setting of official rates in what is effectively a reaction function of the central bank (see Duisenberg (1984)). Finally, Type *e* models are used for equations in which a particular interest rate is related to another rate of interest, without being significantly influenced by other explanatory variables. This approach is generally based on either term structure considerations or arbitrage between segmented financial markets.

The survey below begins with a stylized tabular overview of interest rate equations, used in a number of well-known Dutch empirical macroeconomic models. The literature on independent interest rate equations is then dealt with in the following subsection. The section concludes with a discussion of what the various models tell us about how Dutch interest rates compare with those applied in other countries.

9.4.1 Interest Rate Equations in Empirical Macroeconomic Models

Table 9.3 provides a schematic overview of interest rate equations in eleven empirical macroeconomic models for The Netherlands. The models are listed in the order in which they were published.

The models in question are the Driehuis (1972) quarterly model, the Korteweg and Loo (1977) model, the Knoester (1980) model, MOKMON-1-81 (Fase 1981a), the Loo (1983) model, MORKMON I (De Nederlandsche Bank (1984) and Fase (1984)), RASMUS (Groene, Siebrand, and Windt 1984), CESAM (Kuipers, Jongbloed, Kuper, and Sterken 1988), FREIA-KOMPAS (Erp, Hasselman, Nibbelink, and Timmer 1989), HERMES (Mot, Noord, Schelt-Scheele, and Koning 1989), DUFIS (Sterken

1990) and MORKMON II (Fase, Kramer, and Boeschoten 1990). Those models which do not have a name of their own are referred to below by the name of the relevant author. Where reference is made to the MORKMON models, this phrase covers MOKMON-1-81, MORKMON I and MORKMON II.

At the outset, it should be pointed out that the interest rate nomenclature used in the various models is not consistent. In spite of this, I have endeavoured to find common denominators so that comparisons could be made between the models. Nevertheless, the reader should bear in mind the fact that the definition of, say, short-term interest used for one model is not necessarily identical to that used for another. (For an overview of the interest rate equations in the various models, see Keijzer and Schuit (1991).)

As Table 9.3 shows, the most frequently modelled interest rates are the discount rate, the interest on short-term and long-term government debts, interest on savings accounts and interest on bank credits. The differences in the specifications employed in the models are outlined in the following sections.

Short-term interest Short-term interest is usually taken as the yield on short-term government debt (three-month Treasury paper). This is modelled implicitly in three of the models: Loo, CESAM and FREIA-KOMPAS. The MORKMON models assume a reaction equation of the central bank to movement in the guilder-Deutsche Mark exchange rate. This is modelled by including a variable which reflects the ratio between the exchange rate and parity. In these models, the market expectation regarding the exchange rate is represented by the balance on the current account. In RASMUS and HERMES, short-term interest is described by a reduced form. RASMUS uses the discount rate and the liquidity position of the banks as the explanatory variables, with the discount rate reflecting foreign influences. In HERMES, short-term rates in the US, the guilder-dollar exchange rate, that is interest parity, inflation or the Fisher effect, the current account balance and a cyclical indicator all play a part. Finally, in DUFIS, short-term interest depends directly on the official discount rate.

Long-term interest In The Netherlands, the long-term or capital market interest rate is generally taken as the yield on the three longest-term government loans. Like short-term interest, long-term interest is modelled implicitly by Loo, CESAM and FREIA-KOMPAS. In Knoester, long-term interest is linked to the call money rate. In the other models (Driehuis, MORKMON (3×), RASMUS and HERMES), long-term interest is described by means of a reduced form equation. Short-

Table 9.3: Interest rate comparisons in empirical macroeconomic models

Authors/model	Number of endogenous rates	Financial market	Model type
Driehuis (1972)	1	Long-term government debt	*b*
Korteweg and Loo (1977)	3	Savings	*c*
		Domestic assets	*a*
		Domestic capital	*a*
Knoester (1980)	3	Call money	*a*
		Long-term government debt	*e*
		Short-term savings	*e*
Fase (1981a), MOKMON-1-81	6	Short-term government debt	*d*
		Long-term government debt	*b*
		Current account balances	*c*
		Savings	*c*
		Bank credit	*c*
		Treasury paper	*e*
Loo (1983)	12	Short-term government debt	*a*
		Long-term government debt	*a*
		Savings	*c*
		Short-term savings	*c*
		Long-term savings	*e*
		Short-term bank credit	*c*
		Mortgage rates (2×)	*b*
		Capital market loans (2×)	*b*, *e*
		Other rates (2×)	*e*
De Nederlandsche Bank (1984), Fase (1984), MORKMON I	6	Short-term government debt	*d*
		Long-term government debt	*b*
		Current account balances	*c*
		Savings	*c*
		Short-term bank credit	*c*
		Treasury paper	*e*
Groene *et al.* (1984), RASMUS	3	Short-term government debt	*b*
		Long-term government debt	*b*
		Savings	*c*
Kuipers *et al.* (1988), CESAM	6	Short-term government debt	*a*
		Long-term government debt	*a*
		Short-term savings	*c*
		Long-term savings	*c*
		Short-term bank credit	*a*
		Long-term bank credit	*a*

Table 9.3: (continued)

Authors/model	Number of endogenous rates	Financial market	*Model type*
Erp *et al.* (1989), FREIA-KOMPAS	5	Discount	*d*
		Short-term government debt	*a*
		Long-term government debt	*a*
		Savings	*c*
		Short-term bank credit	*c*
Mot *et al.* (1989), HERMES	3	Short-term government debt	*b*
		Long-term government debt	*b*
		Short-term savings	*b*
Sterken (1990), DUFIS	10	Discount	*d*
		Liquidities	*e*
		Short-term government debt	*e*
		Short-term savings	*c*
		Long-term savings	*c*
		Short-term bank credit	*c*
		Private loans	*c*
		Mortgage rates	*c*
		Bonds	*a*
		Shares	*a*
Fase *et al.* (1990), MORKMON II	7	Discount	*e*
		Short-term government debt	*d*
		Long-term government debt	*b*
		Current account balances	*c*
		Savings	*c*
		Short-term bank credit	*c*
		Treasury paper	*e*

Note: The model types are as follows: *a* the implicit model, *b* reduced form, *c* interest rate setting, *d* central bank reaction function, *e* linked interest rate.

term interest is a determinant of long-term interest in all these models. Driehuis is the only model not to include one or more foreign long-term interest rates as explanatory variables in the equation. The inclusion of foreign rates reflects the internationalization of the capital market. The other important explanatory variables are the anticipated rate of inflation and the anticipated exchange rate. Only RASMUS does not include inflation as an explanatory variable. MOKMON originally incorporated the anticipated inflation rate, but in later versions this was replaced by the differential between the Dutch and German inflation rates: a proxy for anticipated exchange rate. In the first two versions of MORKMON, the anticipated dollar exchange rate was also included. HERMES and Driehuis use somewhat different modelling techniques. HERMES takes explicit account of the influence of the liquidity ratio and the current account balance, while Driehuis allows for unemployment and the 'normal' real rate of interest to explain the long-term interest rate. Driehuis' 'normal' real interest rate variable is based on the speculation motive in the Keynesian theory on the demand for money.

Discount rate In FREIA-KOMPAS and DUFIS, the discount rate is related to the German discount rate and to the differential between the actual exchange rate and parity. In this way, the discount rate is accorded a degree of control over the money market rate. By contrast, in MORKMON II, the discount rate follows the money market rate; in other words, the assumed causal relationship is the opposite of that assumed in FREIA-KOMPAS and DUFIS.

Savings Interest on savings is modelled using interest equations for short-term and long-term savings and for overall savings. The way this is done differs significantly from one model to another, but in nearly all cases the rate of interest is taken as the outcome of interest rate setting.

In Knoester, Loo, CESAM and HERMES, short-term savings rates depend on a short-term interest rate or the official discount rate. In CESAM and DUFIS, the interest rate on short-term savings is partly determined by the long-term savings rate and partly by the rate payable on demand deposits. DUFIS also takes account of the bond yield.

Loo makes interest on long-term savings dependent on the short-term rate. In CESAM, the long-term savings rate depends both on the interest rate on net foreign assets and on the discount rate, while in DUFIS the interest on long-term savings is dependent on the official discount rate and the short-term savings rate.

Interest on all savings collectively is also modelled in a number of different ways. However, in all the models except Korteweg and Loo, the overall savings rate depends on a short-term interest rate. Furthermore, FREIA-KOMPAS and MORKMON II include the long-term interest rate as an explanatory variable. In the MORKMON models and in Loo, the share of the banks' balance sheet accounted for by savings is also an explanatory variable. RASMUS additionally includes a monetary tension variable.

Bank credits With regard to the bank credit rate, a distinction is made between short-term and long-term credit. The long-term bank credit rate is only modelled in CESAM, but Loo, MORKMON, CESAM, FREIA-KOMPAS and DUFIS all model the short-term bank credit rate. Both rates are modelled implicitly by CESAM; in the other models, interest on bank credit depends on the official discount rate and the short-term interest rate. The MORKMON models also allow for the share of the balance sheet total accounted for by bank credit as explanatory variable. Loo makes explicit allowance for a credit ceiling.

From the information above, it will be clear that the interest rate equations in the models under consideration differ from one another considerably. Nevertheless, the various equations frequently make use of the same explanatory variables. Furthermore, the various authors tend to use similar models for similar purposes. Interest on savings and bank credit, for instance, is in most cases modelled on the assumption of interest rate setting. Interest rate setting models are the most commonly used type, followed at some distance by implicit interest rate equation models. Where an implicit model is not used, long-term interest is generally modelled by means of a reduced form equation. In such models, foreign long-term interest and inflation, or anticipated inflation, are the chief determinants. Where short-term interest is concerned, it is notable that the MORKMON models treat the rate as the outcome of central bank policy, while the other models use either an implicit approach or a reduced form equation. Another interesting fact is that MORKMON II makes the discount rate a function of the short-term interest rate, whereas the other two models in which the discount rate is endogenous, FREIA-KOMPAS and DUFIS, assume that the Dutch official discount rate is dependent on comparable rates abroad. In relation to foreign discount rates, it is worth noting that the symbols used may be confusing. In the DUFIS model, for instance, the variable 'rcb' is used to refer both to the official discount rate and to the money market interest rate.

The Loo and Sterken models are characterized by a rather drastic disaggregation of the capital market and consequently include a relatively large number of empirical equations, with twelve and thirteen different rates of interest, respectively.

9.4.2 Interest Rate Equations for Long-term Rates

Table 9.4 provides an overview of several interest rate equations taken from single interest rate studies, *i.e.* equations which did not form part of a large macroeconomic model. The only exceptions are the reduced form equations used in the studies by Fase and Nieuwkerk (1975) and by Butter, Dongelmans, and Fase (1977). The first of these equations was ultimately derived from a small, explicitly formulated structural model

Table 9.4: Interest rate equations in single studies

	Categories of explanatory variable							
	1	2	3	4	5	6	7	8
Stevers (1963)	×	×	×					
Nieuwenburg and Koeman (1969)	×	×	×					
Fase (1972a)					×			
Post (1973)		×			×			
Nieuwenburg and Leemreize (1974)	×	×	×	×	×			
Fase and Nieuwkerk (1975)	×	×	×	×	×			×
Butter *et al.* (1977)	×	×	×					
Bomhoff (1983)	×	×		×	×	×		×
Prins (1983)		×	×	×	×		×	
Stokman (1990)		×	×	×				

Notes:
Category 1: measures of monetary tension; category 2: cyclical indicators; category 3: domestic interest rates; category 4: foreign interest rates; category 5: anticipated inflation; category 6: budgetary deficit; category 7: exchange rate; category 8: relative inflation.

for an open economy. The equation estimated by Butter, Dongelmans, and Fase, for the interest margin on mortgage lending, was part of a simultaneous model of the mortgage lending market.

The considered interest rate is the capital market interest rate. As with interest rate equations which are part of a macroeconomic model, various interest rate definitions are used. In the studies by Stevers (1963), Nieuwenburg and Koeman (1969) and Nieuwenburg and Leemreize (1974), the capital market interest rate is defined as the interest on a representative loan. Butter, Dongelmans, and Fase use the mortgage rate. According to established thinking, mortgage interest is a form of private capital market interest. The other studies work on the basis of bond yield rates. In Fase (1972c), Post (1973), Fase and Nieuwkerk (1975), Bomhoff (1983) and Prins (1983), the rate of interest is taken to be the yield on the three longest-term government loans, while in Stokman (1990), it is taken to be the yield on the five longest-term government loans.

The explanatory variables used by the various authors can be placed in eight broad categories. The first category includes all the variables which reflect the influence of the money supply. The second category consists of cyclical indicators. This is quite a broad category, since various indicators are used in the studies reviewed, including the level of corporate investment in plant (used by Stevers (1963)), the industrial production volume index (used by Nieuwenburg and Leemreize (1974)), the mortgage supply (used by Butter, Dongelmans, and Fase (1977)) and the level of unexpected variation in global trade (used by Bomhoff (1983)).

Anticipated inflation is calculated in various ways, the most common approach being to adopt the adaptive expectation hypothesis (Stevers, Nieuwenburg and Koeman, Fase, Nieuwenburg and Leemreize, Post and Prins). Fase and Nieuwkerk, on the other hand, use an ARIMA model to estimate the anticipated rate of inflation. The budgetary deficit, expressed as a percentage of gross national product, is taken into account only by Bomhoff. Of the authors whose studies are reviewed here, Prins was the only one to treat the appreciation of the guilder against the dollar as an explanatory variable. However, it is worth noting that, in principle, the effect of including the relative inflation rate, as in the studies by Fase, Kramer, and Boeschoten and by Bomhoff, is the same as that of including appreciation. Most of the studies listed in Table 9.4 sought both to explain interest rate movement in quantitative terms and to provide predictions. This was not the case, however, with the studies by Fase, by Post and by Fase and Nieuwkerk, which were primarily intended to test the so-called Fisher hypothesis or Gibson paradox. It is interesting to note that these studies indicated that the Fisher hypothesis requires substantial amendment for an open economy such as that of The Netherlands, since foreign interest rates prove to be one of the main determinants of the domestic interest rate level.

9.4.3 Foreign Influences

With a view to adding some detail to the picture presented in Table 9.4, Table 9.5 provides, by way of illustration, an overview of the effect on domestic rates of a rise in foreign interest rates. The interest rate considered is the capital market interest rate. Two points are worthy of note in this context. First, far more attention is given to the international aspects of the interest rate determination in the empirical literature than in the theoretical literature. The consequences for interest rates of abandoning the assumption of a closed economy, are barely addressed in published research. Second, the results of the single interest rate equations are not readily comparable with those from the simultaneous models, on account of the more complex endogenous effect of shocks in the simultaneous models.

From this table, it is clear that the single interest rate equations generally suggest that the influence of foreign rates on domestic rates is smaller in the short-run. In the long-run, a particular percentage-point rise in foreign interest rates appears to put domestic rates up

Table 9.5: Influence of a one percentage-point rise in foreign interest rates on the domestic capital market interest rate

	Short-term	Long-term
Interest rate equations in simultaneous models		
Loo (1983)	0.68	0.92
Fase (1984), De Nederlandsche Bank (1984), MORKMON I	0.70	0.80
Groene, Siebrand, and Windt (1984), RASMUS	0.59	1.10
Kuipers *et al.* (1988), CESAM	1.1	1.1
Sterken (1990)	1.47	1.17
Fase *et al.* (1990), MORKMON II	0.95	0.85
Single interest rate equations		
Nieuwenburg and Leemreize (1974)	0.13	0.68
Fase and Nieuwkerk (1975)	0.39	1.00
Bomhoff (1983)	0.74	0.74
Prins (1983)	0.24	0.66

Note: Including the effect of other variables, among which domestic interest rates, within a structural model.

by a similar percentage. Again, however, the effect indicated by the single equations is less than that suggested by the simultaneous models. This is probably due to the fact that the single interest rate equations were generally estimated in relatively early studies, when international developments had less influence on domestic capital markets and the policy of shadowing the Deutsche Mark had yet to be introduced.

9.5 Conclusions

This chapter sketches the evolution in interest theory and empirical interest rate research for The Netherlands over three-quarters of a century. The greatest theoretical advance in the last seventy years has undoubtedly been the integration of the monetary and non-monetary theory of interest within the general equilibrium framework. Embodied in the so-called IS-LM paradigm, this development is mainly due to the work of Hicks (1939). Another important new feature of the theory of interest rates is the theory of the term structure of interest rates. Also noteworthy is the shift in emphasis towards empirical, and in particular econometric, studies of interest rate determination. The importance of the empirical econometric approach is due mainly to its usefulness in the verification of theory; it does not have any real prognostic value. One must also conclude that, since 1920, nominal interest rates have persistently, though not constantly, followed an upward course. It is clear that persistent inflation has forced up not only nominal interest rates, but also the real rate of interest. The explanation for this phenomenon, I would conclude, is debatable, but involves factors such as shortage of capital, productivity development, demographic change and a shortage of savings. Given its importance, not least in relation to business economics, it is precisely upon this area of interest theory that future studies should focus.

PART TWO

On Asset Prices

An efficient capital market is an important component of a capitalist system [...] if the capital market is to function smoothly in allocating resources, prices of securities must be good indicators of value.

Fama (1966, p. 133)

It is a capital mistake to theorise before one has data. Insensibly one begins to twist facts to suit theories, instead of theories to suit facts.

A. Conan Doyle, *A Scandal in Bohemia*

We do not yet have a model of expected returns that fits the data.

Hodrick (1987)

Among the many misfortunes which bring ruin to entire state [...] four are the most serious: internal dissension, a high death rate, poor harvests and the corruption of money.

Nicholas Copernicus (1528), *A Method of Coining Money*

10. Index-linked Bonds and Inflation Risk in EMU

10.1 Introduction

Knowledge of expected inflation is of crucial importance to the design of monetary policy. This is especially true when policy aims at an inflation target. In practice, the expected inflation rate cannot be observed directly. However, index-linked bonds may yield important information on inflation expectations.

Index-linked bonds are financial instruments, which fully protect the holder from erosion of the principal or of interest payments, resulting from inflation. This is achieved by having the specified coupon rate or principal payments adjusted periodically for changes in the general price index. Conventional (nominal) bonds do not offer this protection against inflation, which is why investors require a higher coupon rate. As a result of this fundamental difference regarding the protection against the risk of inflation, and assuming no other risk premiums, it is possible to calculate inflation expectations by comparing the price of conventional bonds to index-linked bonds. The United Kingdom is currently an interesting example of the possible use of this method in practice. The Bank of England uses the price formation of index-linked bonds to measure inflation expectations. These are published quarterly in the Bank's Inflation Report, an important document, in view of the Bank's policy of direct inflation targeting.

The method is best illustrated by a fictitious example. Take an index-linked 'zero-coupon bond' of £ 1,000, with a term of one year, where price adjustment takes place on the basis of the consumer price index, and the issue price is £ 960. Basically, this implies a real interest rate of 4%.

If, at the same time, the issue price for a comparable conventional bond is £ 930, the yield gap between the two is 3 percentage points. This can be interpreted to be an estimation of expected inflation, provided

Translation of 'Indexleningen en inflatierisico in de EMU' by M.M.G. Fase and E. Shtrasburg, *Economisch Statistische Berichten*, **82** (August 13, 1997), 604–608.

there is no inflation risk premium involved (or tax on interest-generated income).[1]

The length of time — fifteen years — for which indexed bonds have existed in the United Kingdom permits an empirical analysis of the relationship between nominal (and real) interest rates, inflation and inflation rate uncertainty. The relationship between nominal interest rates and inflation expectations is described in the well-known Fisher equation, which for brevity, will not be further elaborated upon here. Uncertainty about future inflation distorts the relationship between nominal interest rates and inflation expectations, justifying an additional compensation. This is known as the inflation risk premium. Using UK data for the 1982–1996 period, this chapter will examine whether, besides the compensation for expected inflation (the traditional Fisher equation), nominal interest rates also include a compensation for uncertainty concerning inflation expectations. The rationale for examining this is that the usefulness of indexed bonds in measuring inflation expectations is somewhat limited if indeed such a compensation exists.

10.2 Inflation Expectations and Monetary Policy

Information about inflation expectations is all the more important if the central bank bases its strategy on inflation targeting, as is currently the case in the UK and an increasing number of other EMU countries.[2] Under this system of so-called direct inflation targeting, monetary policy is aimed directly at the ultimate goal, the inflation rate. This is in contrast to a policy of monetary or exchange rate targeting. In these cases the central bank focuses on intermediate targets such as the money supply or the exchange rate.

Within the framework of direct inflation targeting, policy decisions are based on the differences between the announced target zone and the forecasts for inflation. Actual inflation cannot serve as a measure for future inflation, as policy actions affect it with a considerable time lag. A large number of economic indicators are used to assess expected inflation. These include the time structure of interest rates, the money supply and the exchange rate. Directly observable inflation expectations would be a more powerful monetary policy indicator, however. Besides, changes in inflation expectations would reflect the effectiveness and credibility of monetary policy.

---

1 Cf. Hetzel (1992).

2 See European Monetary Institute (1996, pp. 66 et seq.).

There are several ways to assess inflation expectations.[3] Popular amongst theoretical economists is the use of statistical time series models. A drawback is that these can only be tested using authentic data concerning inflation expectations. A further complication is that the process of inflation could change over time. This could adversely affect the consistency of inflation expectations and actual inflation.

Another way of establishing inflation expectations is by conducting surveys, to ask people what they expect of future inflation. However, this method has a number of distinct disadvantages. For example, surveys are seldom based on observable behaviour, and the people surveyed rarely have an incentive to give serious answers. In addition, questions can be misunderstood. A question about the expected change in the price level could, for example, be misinterpreted as a question about the change in the inflation rate. Furthermore, information based on surveys is not always timely. The intervals between surveys is often considerable, whereas the results usually cover the very short-term.

A comparison of various ways of measuring inflation expectations has been carried out by the Bank of Canada, for the 1975–1995 period.[4] The study shows differences to be small when inflation is low and stable, but to increase when the rate of inflation is subject to considerable change. In a recent study, the Bank of Finland arrives at similar findings.[5]

Information on inflation expectations, derived directly from financial markets, has a number of advantages over the methods discussed above. Such a direct observation is possible if conventional bonds and indexed bonds are simultaneously traded on the capital market. Inflation expectations can then be derived from market prices (as shown in the example described earlier). This makes inflation expectations available on a timely and continuous basis. In addition, as they are the result of market behaviour, they are more interesting than the generally, non-committal answers in surveys.

The price, and hence the yield of a bond, depend partly on the coupon, life to maturity, the tax regime and market liquidity. In addition, the mechanics of indexation are important. In the UK, for example, indexation is based on the Retail Price Index, with an eight-month delay. As a result, the price of the bond does not only reflect the expected real interest rate, but also includes inflation expectations covering the period during which the bond is not indexed.[6]

Another way of calculating inflation expectations is to take the dif-

---

[3] For an overview, see, for example, Fase (1981c).

[4] Ricketts (1996)

[5] Spolander and Kuismanen (1994).

[6] This additional complication involved in estimating expected inflation is discussed in Deacon and Derry (1994a).

ference in yield, based on market prices, of a conventional bond and an index-linked bond. The weak point of this approach is that it only involves two bonds and it is not always possible to find two with the same maturity. An alternative method, used by the Bank of England, involves a comparison of the term structure of interest rates as implied by conventional and index-linked bonds, respectively.

Apart from the problems discussed above, the resulting series of calculated inflation expectations may deviate from the 'true' expectations because of risk and liquidity premiums. The inflation risk premium reflects investors' demands for a compensation for unexpected changes in inflation. This risk premium applies to bonds on which the real yield is not guaranteed, such as with conventional bonds. This will result in an upward-biased estimate of the 'true' expectations.[7]

The liquidity premium on indexed debt will most probably be higher, as the market for index-linked bonds is less liquid than for conventional bonds. This results in a downward distortion of expected inflation. The overall direction or the magnitude of the factors mentioned here is unclear. Research suggests (see footnote 5) that calculated inflation expectations will be higher than real expectations, owing to the inflation risk premium in nominal yields, and possibly also resulting from differences in tax treatment. The calculated inflation expectations, or changes in them, are more reliable the more stable the inflation risk premium and tax effects are.

10.3 The UK as an Illustration

The *direct* approach described above results in a series of estimated inflation expectations for the UK for the next 25 years. Figure 10.1 shows a comparison of the estimated expectations with actual inflation, for two- and five-year periods. The graph unmistakably demonstrates that inflation expectations are heavily influenced by current inflation, particularly for a short-term time horizon. The figure shows that, in general, inflation expectations tend to overestimate actual inflation.

Figure 10.2 shows the changes in actual and expected inflation. The change in expected inflation is calculated as the difference between current actual inflation and inflation expectations. In general, inflation expectations appear to be a good indicator of future changes in inflation. However, there are remarkable discrepancies in the case of planned policy changes, as was the case in the UK in second half of the 1980s. In addition, it appears that calculated inflation expectations, indeed,

---

[7] Deacon and Derry (1994b).

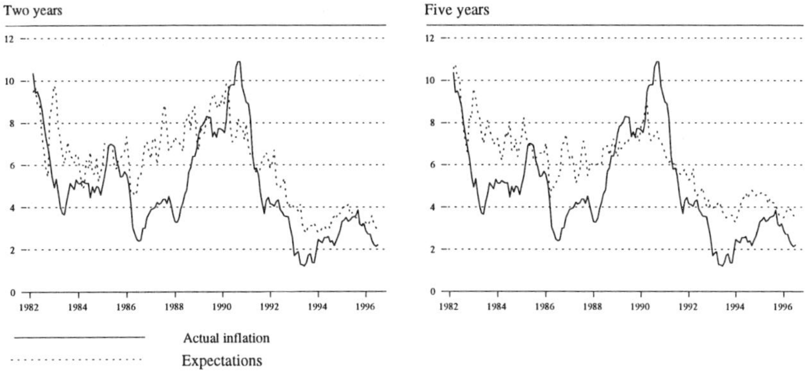

Figure 10.1: Inflation and inflation expectations at two different maturities

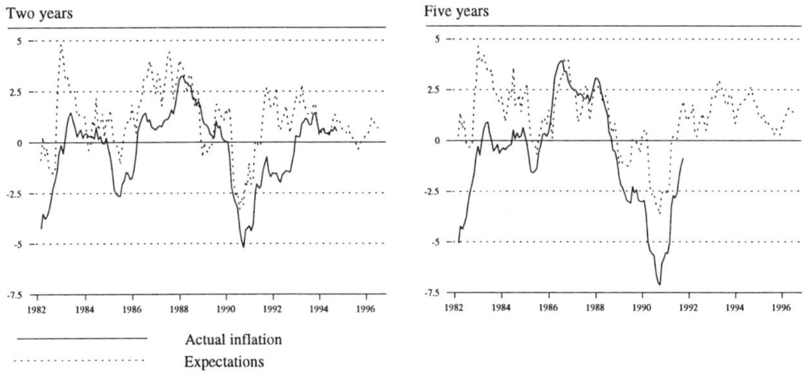

Figure 10.2: Expected and actual changes in inflation

overestimate future inflation; the expected change in inflation is usually greater than the actual change.

The series of inflation expectations contain the 'true' inflation expectations and a possible inflation risk premium. From both a theoretical and a practical point of view, it is interesting that research shows that the inflation risk premium in the US and the UK, for various time periods, is between 0.2% and 2%.[8]

If the inflation risk premium offers compensation for the uncertainty of future inflation, then there must be a relationship with this uncer-

[8] See Campbell and Shiller (1996) and MacFarlane and Brown (1995).

tainty. The standard deviation of inflation is the most common proxy of this uncertainty. However, the relationship is not statistically significant. Intuitively speaking, this is not surprising. The standard deviation of actual inflation measures the deviation of actual inflation from the average and, therefore, does not appear to be the most appropriate measure for future inflation uncertainty.

Volatility of inflation expectations themselves is perhaps a better measure for the inflation risk premium. This indicator corrects for the changes in the difference between nominal and real interest rates. As a result, expectations concerning real developments are irrelevant. This assumption is supported by the regression analysis discussed below.

The inflation risk premium in the UK has been analysed using a regression equation. The estimation results are summarized in Table 10.1. The regression equation distinguishes between the long-term equilibrium on the one hand and short-term deviations on the other, as a reflection of temporary adjustment processes. In the regression equation used here, the latter is described by the so-called error correction term. The short-term is described here merely by the uncertainty over future inflation. Coefficient β_2 is the adjustment coefficient of the so-called *error correction term*, here representing the long-term Fisher relationship.

When interpreting the constant α of the above mentioned equation, a distinction must be made between the shorter maturities (2 and 5 years) and the longer maturities (10 and 15 years). The expectations concerning the shorter periods follow the actual current and future inflation rates closely (as shown in Figure 10.1). This is less so for the longer time horizons of 10 and 15 years. Therefore we have only included average inflation in our regression equation, in the case of maturities of 2 and 5 years. As regards the longer maturities, the long-term level of the gap between nominal and real interest rates is modelled merely by a constant.

The constant can be seen as the long-term difference between the interest rates. In theory, this equals the sum of inflation expectations and risk premium. As far as the short maturities are concerned, part of the 'true' expectations can be explained by average actual inflation. The share of inflation expectations reflected in the constant is, therefore, smaller than is the case with longer maturities. In other words, the share of the risk premium in the constant is larger in the case of short maturities than in the case of long maturities.

In the case of the 2-year maturity, coefficient β_3 can be assumed to be 1 (on the basis of a Wald-test). This restriction implies that the long-term Fisher effect applies fully. In that case, average inflation is fully reflected in nominal interest rates. A re-estimation, using this restriction

Table 10.1: Estimation results for the period March 1982 to August 1994

	Maturities in years			
	2	5	10	15
β_1	1.10	1.79	3.00	3.66
	(2.44)	(4.35)	(8.32)	(11.3)
β_2	−0.19	−0.13	−0.05	−0.04
	(4.24)	(3.93)	(2.64)	(2.73)
β_3	0.78	0.58	–	–
	(5.23)	(3.28)		
α	2.39	3.28	5.62	5.36
	(3.04)	(3.83)	(8.92)	(9.70)
$\bar{R}^2$	0.13	0.20	0.35	0.49
DW	1.82	2.01	2.24	2.31
LM(12)	1.00	0.96	1.19	1.03
p-value	0.45	0.49	0.29	0.42
Q(12)	12.0	11.4	12.6	11.4
p-value	0.44	0.49	0.40	0.49

Notes:
The regression equation used is as follows:

$$\Delta \text{gap}^i = \beta_1 \Delta \sigma^i_{\text{gap}} + \beta_2 \left(\text{gap}^i_{-1} - \beta_3 \pi^g_{-1} - \alpha_i \right),$$

where: gap is the difference between nominal and real rates of interest on a security with maturity i, where $i = 2$, 5, 10 and 15 years; σ_{gap^i} is the standard deviation of the gap, calculated over the next 12 months at maturity i; π^g is the two-year average of current and future inflation, included in the equations for $i = 2$ and 5.
t-values are in brackets; DW is the Durbin-Watson test statistic for first order autocorrelation; LM(12) and Q(12) are the Lagrange multiplier and the Ljung-Box test statistics for autocorrelation, respectively. The numbers underneath are p-values.

of $\beta_3 = 1$, leads to the result that α equals 1.3. [9] Based on the above, this implies that the long-term risk premium on a security with a maturity of two years equals 1.3%. This restriction cannot be made for the five years time horizon, which makes it difficult to say whether the higher constant reflects a higher risk premium or higher inflation expectations.

[9] The relevant estimated regression equation is:

$$\Delta \text{gap}^2 = 1.10 \Delta \sigma^2_{\text{gap}} - 0.19 \left(\text{gap}^2_{-1} - \pi^g_{-1} - 1.29 \right),$$

in which the test variables do not materially differ from the unrestricted estimated equation.

It is interesting to note that average inflation for the whole sample period equals 4.9%, which is close to the implied long-term inflation expectations for the 10 and 15 year maturities. However, the implied long-term inflation expectations — coefficient α — are some 0.5 to 0.7% higher than the average actual inflation rate. This may suggest that long-term nominal interest rates include an average risk premium of this magnitude. The averages would appear to confirm this. The average interest rate gap for all maturities is some 6%, while average inflation is 4.9%. The average gap is therefore 1.1%. It is unlikely that financial markets consistently overestimate inflation.

Although no definite conclusion can be drawn about the magnitude of the risk premium, the equation for the 2-year nominal interest rate implies, assuming the Fisher hypothesis, a magnitude of 1.3%. For the longer maturities, the difference between the interest rate gap and actual inflation suggests the existence of a positive risk premium of some 0.5 to 0.7%. Finally, the increasing $\bar{R}^2$ suggests a better explanation for the variation of the interest rate gap in the case of the longer maturities.

The results of our estimates show a positive and statistically significant relationship between the interest rate gap (the difference between nominal and real interest rates) and inflation uncertainty. This points to the existence of an inflation risk premium in nominal interest rates. In the short-term, increasing uncertainty will lead to a widening of the interest gap. The relevant coefficient becomes larger and statistically more precise, the longer the period considered. This suggests that inflation uncertainty, and the premium for it, is an important explanatory variable, particularly for interest rate differentials for longer maturities.

10.4 Implications for EMU

Several authors have concluded that issuing index-linked bonds is not an attractive idea for The Netherlands.[10] This conclusion is based both on the very modest expected cost saving on the part of the government and the resulting budgetary uncertainty. When inflation is low, as is currently the case in The Netherlands and many other EMU countries, the choice between issuing conventional and index-linked bonds is not particularly interesting. This is especially true because a credible monetary policy, which is the case in The Netherlands as a consequence of the link of the guilder to the Deutsche Mark, leads to a low risk premium. Although the risk premium is unlikely to be negligible for bonds with longer maturities, the advantages will not offset the budget-

[10] See Vlaar (1996) and Brits and Oort (1997).

ary uncertainty that index-linked bonds bring about. In addition, Dutch monetary policy is not fully autonomous, which makes information on inflation expectations less convincing. More interesting, therefore, is the question whether index-linked bonds could be meaningful in EMU, especially in view of its monetary policy.

It is important to bear in mind that the issuance of index-linked bonds is part of fiscal and budgetary policy. As opposed to monetary policy, fiscal and budgetary policy will continue to be determined autonomously by the member states. Some European governments will probably benefit more from issuing index-linked bonds than others. As a consequence, EMU could see the development of a range of bonds offering the possibility of an empirical approach to directly determining inflation expectations within EMU, as is currently the case in the UK.

Index-linked bonds, and their relationship with conventional bonds, will provide important additional policy information, if the ECB makes direct inflation targeting its strategy of monetary policy. Sufficient liquidity of the market for indexed debt is a condition for the usefulness and reliability of this information. This requires a certain amount of issuing activity. Uniform procedures and equal treatment of bond issuance throughout the EU can foster this.

Another aspect deserves attention here. It is sometimes said that nominal interest rates include an 'EMU premium' owing to uncertainty over future European inflation. This risk premium could lead to interest rate differentials, particularly in countries whose policies do not have a particularly good reputation and who have a relatively large public debt. In those cases, the issuance of index-linked debt could be a sign of commitment on the part of national governments. This can be important because budgetary decision-making will, as indicated above, remain decentralized in EMU.

10.5 Conclusions

The side-by-side existence of markets for conventional and for index-linked bonds has an important informative function from a monetary policy perspective. However, the fact that nominal interest rates contain a risk premium, reflecting the compensation for unforeseen inflation, is a complicating element. The exact magnitude of this inflation risk premium is unclear, but its existence is beyond doubt. The differential between nominal and real interest rates shows a statistically significant relationship with this inflation uncertainty.

All arguments, both in favour of and against the desirability of issuing index-linked bonds, come into consideration in the debate against the background of these findings. The government can achieve cost savings given the inflation risk premium. The inflation risk premium and the interest cost savings decline, however, if the government manages to reduce inflation uncertainty. It can be assumed that the effect index-linked bonds will have on budgetary developments will depend on the degree to which the government can lower inflation. When deciding whether to issue index-linked bonds or not, governments must weigh up the cost savings and the budgetary uncertainty, taking the specific circumstances of a particular country into account.

No consensus exists as regards one other aspect of indexed bonds: the additional information they provide on the development of inflation expectations. This is of great importance to a policy of direct inflation targeting. Following the UK's example, it should receive greater weight in the relevant decision-making.

11. Price Determination on the Equity Market: A Macroeconomic View

11.1 Introduction

In his superb *The great crash of 1929* the American economist, J.K. Galbraith, famous also for his literary abilities and talent for analysis, writes about that dramatic October of 1929: 'That autumn Professor Irving Fisher of Yale made his immortal estimate: "Stock prices have reached what looks like a permanently high plateau".'

To prevent any misunderstanding about his respect for the still highly regarded economist, Galbraith added: 'Irving Fisher was the most original of American economists. Happily there are better things — his contributions to index numbers, technical economic theory, and monetary theory — for which he is remembered.'

It is clear that Galbraith's words on Fisher show that modesty is called for. In addition and apart from that, it is obvious that an economist writing about equity prices can only talk in general terms. Should he really be able to predict anything that might make money, he will keep quiet and use this knowledge for his own gains. Be that as it may, I do not intend to provide you with a forecast for equity prices; I do not consider that to be practicably possible.

What this chapter will give you instead is some thoughts that fit into the modern economic tradition of price determination. Thus, it is a reflection by a macroeconomist, who, in his work on monetary economics, occasionally also devotes some attention to the equity market.

The argument is built up from three different angles. The first is monetary economics. This is a very general angle, but not uninteresting. The second angle is much more specific and focuses on four views of

Translation of 'Koersvorming op de aandelenmarkt in macro-economisch perspectief' by M.M.G. Fase, *Bank- en Effectenbedrijf*, **39** (September 1990), 14–19. The translation is reprinted by permission.

price determination that can be found in economic literature. The third angle is, again, purely macroeconomic and looks at the extent to which equity prices are relevant for the general economic situation, that is macroeconomic spending and production.

11.2 Money Stock and Equity Prices

An old macroeconomic line of thought, particularly popular for some time among monetarists, sees a relationship between the growth of the money supply on the one hand and the general trend of equity prices on the other. Evidence can be obtained from a graphical inspection of both time series, put in a historic perspective, and also from correlation calculations. This has been done both for The Netherlands and for the US. In this respect, the work of Milton Friedman is well known; he established a positive relationship between the real growth of the money supply — which is the money supply growth in a certain time period minus the inflation rate over that period — and changes in equity prices.

Such analyses are not very convincing for at least three reasons. First, a robust economic argument cannot be built to support such a relationship. Second, it could also be argued that the relationship runs the other way around. Indeed, empirical research concerning the demand for money or liquidity would appear to support this 'reverse causation', as it is often called. The considerations involved concern not only investment returns, but also the volume of transactions: a higher level of activity on the equity market demands larger transaction balances, which justifies a larger money supply or liquidity volume. A third factor, which is certainly true in the case of a small country such as The Netherlands — but perhaps also on a world-wide scale, given increased financial internationalization — is that there often appears to be a global correlation of equity prices. This is demonstrated unequivocally by statistical analyses of equity prices on the various national stock markets throughout the world.[1]

Despite the validity of these three objections, it is worth looking into a possible relationship between money supply and equity prices in The Netherlands.

For this purpose, we have investigated the relationship between monetary aggregates M1 and M2 on the one hand, and the development of the overall stock market index on the other. The most important conclusion of this statistical analysis is that changes in M1 have some impact on the stock market index, albeit with a lag. Such an impact could not

[1] See, for example, Fase and Berg (1979), Fase (1981b), Fase and Huijser (1988).

be observed in the case of M2. It is remarkable that the statistically weaker equation shows a better predictive power for equity prices than the statistically superior relationship (details of the statistical analysis on which this brief description is based can be found in Appendix 11.A).

Another point concerns the fact, that, for a long time, particularly in the US, the market was convinced that growth of the money supply was important for, among other things, the stock market. Equity prices on Wall Street reacted every time money supply numbers released did not match expectations. However, this is no longer the case. The role appears to have been taken over — at least in the US — by figures on the current account deficit, interest rates and unemployment. They are important indicators of the state of, and expectations for, the economy, insofar as the market perceives the information, that becomes available periodically, to be newsworthy. The fact that the market reacts to such figures is telling and therefore important. However, it would be extreme to assert that a solid argument for this phenomenon can be found in macroeconomic theory, even though it could easily be incorporated and rationalized within the neo-classical school of thought in economics.

11.3 Price Determination and Tinbergen's Analysis

Following this general, and thus real, macroeconomic approach I would like to discuss four more or less independent examples of thinking about equity price formation. The first is chiefly of historic interest; the other three have more immediate relevance and have been put forward as explanations for the crash in 1987, and have also been used to rationalize the 1989 mini-crash.

As far as I am aware, the oldest study into equity prices from a macroeconomic viewpoint was that of Tinbergen (1932). Before discussing the contents of this study, I would like to point out that the term 'macroeconomic' did not exist in those days.

Tinbergen's over 65-year-old analysis of the stock market had two aims. First, he considered an analysis of the price determination on the stock market to be of great importance for the analysis of the business cycle. Equity prices, according to Tinbergen, have a certain role in forecasting business cycle developments: in his view they were a kind of barometer of economic activity. Here he had a practical aim. A second reason for analyzing the stock market was because he saw it as a good example of supply and demand determining prices; in other words he had an intellectual aim.

In my opinion, what makes Tinbergen's approach special is his attempt to quantify his analysis by adding a statistical analysis. He carries out a multiple correlation calculation. What is the outcome of this? Before discussing the results, it is useful to recall the historical situation on the Amsterdam stock exchange. In those days (the 1920s and 1930s), rubber companies were important stocks quoted in Amsterdam. That is why Tinbergen saw them as representative of the market as a whole and used them in his analysis, trying to explain price trends.

Tinbergen noticed that share prices of rubber companies could be explained on the basis of the price of rubber on the world market, and by the trend of the overall stock market index in Amsterdam, in a relation of 1.3:1. (So, from a quantitative perspective, the price of rubber, affecting the profitability turned out to be the dominant factor. The general trend of equity prices — indicator of economic activity — was the second determinant). Tinbergen was quite successful in his statistical description of historic share price trends of rubber companies on the Amsterdam stock market. This is borne out by the fact that he calculated a correlation coefficient of 0.8.

Three things are noteworthy in this result. Firstly, Tinbergen actually constructed a formula for forecasting the price trend of one individual stock. Second, he saw the general trend of equity prices as a macroeconomic indicator of economic activity. Third, Tinbergen does not even mention the possibility of using his formula to make money. Do we therefore have to conclude that it is not possible? I am afraid that is, indeed, the current view embodied in the school of rational expectations and its (logical) counterpart, efficient markets.

11.4 Modern Views

Within modern economic thinking, there are two rival theoretical views on equity price determination, which attracted renewed interest, following the crash of October 1987. In addition, an institutional approach was developed as a by-product of what happened on the New York stock exchange in October 1987. The crash strongly boosted the interest of academic economists. Their attention focused primarily on the merits of both theoretical views, while the people directly involved, the stock market people themselves, focused on the institutional approach.

The theoretical lines of thought concerned are the efficient market theory, and the diametrically opposed, 'bubble' theory.[2]

---

[2] Cf., *e.g.* Diba and Grossman (1988), Grauwe and Matthews (1988), Hardouvelis (1988).

The former attaches great significance to rational behaviour of market participants, who instantly process every new piece of information. The second approach puts the emphasis on the intuitive behaviour of the participants of the stock market. The third approach is devoid of any theoretical consideration but emphasizes the role of the market organization.

11.4.1 The Efficient Market Theory

To summarize it briefly and practically, the efficient market theory states that the expected share price equals the present value of all future dividend payments after taxes. This implies that the market must make an assessment of expected dividend payments and interest rates, and of the general financial-economic and political climate in which share price formation takes place. These are, so to speak, the 'fundamentals'. Rationally operating market participants use all available information to assess the future dividend payments and other fundamentals such as profits and interest rates, inflation expectations and general economic activity. New facts concerning the fundamentals reaching the market will immediately affect the price formation process, according to the efficient market theory. Market participants are efficient processors of information.

What does this theory mean for the explanation of, for example, the stock market crash of 1987? To put it differently, can this highly abstract and interesting view adequately describe the facts of 1987?

According to this fundamentalist approach, the crash of 19 October 1987 must have been the market's response to either a deterioration of dividends or the general level of economic activity, or to an expected rise in interest rates (relevant in determining the present value). What does this mean?

The actual drop in share prices amounted to some 25%. If the theory holds, expected future dividend payments must have suddenly dropped 25%, or interest rates (used for discounting) must have risen by some 25%. In addition, a combination of the two is possible. An expected recession would therefore have been the underlying cause. It is clear that the actual circumstances at the time do not provide arguments for such a view.

11.4.2 The Bubble Theory

The second line of thought that I distinguish here assumes that the stock market is subject to speculative behaviour unrelated to 'fundamentals'. This is not to say that investors operate irrationally if they, for example, dump their holdings when their insights prompt them to do so. However, this line of thought sees the market as an expression of speculative bubbles, with intuition or market sentiment being an important driving force. This much less fundamentalist, or perhaps post-modernist, approach implies that a stock market crash is not the result of a change in economic fundamentals and thus, cannot be seen as a change of expectations of future economic developments. Instead, in this view, a crash is the result of a number of coincidental factors, which cause the speculative bubbles to burst. In the case of October 1987, several different events, which took place then, can be mentioned: the conflict in the Gulf, statements made by the US Treasury Secretary and the German Finance Minister. It is interesting to note that this post-modernist view is featured, among other places, in the 1987 annual report of the BIS, in the analysis of the stock market crash of that year. It seems clear from the above that the bubble theory appears to be overtaking the efficient market theory in explaining the 1987 stock market crash. However, as a view on the price formation process this is not particularly encouraging and does not tell a lot about the future.

11.4.3 The Cascade Theory

Before moving on to the next topic of this chapter, the macroeconomic meaning of the stock market, it may be useful to dwell briefly on the third view. This view is undoubtedly less academic and is referred to above as the 'institutional view'. According to this line of thought, institutional circumstances were the main cause of the 19 October 1987 stock market crash, and in a certain sense, also of the mini-crash in 1989. These circumstances include the way in which the markets are organized and regulated by the various parties, in other words, the trading practices. This view is known by the expressive name of the 'cascade theory'.[3]

The cascade theory is primarily an institutional view of price trends on stock markets. The key element is a mechanical explanation for the fall in equity prices, focusing on the mechanical trading strategies that had become common on the New York stock market. Portfolio protection strategies and forward contracts, together with arbitrage between the spot and forward markets, played an important role here. So-called 'program trading' was, allegedly, the driving force. The scope of this chapter does not permit a detailed discussion, but it is, nevertheless, remarkable that the cascade theory became widely known because of the so-called Brady report.

---

[3] Santoni (1988).

In 1988, following a presidential request, Brady started an investigation into the causes of the October 1987 stock market crash. The commission concluded that the panic on the stock market could best be explained by existing market practices. On the basis of this conclusion, the Brady report recommended the introduction of circuit-breakers as a preventive measure.[4]

How realistic is this explanation? Several facts and views argue against the cascade theory. First, it can be shown that the developments on the New York stock market in the week of 19 October 1987 can easily be explained by other factors. Some simple calculations — that of Santoni, for example — illustrate this. Second, the drop in stock prices also occurred on markets where the sophisticated trading practices, such as program trading and portfolio protection strategies — the alleged culprits — did not exist. Third, it cannot be ignored that this theory does not explain earlier periods of sharp falls in equity prices, such as 1962 or 1929, nor that it fails to explain the unequal scale of the almost world-wide equity price declines in 1987 (French and German share prices fell much less than those of the US). Nevertheless, there is an element of truth in the cascade theory, in the sense that market organization is not irrelevant to price determination.

The key question is, what lessons can be drawn from these three alternative explanations, or hypotheses, as statisticians would say. The main lesson is we should bear in mind is that some sort of general interdependence exists, making an isolated and thus monistic explanation questionable. This was mentioned already, when we discussed the monetarist view on stock market price trends. The second lesson is to be open-minded about an explanation and not to rule out any possibility in advance. The third lesson is that one must not expect too much of attempts to forecast stock market fluctuations. This lesson is supported by empirical evidence of market efficiency on the Amsterdam stock market.[5] Both macroeconomists and people actually involved in the stock market can say sensible things about share prices, but real forecasting is not really possible.

11.5 EQUITY PRICES AND SPENDING

In addition to their effect on other asset prices or savings, equity prices affect spending and, therefore, have important macroeconomic implications. Equities, bonds, property, gold, cash or antiques, are examples of

---

[4] For an assessment of the Brady report see Greenwald and Stein (1988).

[5] Mourik (1988).

assets in which private households, companies and financial institutions hold their wealth. From a macroeconomic perspective, price fluctuations do not only encourage substitution processes between the different assets, they also affect the overall wealth effect. For the macroeconomist, the size of wealth is one of the explanatory variables of consumer spending. It is therefore likely that, for example, a rise or fall of equity prices may result in an increase or fall in spending.

In October 1987 (and with the crisis in Asia of 1997/98) this fear preoccupied the world, although its highly asymmetrical nature was overlooked at the time. What was also forgotten was that the effect on spending is smaller the more equities are held by so-called 'dead hands', as was the case in The Netherlands as opposed to the US. The crash in the last quarter of 1987 implied a decline in wealth of some 8% for Dutch private households. According to the consumption equation of De Nederlandsche Bank's macroeconomic MORKMON II model, this should eventually lead to a drop in private consumption of around 1%. The immediate, that is short-term, spending effect following the 1987 stock market crash was estimated to amount to less than *f* 1 billion, or just over 1/3%. This is very minor indeed and scarcely justifies any excitement. The value of the housing stock rose appreciably during the same period, making the overall wealth effect extremely small. As a result, it is not surprising that the effect on spending was small.

The non-quantifiable effects are more important than the wealth effects discussed above. By this is meant the loss of confidence in the entire economy that may result from the crash (or from the foreign exchange market, a bank collapse, or from the inflation that followed German reunification). Awareness of confidence effects is very important, not least to those operating on the stock market or the options market.

It was clear in October 1987 that policy makers were also very aware of such confidence factors. Contrary to, for example, 1929, monetary authorities were able to prevent panic by decisively producing a policy response. This included supplying liquidity by the central banks, and issuing new market rules on stock exchanges to prevent chain reactions.

11.6 Conclusion

The above was primarily an effort to reflect in broad terms on a very concrete phenomenon. The emphasis was put specifically on the larger picture of possible relationships. Three different approaches were taken. Whatever lessons can be drawn from this reflection, it is beyond doubt that they can at best only be modest. It is equally clear that the conclusion will not provide opportunities to make a lot of money. Perhaps the above discussion can best be summarized in three statements:

1. bear in mind that interdependencies characterize economics and that typically macroeconomic relationships can, in certain circumstances, be very important for the assessment of future price trends on the stock market;
2. information and expectations are of fundamental importance, and knowledge of macroeconomics and macroeconomic facts can be very helpful. Newspapers, in particular, cover these facts extensively;
3. finally, any assessment must be based on common sense. That applies to macroeconomists as well. For the explanation of equity prices at a particular point in time, this is more important than economic theory; although that does not make economic theory less interesting.

APPENDIX 11.A STATISTICAL ANALYSIS

There is no consensus on theoretical views of the qualitative character of the impact that the money supply has on equity prices. This is because the transmission mechanism can run either through interest rates, the production and profits of companies, or inflation expectations, while the openness of the economy and the capacity utilization of production factors are also important. Assuming that inflation in an open economy is not very sensitive to the money supply, a positive relationship between money supply and equity prices would appear most likely. That relationship should be expected to be weak because of the quantitatively limited short-term interaction between money and income. In addition, the money supply does not fulfil the role of signal for policy intentions of the monetary authorities in The Netherlands.

This implies that expectations for inflation and interest rates are not very sensitive to the money supply or to deviations of money supply growth from the expected growth rate. As far as such a signal function does exist, it weakens the above-mentioned positive relationship between equity prices and money supply.

Transfer functions were used to determine differences and lags, which are important to the relationship studied. As regards the money supply, both M1 and M2 were used (in both cases real and nominal aggregates were involved in the study). In order to do so, the ARIMA models of the relevant series were first constructed. Subsequently, cross-correlations have been calculated for the sample period April 1980–June 1989 using monthly data. 111 observations were thus available for the estimation. On this basis, it was determined that the transfer function matched a simple regression equation, which therefore has been estimated.

Table 11.A.1 summarizes the estimation results. Judging by the correlation coefficient R, the relationship is weak. For M1 a statistically significant, lagged impact on the stock market index was found over the April 1980–June 1989 period. The impact of M2 proved not statistically significant. The two equations with nominal and real M1, respectively, as explaining variables are (apart from the dummy variable):

$$\text{percentage change of the stock market index (t)} = 0.02 + 0.36\Delta \ln \text{M1}_{t-1} + 0.55\Delta \ln \text{M1}_{t-2} - 0.30\text{dummy},$$

and

$$\text{percentage change of the stock market index (t)} = 0.01 + 0.09\Delta \ln \text{M1}_{t-1} + 0.12\Delta \ln \text{M1}_{t-2} - 0.06\text{dummy}.$$

Table 11.A.1: Results of statistical analysis

	Constant	Lagged money supply 1	Lagged money supply 2	Dummy October 1987	R^2	SE	DW	Q(1)	Q(12)	Q(24)
Nominal M1	0.0189	0.363	0.551	−0.302	0.30	0.046	2.14	0.57	7.52	16.99
	(1.24)	(1.56)	(2.41)	(6.18)						
Nominal M2	0.0206		0.271	−0.288	0.27	0.047	2.08	0.22	8.06	16.61
	(1.32)		(0.90)	(5.79)						
Real M1	0.0054	0.094	0.122	−0.059	0.28	0.011	2.06	0.09	7.41	16.28
	(1.53)	(1.84)	(2.43)	(5.21)						
Real M2	0.0055		0.061	−0.055	0.25	0.011	1.96	0.04	9.01	15.81
	(1.50)		(0.90)	(4.78)						

Notes:
The variable to be explained is the change of the general CBS stock market index on a log scale; the money supply has also been measured by the change on a log scale. The sample period is April 1980–June 1989. The dummy October 1987 measures the impact of the stock market crash of October 1987. The coefficients of the 11 seasonal dummies are not reported. t-values in brackets. Q(n) is the Box-Pierce test on the residual pattern of the disturbances which is χ^2 distributed with n degrees of freedom; $\bar{R}^2$ is the corrected correlation coefficient; SE is the standard error of the residuals; DW is the Durbin-Watson statistic.

The estimated regressions were used to forecast the stock market over the period July 1989–December 1989, which is outside the sample period. Measured by the so-called RMSE, the forecasting error of the first equation is 0.035, for the second equation 0.0072. The forecasting errors are thus a little smaller than would have been expected on the basis of the residuals of the equations used, presented in Table 11.A.1 (0.046 and 0.011, respectively). A graphical inspection, which is not given here, shows a declining trend for both the forecast series and the actual series of the growth rate of the stock market index and a recovery in December 1989. In fact, a strong recovery had started already in November 1989, following a stronger decline than forecast by the model. It is not surprising that such a simple model does not produce more accurate predictions.

The conclusion has to be that the trend of the stock market index cannot be accurately forecast using either the nominal or real version of the growth of money supply M1. Friedman's view cannot, therefore, be supported by this simple statistical exercise.

12. The Linkage of Stock Exchange Markets between Countries

12.1 INTRODUCTION

Economic theory often assumes complete or virtually complete capital mobility. Consequently, a policy of, for instance, increasing interest rates under a system of fixed exchange rates induces capital flows to the country concerned, which will continue until spontaneous adjustment has caused the domestic level of interest rates to become equal to the world level. So the ultimate result is merely a change in the composition of the portfolio. At the other end of the scale, there is the view that national capital markets are segmented markets because of a lack of capital mobility brought about by, for instance, divergent expectations or risk perceptions. Consequently, within a fixed exchange rate regime, monetary policy is a powerful instrument. To the extent that there is capital mobility, it is reflected in convergence of international interest rates or in strong share price co-movements. Regarding interest rates, the findings obtained by Fase (1976) and Volker (1980) suggest a high degree of financial integration under a system of fixed exchange rates. The results of studies, based on share prices, are less clear. Contrary to the results of Ripley (1973) and Fase and Berg (1979), those of Agmon (1972) and Société Générale de Banque (1973) lend support to the hypothesis of an integrated financial market.

This chapter reports the results of a Pierce-Haugh dependency test to examine the degree of integration or segmentation of stock markets in 11 industrial countries. In addition, a Granger-Sims type causality test is performed to identify the dependency of the Amsterdam stock exchange on Wall Street. Unlike earlier studies, this chapter concentrates on the lag and error structure, as many results are suspect in terms of spurious relationships. The data used are mid-week figures for the period 1971–

Reprinted from *Economics Letters* **7** (1981), M.M.G. Fase, 'The linkage of stock exchange markets between countries: An empirical study of share price co-movements in eleven industrial countries', 363–369

1976, taken from Fase and Berg (1979). These figures are all share price indices as supplied by the national agencies and published in, for example, the *Financial Times*.

12.2 Methodology and Results

The individual series for each country, z_t, have been cleared of spurious relationships by filtering, as suggested by Haugh (1976) and Pierce (1977). To this end, for each series an ARIMA (p, d, q) model has been estimated. This model takes the form of $\phi_p(L)\nabla^d z_t = \theta_q(L)a_t$, where $\phi_p(L)$ and $\theta_q(L)$ are polynomials in L of order p and q, while $\nabla^d = (1 - L)^d$ is the dth difference operator and a_t is white noise. The estimated ARIMA models, along with the Box-Pierce portmanteau statistics against serial correlation of residuals, are shown in Table 12.1.

Filtering the series by the estimated models removes serial correlation. Cross-correlations $\hat{r}_{ij}(k)$ at lag k between the two residual white noise series $\hat{a}_i$ and $\hat{a}_j$ are calculated in accordance with

$$\hat{r}_{ij}(k) = \frac{\sum \hat{a}_{i\,t-k}\hat{a}_{jt}}{\sqrt{\sum \hat{a}_{jt}^2 \sum \hat{a}_{it}^2}}.$$

Following Haugh (1976) an overall measure of dependence between the series i and j is obtained by the statistics S_{ij} with

$$S_{ij} = n^2 \sum_{k=-m_1}^{m_2} (n - |k|)^{-1} \hat{r}_{ij}^2(k),$$

where $S_{ij} \simeq \chi^2_{m_1+m_2+1}$ and n is the length of the series. Thus, our approach in examining the question of international stock market segmentation is equivalent to looking at the extent of covariation among pre-whitened share prices in different countries.

The results in Table 12.2 indicate that, with the notable exception of Italy, all the S-statistics for two-sided lag length of 13 exceed the 95% critical level of 40.11 with 27 degrees of freedom. This means that, Italy apart, none of the national stock prices indices varies independently of the other national indices. This result holds true, although not reported here, for two-sided lag length of 23 as well as for a lag length of 0, that is contemporaneous correlation. Therefore, we may conclude that the national stock markets are closely linked, indicating a considerable degree of financial integration.

Table 12.1: ARIMA models and diagnostic check for share prices in eleven industrial countries, 1971–1976 (midweek observations)

i	Country	Estimated ARIMA models	Box-Pierce statistics
1	The Netherlands	$\nabla z_t = (1 + \underset{(2.6)}{0.144}L^2)a_t$	$\chi^2_{11} = 9.8$
2	United Kingdom	$\nabla z_t = (1 + \underset{(2.9)}{0.160}L^2)a_t$	$\chi^2_{11} = 9.0$
3	US	$\nabla z_t = a_t$	$\chi^2_{12} = 5.6$
4	Belgium	$(1 - \underset{(5.5)}{0.297}L)\nabla z_t = a_t$	$\chi^2_{11} = 8.0$
5	France	$(1 - \underset{(4.1)}{0.227}L)\nabla z_t = (1 + \underset{(2.6)}{1.146}L^7)a_t$	$\chi^2_{10} = 8.9$
6	Japan	$\nabla z_t = (1 - \underset{(1.9)}{0.015}L^2 + \underset{(2.7)}{0.153}L^3)a_t$	$\chi^2_{10} = 9.9$
7	Canada	$(1 - \underset{(3.1)}{0.174}L)\nabla z_t = a_t$	$\chi^2_{11} = 13.5$
8	Australia	$\nabla z_t = (1 + \underset{(3.9)}{0.218}L^2)a_t$	$\chi^2_{11} = 11.7$
9	Switzerland	$\nabla z_t = (1 + \underset{(2.7)}{0.151}L^3)a_t$	$\chi^2_{11} = 6.9$
10	West Germany	$\nabla z_t = (1 + \underset{(2.7)}{0.151}L^2 - \underset{(1.9)}{0.104}L^6)a_t$	$\chi^2_{10} = 8.7$
11	Italy	$\nabla z_t = (1 + \underset{(2.5)}{0.141}L^3 - \underset{(3.1)}{0.172}L^7)a_t$	$\chi^2_{10} = 10.4$

Note: Figures in parentheses are t-statistics; the suffix n in χ^2_n indicates degrees of freedom.

12.3 WALL STREET AND DAMRAK

Statistical evidence for the view that the share prices on the Amsterdam stock exchange, that is Damrak, are mainly determined by foreign stock markets, goes back to the prewar studies of Donner (1934) and Tinbergen (1939). The statistical methodology employed in this chapter also offers a means to examine the direction of causality. Cross-correlation of ARIMA residuals at any negative lag would indicate that country i may lead Dutch stock market prices or, following Pierce (1977) that country i 'causes' movement on the Amsterdam stock market.

Table 12.2: Test statistic S_{ij}, for $m_1 = m_2 = 13$

	j									
i	1	2	3	4	5	6	7	8	9	10
2	59.25									
3	75.22	53.31								
4	111.00	49.17	51.50							
5	86.57	42.53	55.63	91.16						
6	65.41	40.36	48.54	42.85	31.73					
7	73.07	47.49	174.72	65.20	67.99	41.04				
8	58.45	54.68	50.36	35.79	44.12	54.07	45.60			
9	98.29	49.93	77.09	92.61	82.71	51.32	72.90	60.05		
10	95.43	48.05	30.08	51.38	63.28	40.80	26.72	40.34	76.63	
11	46.49	35.83	37.09	81.54	32.69	40.90	22.75	42.93	37.26	35.78

Note: i, j indicate the countries according to Table 12.1.

Table 12.3 sets out the lags of univariate residual cross-correlation among the countries studied vis-à-vis The Netherlands, which were significant at 95% confidence interval. This pattern is hardly affected if we consider 97.5% and 99% confidence intervals. The results indicate only negative lags for the US and Japan with respect to Dutch share prices, and predominantly negative lags for Australia, Belgium, Canada and

Table 12.3: Pattern of significant lags among Dutch and country i's share prices

i	Country	Length of lags in weeks											
2	United Kingdom				−18			0	7	23	32	34
3	US	−35	−27	−23	−18	−13	−1	0				
4	Belgium	−35	−34				−1	0				35
5	France				−17		−1	0	2	23		
6	Japan					−9	−3	0				
7	Canada	−35	−27			−13	−1	0				30
8	Australia	−36	−28	−17	−13	−12	−3		1			
9	Switserland			−25			−3	0				36
10	West Germany				−9	−3	−1	0	1	3	20	31
11	Italy	−35	−26	−24			−1	0	6		35	36

Switzerland; while for UK, France, West Germany and Italy feedback relationships seem to exist. In view of this pattern, we may conclude that Wall street 'causes' share price movements in Damrak. Interestingly enough, significant contemporaneous correlation seems to exist with all countries considered, with the exception of Australia which may be considered 'causal' to Damrak too. However, this is not what we plan to investigate here, as we are mainly interested in Wall Street.

The results obtained seem to corroborate the fact that the majority of national shares are non-tradables outside the country. However, because in each country domestic shares are substitutes for a few internationals, the substitutability carries over internationally. Our results offer strong statistical evidence for the hypothesis of internationally linked stock markets.

13. The Interaction between Trading Volume of Stocks and Options: Some Statistical Evidence

The finance literature — see, for example. Black (1975), Jennings and Starks (1986), Manaster and Rendleman (1982) — provides several examples of research into the interaction between stock and option prices. This research examines the hypothesis that option prices include incremental information on stock prices. Other researchers, such as Copeland (1976, pp. 1149–1168) and more recently Anthony (1988, pp. 949–964), have analysed trading volume on stock and option markets to test the sequential-information-arrival hypothesis, using trading volume as a proxy for the rate of information arrival. The main difference between these two studies concerns both the markets considered and the statistical methodology employed. For the latter, Anthony employs Granger-Sims causality tests based on regression analysis and univariate autoregressive time series models. Unlike finance theorists, practitioners have no doubt that option trading encourages stock trading, although they are less unanimous on the feedback. To study this question, the multivariate time series model or vector ARIMA model offers an appropriate framework to examine the Granger-Sims causality. The feedback or causality question became of paramount practical importance in discussions on the October 1987 stock market crash, when options and futures trading were blamed for causing part of the trouble, and serious doubts were raised on the market mechanisms for financial derivatives as options. In the US, this led to the well-known Brady report of January 1988. Similar studies were made for European financial centres like Amsterdam.

This chapter addresses the feedback hypothesis by postulating a general bivariate autoregressive time series model as a tool for analysis, which was applied to daily data for the Amsterdam stock and options markets. Thus, it enables one to operationalize the feedback assump-

Reprinted from *Journal of International Money and Finance* **13**(5) (October 1994), M.M.G. Fase, 'The interaction between trading volume of stocks and options: Some statistical evidence', 587–601 ©1994 with kind permission from Elsevier Science.

tion and to derive conclusions on the type of causality in a generalized Granger-Sims framework.

As indicated above, the present analysis is akin to an extension of Anthony. The results are generally consistent with Anthony's findings, that option trading often leads stock trading. However, this chapter offers several incremental contributions. These are both technical and substantial. As to the first, they are the use of the bivariate ARMA model, the evidence from a different market from the US market, and the coverage of a more extensive sample period. As a matter of substance, the finding that the results are unstable over the longer time period considered here, is of particular interest. Unlike Anthony, the reported results include all traded options, not only near the money options. Thus, the results offer corroborating evidence from a European market.

Section 13.1 introduces the statistical model and discusses the data used in estimating this model. Section 13.2 summarizes the results of this statistical analysis of the transactions volume data of the stock and option market. The final section draws the main conclusions of this exercise.

13.1 Statistical Methodology

13.1.1 The Stochastic Multivariate Time Series Model

The behaviour of a univariate time series x_t is often described by stochastic difference equations or ARIMA (p,d,q) models of the form:

$$\phi_p(B)\nabla^d x_t = \theta_0 + \theta_q(B)a_t, \tag{13.1}$$

where $\phi_p(B) = \phi_1 B - \phi_2 B^2 - \cdots - \phi_p B^p, \theta_q(B) = 1 - \theta_1 B - \theta_2 B^2 - \cdots - \theta_q B^q$ are scalar polynomials in B, θ_0 is a constant. B is the backshift operator such that $Bx_t = x_{t-1}, \nabla$ the difference operator such that $\nabla = 1 - B$, and p, d, q are non-negative integers. In (13.1) the a_t are stochastically independent, normally distributed random shocks with zero mean and constant variance σ_a^2.

Apart from differencing the straightforward generalization of (13.1) is the $m \times m$ vector or multivariate stochastic difference equation:

$$\phi(B)x_t = \theta_0 + \theta(B)a_t, \tag{13.2}$$

where $\phi(B) = I - \phi_1 B - \phi_2 B^2 - \cdots - \phi_p B^p, \theta(B) = I - \theta_1 B - \theta_2 B^2 - \cdots - \theta_q B^q$ are matrix polynomials in the backshift operator B, the ϕ and θ matrices of order $m \times m$, I the $m \times m$ identity matrix, θ_0 a $m \times 1$ vector of constants, $x_t = (x_{1t}, x_{2t}, \ldots, x_{mt})^\top$ a $m \times 1$ vector of observations at time t on a set of m univariate jointly stationary time series, $a_t = (a_{1t}, a_{2t}, \ldots, a_{mt})^\top$, a $m \times 1$ vector of stochastically independent and normally distributed random shocks with zero mean and covariance matrix Σ_a, that is $\mathrm{E}a_t = 0$ and $\mathrm{E}(a_t, a_t^\top) = \Sigma_a$ where Σ_a is a positive definite matrix of order $m \times m$. Equation (13.2) is called a vector ARMA model. It is well-known that the parameters of the vector ARMA model must meet certain conditions to ensure stationarity and invertibility, namely that the roots of the determinantal equation of both $|\phi(B)| = 0$ and $|\theta(B)| = 0$ should all lie outside the unit circle.

An alternative but equivalent representation of (13.2) is:

$$\begin{pmatrix} \phi_{11}(B) & \cdots & \phi_{1m}(B) \\ \vdots & & \vdots \\ \phi_{m1}(B) & \cdots & \phi_{mm}(B) \end{pmatrix} = \begin{pmatrix} x_{1t} \\ \vdots \\ x_{mt} \end{pmatrix}$$
$$\begin{pmatrix} \theta_1 \\ \vdots \\ \theta_m \end{pmatrix} + \begin{pmatrix} \theta_{11}(B) & \cdots & \theta_{1m}(B) \\ \vdots & & \vdots \\ \theta_{m1}(B) & \cdots & \theta_{mm}(B) \end{pmatrix} \begin{pmatrix} a_{1t} \\ \vdots \\ a_{mt} \end{pmatrix}, \tag{13.3}$$

with $\phi_{ij}(B)$ and $\theta_{ij}(B)$ scalar polynomials in B of degree p_{ij} and q_{ij} respectively. The polynomials in the diagonal position start with unity, while the polynomials in the off-diagonal position start with terms which are some power of B.

To illustrate the above notation and for future reference I consider here the bivariate ARMA (1,1) model:

$$\begin{pmatrix} 1-\phi_{11}B & -\phi_{12}B \\ -\phi_{21}B & 1-\phi_{22}B \end{pmatrix} \begin{pmatrix} x_{1t} \\ x_{2t} \end{pmatrix} = \begin{pmatrix} 1-\theta_{11}B & -\theta_{12}B \\ -\theta_{21}B & 1-\theta_{22}B \end{pmatrix} \begin{pmatrix} a_1 \\ a_2 \end{pmatrix} \tag{13.4}$$

13.1.2 Conditions for Causality

Since Sims's (1972) seminal article on the causality between money and income the time series framework has become an important statistical tool for empirical causality analysis in economics along the lines suggested by Granger (1969).

Of course, this does not mean that there is full agreement among economists about the appropriateness of Granger's definition of causality (see Zellner (1979)). The multivariate time series model offers a natural generalization for this purpose. Following Kang (1981), Hsiao (1982) and Osborn (1984), necessary and sufficient conditions for causality in the multivariate ARMA process can be formulated. These formal conditions are formalizations of the intuitive notion that in a multivariate framework causality means something like an upper-block-triangular structure of the matrices $\phi(B)$ and $\theta(B)$ in equation (13.3). Suppose that in this general multivariate ARMA model the vectors x and a can be partitioned so that x_1 and a_1 are $g \times 1$ vectors and x_2 and a_2 are $h \times 1$ vectors, $g + h = m$, with submatrices $\phi(B)_{ij}$ and $\theta(B)_{ij}$ conformably partitioned. Then, according to Osborn, the variables in the vector x_1 do not cause the variables in the vector x_2 if, and only if, there is a representation of the multivariate ARMA system (13.3) in which the submatrices $\phi(B)_{21} = \theta(B)_{21} = 0$. In other words, x_1 does not cause x_2 if, and only if, in $x = \phi(B)^{-1}\theta(B)a$ either the polynomial matrix $\phi(B)^{-1}\phi(B)$ is upper-block-triangular, when partitioned conformably to x and a, or equivalently, in $a = \theta(B)^{-1}\phi(B)x$ the polynomial matrix $\theta(B)^{-1}\phi(B)$ is upper-block-triangular, when partitioned conformably.

Using the bivariate ARMA model (13.4) to illustrate the above, the necessary and sufficient condition for x_1 not to cause x_2 is:

$$-\theta_{21} + \phi_{11}\theta_{21} - \phi_{21}\theta_{11} + \phi_{21} = 0, \tag{13.5}$$

with ϕ_{ij} and θ_{ji} elements of the coefficient matrices in (13.4). Note that this condition is weaker than the condition $\phi_{21} = \theta_{21} = 0$ which is of course sufficient, but, in spite of its strong intuitive appeal, not necessary. A similar reasoning holds to determine the necessary and sufficient conditions for x_2 not to cause x_1.

13.1.3 Specification and Estimation

The class of vector ARMA models contains a large number of possibilities. Therefore, my aim is to specify a parsimonious model representing the data as adequately as possible. The main instrument of model selection, that is choosing numerical values of the integers p and q of the polynomials in the backshift operator B, includes the sample cross-correlation and partial-autocorrelation matrices, which have to be estimated from the data. A useful device for determining the order of the model, is the pattern of the indicator symbols of the sample cross-correlations and of the partial-autoregressive matrices and related statistics suggested by Tiao and Box (1981) and technically simplified for practical use in Tiao and Tsay (1983).

As soon as a suitable tentative specification has been chosen, efficient estimates of the parameter matrices ϕ, θ and Σ_a are obtained by maximizing the exact likelihood function L with

$$L(\phi, \theta, \Sigma_a|x) \propto L_c(\phi, \theta, \Sigma|x)L_1(\phi, \theta, \Sigma|x),$$

where

$$L_c(\phi, \theta, \Sigma_a|x) \propto |\Sigma_a|^{(-n-p)/2} \exp\Big\{-\frac{1}{2}\mathrm{tr}\Sigma_a^{-1} S(\phi, \theta)\Big\}$$

is the conditional likelihood function with $S(\phi, \theta) = \Sigma_{t=p+1}^{n} a_t a_t^\top$, the a_t following from the vector ARMA (p,q) model to be estimated and L_1 depending only on the data vectors $x_1, \ldots, x_p$ if all $q = 0$ or on all data vectors $x_1, \ldots, x_n$ if $q \neq 0$ with n the number of vector observations. Because estimation by using the exact likelihood function is rather slow, the conditional likelihood function is used in the preliminary stage of model building, and the exact method is used mainly towards the end (see also Tiao and Box (1981, p. 809)).

The test statistic given by (13.5) is easily computed while its variance follows immediately using Cramèr's approximation formula (see Cramèr (1946, pp. 353–354), Klein (1956, p. 258)). It reads as:

$$\begin{aligned}
\mathrm{var} f(\phi, \theta) = & (1-\phi_{11})^2 \mathrm{var}\theta_{21} + \theta_{21}^2 \mathrm{var}\phi_{11} (1-\theta_{11})^2 \mathrm{var}\phi_{21} \\
& + \phi_{21}^2 \mathrm{var}\theta_{11} - 2\theta_{21}(1-\phi_{11})\mathrm{cov}(\theta_{21}, \phi_{11}) \\
& - 2(1-\phi_{11})(1-\theta_{11})\mathrm{cov}(\theta_{21}, \phi_{21}) \\
& + 2(1-\phi_{11})\phi_{21}\mathrm{cov}(\theta_{21}, \theta_{11}) \\
& + 2\theta_{21}(1-\theta_{11})\mathrm{cov}(\phi_{11}, \phi_{21}) - 2\theta_{21}\phi_{21}\mathrm{cov}(\phi_{11}, \theta_{11}) \\
& - 2\phi_{21}(1-\theta_{11})\mathrm{cov}(\phi_{21}, \theta_{11}).
\end{aligned} \tag{13.6}$$

Equations (13.5) and (13.6) are the main statistical ingredients for this statistical testing on feedback in the next section.

13.2 Statistical Analysis of Option Series

13.2.1 The Data

The starting point for the statistical analysis is a sample of five firms listed at the Amsterdam stock exchange and additionally listed for call-and-put option trading at the European Options Exchange. The data are daily trading volumes for the period from January 2, 1985 to December 30, 1989. A listing of the sampled firms, together with a few statistics, is provided in Table 13.1.

The collected data include the daily volume of trade on common shares and the corresponding number of underlying shares for options. For options the data concern volume of all call-and-put options series respectively, and also the subseries: short at-the-money series, short out-of-the-money series, as well as the remaining series. The latter

Table 13.1: Summary statistics sample for 1989

Firm	Stock volume [a]	Option volume [b]	Share of options traded (%)	Share price volatility (%)
Heineken	23.0	11.0	48	17.5
Hoogovens	94.4	135.4	143	32.9
Nedlloyd	37.2	36.3	98	28.2
Philips	283.1	175.9	62	21.4
Royal Dutch	153.3	132.3	86	15.1

Notes:
[a] $\times 10^{-6}$ traded number of shares.
[b] $\times 10^{-6}$ traded number of underlying shares.

include both the short in-the-money series and all long series. An option series is defined as short if the remaining term to maturity is less than three months. At-the-money options are options with an exercise price differing less than 5% from the final quote of the day considered; out-of-the-money call options are options with an exercise price at least 5% above the final quote; out-of-the-money put options are options with an exercise price at least 5% lower than the final quote.

Apart from the five firms, I have considered all stocks for which options exist at the European Options Exchange (EOE) in Amsterdam. The reason I confined the analysis of individual stocks to a sample of only five was a matter of convenience and resources: collecting the daily data for the five stocks over a period of five years was an enormous task. Moreover, with this sample of five out of 23 EOE stock options at the end of 1989 the research covers almost 50% of trade in options and 40% of trade at the Amsterdam stock market. Looking at the spectrum of my sample, I believe that it offers a rather representative picture, having two firms (Hoogovens and Nedlloyd) with a very high share of options traded and the others much more in line with the conventional picture. Also, with respect to share price volatility, the sample seems to be fairly representative with Royal Dutch having a low volatility and Hoogovens the highest. Another way to look at the sample is offered in Table 13.2 showing the number of outstanding shares, the number of shares traded, and the number of underlying shares traded for options, as well as some turnover statistics. Again, it is seen how vulnerable the firms Hoogovens and Nedlloyd are when annual trade is compared with the outstanding stock of shares.

Table 13.2: Number of outstanding shares, shares traded and options traded (in thousands)

	Outstanding shares (1)	Shares traded (2)	(2) as a percentage of (1) (3)	Options traded[a] (4)	(4) as a percentage of (1) (5)
1985					
Heineken	19 267	16 985	88	16 572	86
Hoogovens[b]	10 852	34 133	315	42 821	395
Nedlloyd	3 466	9 822	283	15 423	445
Philips	219 900	169 441	77	108 238	49
Royal Dutch	268 040	109 054	41	91 450	34
1986					
Heineken	23 816	16 680	70	14 539	61
Hoogovens[b]	15 242	62 124	408	98 312	645
Nedlloyd	3 466	7 042	203	16 692	482
Philips	229 500	183 295	80	130 885	57
Royal Dutch	268 040	147 050	55	156 852	59
1987					
Heineken	25 689	17 927	70	16 501	64
Hoogovens[b]	16 013	29 522	184	38 317	239
Nedlloyd	3 466	7 727	223	16 509	476
Philips	243 900	216 531	89	140 152	57
Royal Dutch	268 040	155 367	58	152 573	57
1988					
Heineken	25 689	16 320	64	8 249	32
Hoogovens[b]	15 871	49 853	314	43 915	277
Nedlloyd	3 469	14 252	411	19 139	552
Philips	257 600	180 278	70	71 695	28
Royal Dutch	268 040	99 346	37	91 709	34
1989					
Heineken	30 232	23 019	76	11 035	37
Hoogovens[b]	16 805	94 373	562	135 431	806
Nedlloyd	9 761	37 223	381	36 330	372
Philips	268 200	283 146	106	175 943	66
Royal Dutch	523 596	153 252	29	132 275	25

Notes:

[a] Total of call and put turnovers expressed as numbers of underlying shares.

[b] Adjusted for the interests of the Government and the Municipality of Amsterdam: 35% in 1985, 19% in 1986/87 and 20% in 1988/89.

Table 13.3: Frequency of different ARIMA model specifications, 1985–1989

	Call								Put							
Model type:	(4,0)	(3,1)	(2,1)	(1,1)	(1,2)	(1,3)	(1,4)	other	(4,0)	(3,1)	(2,1)	(1,1)	(1,2)	(1,3)	(1,4)	other
All series																
Heineken	–	–	–	4	–	–	–	1	–	1	1	1	–	–	–	2
Hoogovens	–	–	–	2	1	–	–	2	–	–	–	1	1	1	–	2
Nedloyd	–	–	–	2	1	–	–	2	–	–	–	2	–	–	–	3
Philips	–	–	–	3	2	–	–	–	–	–	–	1	2	1	–	1
Royal Dutch	–	–	1	–	2	1	–	1	–	1	–	–	2	–	–	2
Total	–	–	–	–	2	–	–	1	–	–	–	–	1	–	–	2
At-the-money																
Heineken	–	1	–	2	–	–	–	2	–	–	1	1	–	–	1	2
Hoogovens	–	–	–	2	1	1	–	1	–	–	1	2	–	–	–	2
Nedloyd	2	–	–	2	–	–	–	1	1	–	–	2	–	–	2	–
Philips	–	–	–	3	–	–	–	2	–	–	–	3	–	2	–	–
Royal Dutch	–	–	2	2	–	1	–	–	–	–	–	3	–	1	–	1
Out-of-the-money																
Heineken	1	2	–	2	–	–	–	–	1	–	–	2	–	–	–	2
Hoogovens	–	–	1	3	–	1	–	–	–	–	–	1	–	–	1	3
Nedloyd	–	–	1	3	–	–	–	1	1	1	1	1	–	–	1	–
Philips	–	–	–	2	1	1	–	1	–	1	–	3	–	–	–	1
Royal Dutch	1	–	–	1	–	1	–	2	–	1	2	1	–	1	–	–
Remaining series																
Heineken	1	1	–	–	–	–	–	3	1	2	–	1	–	–	–	1
Hoogovens	–	–	3	2	–	–	–	–	–	–	3	1	–	–	–	1
Nedloyd	1	1	–	2	–	–	–	1	–	–	1	1	–	–	1	2
Philips	–	1	1	1	1	–	–	1	–	1	–	1	1	1	–	1
Royal Dutch	–	1	2	1	–	–	1	–	–	1	–	3	–	–	–	1
Total	6	7	11	39	11	6	1	22	4	9	10	31	7	7	6	29

Note: Model type (p, q) indicates an AR part of order p and a MA part of order q, with first order differences in the variables; 'other' covers 25% of all models.

13.2.2 The Estimated Models

A preliminary analysis of the pattern of the sample cross-correlations as well as of the likelihood-ratio statistic — for the sake of brevity not reported here — for the daily data within each of the years 1985–1989 for each of the series considered suggest bivariate ARIMA models of low order. The number of models to be estimated amounts to 240 (= 6 x 5 x 4 x 2) resulting from six cases, five years and four different series both for calls and puts. This large number of estimated models prohibits full reporting of the estimated results. Table 13.3, therefore, shows a summary of the main characteristics of the estimated ARIMA models and illustrate this with the estimated model of Royal Dutch in the sample year 1988.

As Table 13.3 shows, the majority of the estimated models is of the ARIMA (1, 1, 1) type and a few are of higher order with a maximum of 4. This means that, on the whole, the implied lag structure is simple and that in most cases there is only a one day lag. This holds for the models for all option series as well as for the short at-the-money, short out-of-the-money and the remaining series. An example of a model estimated for the put option series Royal Dutch in 1988 is:

$$\begin{pmatrix} \underset{(0.06)}{1-0.187B} & 0 \\ 0 & \underset{(0.05)}{1+0.70B} \end{pmatrix} \begin{pmatrix} \Delta x_1 \\ \Delta x_2 \end{pmatrix} = \begin{pmatrix} \underset{(0.04)}{1-0.777B} & 0 \\ 0 & \underset{(0.05}{1-0.601B^2} \end{pmatrix} \begin{pmatrix} a_1 \\ a_2 \end{pmatrix},$$

with standard errors in parentheses.

13.2.3 The Causality Analysis

As pointed out before, the number of 240 estimated ARIMA models prohibits a full reporting and discussion of estimation results (see Fase and Mourik (1990)). However, the main purpose of the analysis is to establish the type of feedback between trade on the Amsterdam stock exchange and the EOE option market. Causality testing provides the appropriate framework to establish the feedback relations statistically.

The test results are shown in Table 13.5; the statistics behind this qualitative summary are set out in Table 13.6. The general picture that emerges from Table 13.5 is that, very often, the causality runs from

Table 13.4: Frequency of different ARIMA model specifications, 1985–1989

	Call					Put				
Model type:	(2 ... 4,1)	(1,1)	(1,2 ... 4)	(0,1 ... 4)	other	(2 ... 4,1)	(1,1)	(1,2 ... 4)	(0,1 ... 4)	other
All series										
Heineken	–	4	0	1	–	2	1	–	2	–
Hoogovens	–	2	1	–	2	–	1	2	1	1
Nedloyd	–	2	1	2	–	–	2	–	2	1
Philips	–	3	2	–	–	–	1	3	–	1
Royal Dutch	1	–	3	1	–	1	–	2	2	–
Total	–	–	2	1	–	–	–	1	–	2
At the money										
Heineken	1	2	–	1	1	1	1	1	1	1
Hoogovens	–	2	2	1	–	1	2	–	1	1
Nedloyd	2	2	–	1	–	1	2	2	–	–
Philips	–	3	–	2	–	–	3	2	–	–
Royal Dutch	2	2	1	–	–	–	3	1	–	1
Out-of-the-money										
Heineken	3	2	–	–	–	1	2	–	2	–
Hoogovens	1	3	1	–	–	–	1	1	3	–
Nedloyd	1	3	–	–	1	3	1	1	–	–
Philips	–	2	2	1	–	1	3	–	–	1
Royal Dutch	1	1	1	1	1	3	1	1	–	–
Remaining series										
Heineken	2	–	–	3	–	3	1	–	1	–
Hoogovens	3	2	–	–	–	3	1	–	–	1
Nedloyd	2	2	–	–	1	1	1	1	1	1
Philips	2	1	1	1	–	1	1	2	1	–
Royal Dutch	3	1	1	–	–	1	3	–	1	–
Total	24	39	18	16	6	23	31	20	18	11

Note: Model type (p, q) indicates an AR part of order p and a MA part of order q, with first order differences in the variables; 'other' covers 25% of all models.

trade on the option market to trade on the stock market. This holds, in particular, for the remaining series and for the short at-the-money series. More surprising, however, is that in about 50% of the cases studied, the hypothesis of feedback — that is two-way causality — or any other form of causality, should be rejected. This implies that frequently the stock and options market in Amsterdam operates independently and could not aggravate a potentially unstable situation. However, this general conclusion does not hold for 1987, as Table 13.5 shows, indicating that on this particular occasion, trade on the EOE was the driving force for trade at the Amsterdam stock market.

13.3 Summary and Conclusions

Perhaps the most important finding of this chapter is that the bivariate ARIMA model offers a suitable statistical framework for examining the feedback from trade on the stock and option market. This is the main novelty of this chapter. More interesting from an economic and finance point of view, however, is the fact that causality often runs from options trade to the stock market, which seems to support the feeling of the business profession and the main hypothesis. Nevertheless, in a large number of cases no interaction was established at all. As to the length of lags, most models indicate a one-day lag for options. This seems in accordance with the leading function of option trade with respect to trade in stocks. Statistically, it is interesting that the results obtained indicate most convincingly that the relation reveals no stability over time. This means that perhaps market sentiments and unpredictable behaviour, rather than stringent logical behavioural patterns, would shape the underlying market structure and trade pattern.

Table 13.5: Summary of test results

	1985		1986		1987		1988		1989		1985–89		1987–89	
	call	put	call	put	call	put	call	put	call	put	call	put	call	put
All series														
Heineken	A	A	no	no	O	O	W	O	no	no	A	O	no	O
Hoogovens	W	no	O	O	O	W	no	O	no	no	W	O	O	O
Nedlloyd	no	O	O	W	O	A	O	no	no	W	O	W	O	W
Philips	no	A	A	no	no	no	O	no	no	O	W	W	O	W
Royal Dutch	O	O	A	O	O	O	O	no	O	no	W	O	O	O
Short at-the-money series														
Heineken	O	A	A	no	no	O	A	O	A	no	A	no	W	g
Hoogovens	A	A	no	W	O	O	no	no	A	no	W	W	W	g
Nedlloyd	A	A	O	no	O	no	no	no	W	no	W	O	W	O
Philips	O	no	A	no	no	O	O	no	no	no	A	A	A	W
Royal Dutch	O	no	no	no	no	O	no	no	W	no	W	O	no	g
Short out-of-the-money series														
Heineken	no	W	O	O	A	no	no	O	O	no	O	A	O	A
Hoogovens	A	A	no	no	O	O	no	A	no	W	O	O	no	O
Nedlloyd	O	no	A	A	no	no	no	no	A	W	O	A	O	W
Philips	no	no	A	no	no	O	no	no	no	no	W	W	A	W
Kon. Olie	no	no	no	no	no	no	W	W	W	no	W	A	O	g
Remaining series														
Heineken	no	A	no	no	no	O	A	no	no	no	A	O	O	O
Hoogovens	no	no	A	O	O	O	no	A	O	no	O	W	W	O
Nedlloyd	O	A	O	W	no	W	no	no	A	O	W	W	O	W
Philips	O	no	no	no	no	O	no	no	O	no	O	A	O	O
Royal Dutch	no	no	O	no	O	O	O	no	O	no	O	W	O	O

Notes:
'A' means that the causality runs from stocks to options; 'O' indicates that the causality runs from options to stocks and 'W' that there exists feedback; 'no' means that statistically no interrelationship was found.

Table 13.6: Summary of test results

		1985 call	1985 put	1986 call	1986 put	1987 call	1987 put
All series							
Heineken	S→O	$5.1E-4$	$5.8E-4$	0.0	0.0	18.01	0.0
		$(2.4E-4)$	$(1.9E-4)$	(0.0)	(0.0)	(0.0)	(0.0)
	O→S	0.0	0.0	0.0	0.0	$4.1E-4$	38.2
		(0.0)	(0.0)	(0.0)	(0.0)	(8.43)	(8.69)
Hoogovens	S→O	$-1.3E-4$	0.0	0.0	0.0	0.0	$-3.3E-3$
		$(6.6E-5)$	(0.0)	(0.0)	(0.0)	(0.0)	$(5.7E-4)$
	O→S	48.96	1.42	5.11	25.27	31.63	66.51
		(7.41)	(0.87)	(2.47)	(9.59)	(9.53)	(6.07)
Nedlloyd	S→O	0.0	0.0	0.0	$-1.9E-4$	0.0	$2.4E-5$
		(0.0)	(0.0)	(0.0)	$(6.4E-5)$	(0.0)	$(1.0E-5)$
	O→S	0.0	102.1	125.52	21.21	41.67	0.0
		(0.0)	(40.69)	(27.68)	(9.6)	(18.46)	(0.0)
Philips	S→O	0.0	$6.9E-5$	$1.3E-4$	0.0	0.0	0.0
		(0.0)	$(3.3E-5)$	$(5.3E-5)$	(0.0)	(0.0)	(0.0)
	O→S	2.52	0.0	0.0	0.0	0.0	14.4
		(1.27)	(0.0)	(0.0)	(0.0)	(0.0)	(8.83)
Royal Dutch	S→O	0.0	0.0	$5.4E-4$	0.0	0.0	0.0
		(0.0)	(0.0)	$(2.2E-4)$	(0.0)	(0.0)	(0.0)
	O→S	46.01	37.64	0.0	35.86	59.7	156.95
		(13.25)	(17.83)	(0.0)	(12.99)	(20.99)	(29.85)
Short at-the-money series							
Heineken	S→O	$5.2E-5$	$3.5E-5$	$7.7E-5$	0.0	0.0	0.0
		$(3.1E-5)$	$(1.5E-5)$	$(3.4E-5)$	(0.0)	(0.0)	(0.0)
	O→S	41.22	0.0	0.0	0.0	0.0	12.76
		(14.94)	(0.0)	(0.0)	(0.0)	(0.0)	(6.3)
Hoogovens	S→O	$5.2E-5$	$9.7E-5$	0.0	$9.6E-5$	0.0	0.0
		$(2.1E-5)$	$(5.4E-5)$	(0.0)	$(3.5E-5)$	(0.0)	(0.0)
	O→S	3.1	0.0	0.0	86.95	56.89	100.21
		(1.8)	(0.0)	(0.0)	(36.58)	(24.84)	(18.93)
Nedlloyd	S→O	$2.9E-5$	$1.6E-5$	0.0	0.0	0.0	$2.7E-6$
		$(1.2E-5)$	$(5.2E-5)$	(0.0)	(0.0)	(0.0)	$(1.5E-6)$
	O→S	42.79	0.0	283.58	7.94	23.1	0.0
		(22.9)	(8.68)	(88.65)	(5.12)	(10.63)	(0.0)
Philips	S→O	0.0	0.0	$4.4E-5$	0.0	0.0	$3.9E-5$
		(0.0)	(0.0)	$(1.6E-5)$	(0.0)	(0.0)	$(2.0E-5)$
	O→S	84.64	0.0	0.0	0.0	0.0	193.08
		(33.34)	(0.0)	(0.0)	(0.0)	(0.0)	(67.52)
Royal Dutch	S→O	0.0	0.0	$1.7E-5$	$7.4E-6$	0.0	0.0
		(0.0)	(0.0)	$(1.1E-5)$	$(4.3E-6)$	(0.0)	(0.0)
	O→S	−6.33	3.61	0.0	0.0	0.0	448.99
		(2.64)	(2.4)	(0.0)	(0.0)	(0.0)	(162.17)

Notes:
'A' means that the causality runs from stocks to options; 'O' indicates that the causality runs from options to stocks and 'W' that there exists feedback; 'no' means that statistically no interrelationship was found.

Table 13.6: (continued)

1988		1989		1985–89		1987–89	
call	put	call	put	call	put	call	put
8.36	0.0	0.0	1.7$E-5$	3.9$E-5$	0.0	0.0	0.0
(1.3$E-4$)	(0.0)	(0.0)	(9.7$E-6$)	(1.1$E-5$)	(0.0)	(0.0)	(0.0)
6.51	−45.8	0.0	0.0	0.0	0.5	−0.27	0.44
(2.24)	(13.52)	(0.0)	(0.0)	(0.0)	(0.24)	(0.37)	(0.17)
0.0	2.6$E-6$	0.0	0.0	2.2$E-5$	0.0	0.0	0.0
(0.0)	(2.6$E-6$)	(0.0)	(0.0)	(1.0$E-5$)	(0.0)	(0.0)	(0.0)
0.0	27.41	0.0	0.0	7.96	0.8	8.35	38.79
(0.0)	(12.05)	(0.0)	(0.0)	(1.47)	(0.28)	(1.92)	(4.41)
0.0	0.0	0.0	2.0$E-4$	0.0	4.1$E-6$	0.0	9.4$E-5$
(0.0)	(0.0)	(0.0)	(5.1$E-5$)	(0.0)	(1.6$E-6$)	(0.0)	(2.4$E-5$)
144.33	0.0	0.0	50.65	7.68	1.96	5.42	11.21
(36.94)	(0.0)	(0.0)	(23.8)	(1.89)	(0.92)	(1.67)	(4.02)
0.0	0.0	0.0	0.0	−9.3$E-5$	2.5$E-5$	0.0	3.2$E-8$
(0.0)	(0.0)	(0.0)	(0.0)	(3.4$E-5$)	(8.6$E-6$)	(0.0)	(1.5$E-8$)
7.04	0.0	1.79	−249.0	0.95	32.38	5.3	27.48
(2.91)	(0.0)	(0.93)	(39.25)	(0.4)	(8.39)	(1.46)	(6.44)
0.0	0.0	0.0	0.0	4.4$E-5$	0.0	0.0	0.0
(0.0)	(0.0)	(0.0)	(0.0)	(1.3$E-5$)	(0.0)	(0.0)	(0.0)
4.05	0.0	21.29	0.0	0.3	1.32	3.36	13.36
(1.93)	(0.0)	(4.79)	(0.0)	(0.11)	(0.37)	(1.32)	(3.23)
1.8$E-4$	0.0	1.8$E-5$	0.0	−2.1$E-5$	0.0	2.0$E-5$	0.0
(5.6$E-5$)	(0.0)	(8.8$E-6$)	(0.0)	(6.7$E-6$)	(0.0)	(7.3$E-6$)	(0.0)
3.78	−146.0	0.01	0.0	0.0	0.0	4.56	2.44
(1.96)	(49.47)	(0.2)	(0.0)	(0.0)	(0.0)	(1.58)	(2.21)
4.3$E-5$	0.0	2.4$E-5$	4.9$E-6$	8.5$E-6$	7.7$E-6$	1.5$E-6$	0.0
(5.3$E-5$)	(0.0)	(1.2$E-5$)	(2.8$E-6$)	(2.7$E-6$)	(2.4$E-6$)	(5.2$E-6$)	(0.0)
4.1	15.83	0.0	0.0	2.76	2.33	3.23	−6.65
(2.83)	(9.78)	(0.0)	(0.0)	(0.79)	(0.78)	(1.06)	(8.31)
0.0	0.0	3.3$E-6$	0.0	1.3$E-6$	0.0	2.0$E-6$	0.0
(0.0)	(0.0)	(1.5$E-6$)	(0.0)	(3.5$E-7$)	(0.0)	(6.2$E-7$)	(0.0)
0.0	0.0	125.24	0.0	19.64	8.77	6.78	4.37
(0.0)	(0.0)	(58.15)	(0.0)	(5.15)	(2.97)	(2.69)	(1.64)
−5.0$E-6$	0.0	0.0	2.0$E-6$	−1.7$E-5$	2.8$E-6$	−1.0$E-5$	1.5$E-5$
(3.5$E-6$)	(0.0)	(0.0)	(1.1$E-6$)	(5.2$E-6$)	(9.7$E-7$)	(3.8$E-6$)	(6.4$E-7$)
3.89	0.0	0.59	0.0	0.78	16.9	1.0	3.91
(2.44)	(0.0)	(0.52)	(0.0)	(0.63)	(9.04)	(0.88)	(1.5)
0.0	0.0	−3.1$E-4$	0.0	−8.1$E-5$	0.0	3.3$E-7$	0.0
(0.0)	(0.0)	(8.6$E-5$)	(0.0)	(9.5$E-6$)	(0.0)	(3.3$E-6$)	(0.0)
0.0	0.0	78.59	0.0	38.01	2.11	0.0	0.0
(0.0)	(0.0)	(27.13)	(0.0)	(8.63)	(0.82)	(0.0)	(0.0)

Table 13.6: (continued)

		1985 call	1985 put	1986 call	1986 put	1987 call	1987 put
Short out-of-the-money series							
Heineken	S→O	$-1.9E-5$	$6.6E-5$	0.0	0.0	$2.2E-5$	0.0
		$(2.8E-5)$	$(1.4E-5)$	(0.0)	(0.0)	$(1.1E-5)$	(0.0)
	O→S	0.0	−26.4	602.85	−74.9	0.0	0.0
		(0.0)	(13.09)	(146.38)	(34.19)	(0.0)	(0.0)
Hoogovens	S→O	$6.5E-5$	$5.4E-5$	0.0	0.0	0.0	0.0
		$(2.5E-5)$	$(1.6E-5)$	(9.0)	(0.0)	(0.0)	(0.0)
	O→S	11.68	0.0	0.0	0.0	−128.0	−158.0
		(5.92)	(0.0)	(0.0)	(0.0)	(63.07)	(78.08)
Nedlloyd	S→O	0.0	0.0	$3.2E-5$	$2.4E-5$	0.0	$2.3E-6$
		(0.0)	(0.0)	$(6.3E-6)$	$(7.6E-6)$	(0.0)	$(1.2E-6)$
	O→S	1027.54	0.0	552.1	0.0	0.0	0.0
		(313.47)	(0.0)	(317.03)	(0.0)	(0.0)	(0.0)
Philips	S→O	0.0	0.0	$8.4E-6$	$1.5E-5$	0.0	0.0
		(0.0)	(0.0)	$(3.1E-6)$	$(8.6E-6)$	(0.0)	(0.0)
	O→S	86.31	0.0	0.0	0.0	0.0	117.01
		(43.57)	(0.0)	(0.0)	(0.0)	(0.0)	(44.79)
Royal	S→O	0.0	0.0	$8.6E-6$	$7.1E-6$	0.0	0.0
Dutch		(0.0)	(0.0)	$(4.8E-6)$	(0.0)	(0.0)	(0.0)
	O→S	0.0	−9.65	11.87	0.0	0.0	0.0
		(0.0)	(6.02)	(7.15)	(0.0)	(0.0)	(0.0)
Remaining series							
Heineken	S→O	$3.6E-4$	$2.3E-4$	0.0	0.0	0.0	0.0
		$(1.8E-4)$	$(2.3E-4)$	(0.0)	(0.0)	(0.0)	(0.0)
	O→S	0.0	0.0	0.0	0.0	8.02	0.0
		(0.0)	(0.0)	(0.0)	(0.0)	(3.02)	(0.0)
Hoogovens	S→O	$3.8E-5$	$8.4E-5$	0.0	$1.1E-4$	0.0	0.0
		$(6.5E-5)$	$(1.1E-4)$	(0.0)	$(5.2E-5)$	(0.0)	(0.0)
	O→S	0.0	0.0	4.82	0.0	18.48	3.06
		(0.0)	(0.0)	(1.71)	(0.0)	(3.37)	(1.07)
Nedlloyd	S→O	$3.6E-5$	0.0	$-1.5E-4$	0.0	$3.1E-5$	$1.1E-6$
		$(1.7E-5)$	(0.0)	$(7.7E-5)$	(0.0)	$(1.2E-5)$	$(4.9E-6)$
	O→S	3.65	9.64	50.78	38.59	3.28	15.63
		(2.35)	(4.37)	(24.88)	(13.35)	(1.47)	(8.33)
Philips	S→O	$1.2E-6$	0.0	0.0	$-1.8E-5$	0.0	0.0
		$(2.4E-6)$	(0.0)	(0.0)	$(4.5E-5)$	(0.0)	(0.0)
	O→S	0.0	4.5	0.0	0.0	198.66	0.0
		(0.0)	(2.17)	(0.0)	(0.0)	(27.79)	(8.0)
Royal	S→O	0.0	0.0	0.0	0.0	0.0	0.0
Dutch		(0.0)	(0.0)	(0.0)	(0.0)	(0.0)	(0.0)
	O→S	0.0	0.92	0.0	2.7	95.54	10.79
		(0.0)	(0.87)	(0.0)	(1.19)	(13.6)	(4.0)

Table 13.6: (continued)

1988		1989		1985–89		1987–89	
call	put	call	put	call	put	call	put
0.0	0.0	0.0	0.0	0.0	3.8E−7	0.0	7.9E−7
(0.0)	(0.0)	(0.0)	(0.0)	(0.0)	(1.7E−7)	(0.0)	(3.7E−7)
0.0	−622.0	63.73	0.0	8.83	0.0	0.13	0.0
(0.0)	(238.52)	(25.17)	(0.0)	(3.14)	(0.0)	(0.05)	(0.0)
0.0	7.6E−6	0.0	−1.0E−5	0.0	0.0	0.0	0.0
(0.0)	(2.3E−6)	(0.0)	(4.9E−6)	(0.0)	(0.0)	(0.0)	(0.0)
0.0	36.35	0.0	576.03	16.58	1.84	0.0	68.76
(0.0)	(27.24)	(0.0)	(184.75)	(5.23)	(0.77)	(0.0)	(25.58)
0.0	0.0	3.4E−6	6.0E−7	0.0	3.7E−7	0.0	6.2E−7
(0.0)	(0.0)	(1.1E−6)	(2.9E−7)	(0.0)	(1.3E−7)	(0.0)	(2.1E−7)
0.0	0.0	0.0	324.81	89.63	0.0	39.51	67.63
(0.0)	(0.0)	(0.0)	(136.27)	(24.52)	(0.0)	(16.2)	(13.17)
0.0	2.3E−6	0.0	0.0	7.9E−8	8.6E−7	−1.1E−8	1.3E−6
(0.0)	(1.2E−6)	(0.0)	(0.0)	(3.9E−7)	(3.8E−7)	(5.2E−7)	(5.7E−7)
0.0	0.0	21.26	0.0	7.9	9.67	3.52	16.6
(0.0)	(0.0)	(11.44)	(0.0)	(2.97)	(3.65)	(3.08)	(5.92)
4.5E−5	4.2E−5	−6.6E−6	8.3E−8	1.5E−6	2.7E−7	0.0	2.1E−6
(1.7E−5)	(9.9E−6)	(2.2E−6)	(2.4E−7)	(7.5E−7)	(8.0E−8)	(0.0)	(1.2E−6)
450.2	304.36	36.47	0.0	10.19	0.0	25.39	0.0
(217.67)	(56.97)	(15.87)	(0.0)	(3.21)	(0.0)	(8.25)	(0.0)
0.0	9.9E−5	1.5E−5	0.0	2.5E−6	2.8E−5	7.5E−6	−6.2E−5
(0.0)	(4.8E−5)	(7.9E−6)	(0.0)	(1.7E−6)	(8.7E−6)	(4.0E−6)	(4.9E−5)
0.0	4.66	0.0	0.0	0.5	0.0	0.24	−4.83
(0.0)	(2.9)	(0.0)	(0.0)	(0.24)	(0.0)	(0.06)	(2.18)
2.9E−5	0.0	0.0	0.0	2.0E−5	1.9E−5	0.0	−5.7E−4
(1.0E−5)	(0.0)	(0.0)	(0.0)	(9.7E−6)	(2.9E−5)	(0.0)	(1.2E−4)
0.0	1.48	2.55	7.9	1.9	1.75	46.08	6.34
(0.0)	(0.75)	(1.33)	(3.04)	(0.47)	(48.0)	(5.37)	(1.43)
0.0	0.0	2.9E−5	2.3E−5	5.1E−6	3.1E−6	4.3E−6	0.0
(0.0)	(0.0)	(2.5E−5)	(1.0E−5)	(1.4E−6)	(9.9E−7)	(1.5E−6)	(0.0)
0.0	0.0	13.77	0.0	6.15	2.8	6.8	3.48
(0.0)	(0.0)	(6.4)	(0.0)	(1.54)	(0.74)	(2.26)	(1.33)
−1.5E−5	−2.5E−5	5.3E−6	0.0	7.2E−6	1.0E−6	1.7E−6	−1.5E−6
(9.9E−6)	(1.4E−5)	(2.8E−6)	(0.0)	(2.4E−6)	(8.8E−6)	(4.2E−6)	(5.6E−6)
0.0	5.55	0.0	2.07	0.0	1.84	32.11	1.02
(0.0)	(3.87)	(0.0)	(0.87)	(0.0)	(0.55)	(9.83)	(0.36)
0.0	0.0	0.0	0.0	2.3E−5	0.0	0.0	0.0
(0.0)	(0.0)	(0.0)	(0.0)	(7.6E−6)	(0.0)	(0.0)	(0.0)
0.0	2.33	0.0	0.58	5.7E−3	0.67	6.8	0.89
(0.0)	(1.11)	(0.0)	(0.29)	(2.5E−3)	(0.17)	(2.34)	(0.31)

14. The Equity Premium Puzzle

14.1 Introduction

Investors in equity require a premium to cover their risk. The size of the premium has been the subject of empirical and theoretical debate ever since Mehra and Prescott published a study on the equity premium in the US. Between 1889 and 1978 the average real return on equities in the Standard & Poor 500 index was nearly 7%. The real return over the same period on a risk-free investment in Treasury paper was less than 1%. The difference is a risk premium of nearly 6%.[1]

This premium is considerably higher than predicted by the Consumption Based Capital Asset Pricing Model (CCAP model).[2] The CCAP model is a generally accepted theory. It is based on the assumption that consumers maximize expected utility over time by smoothing consumption outlays. The model draws comparisons between an individual's consumption and saving patterns. The consumer is therefore also an investor. This investment behaviour is determined by two critical factors: the degree of risk aversion and the consumer's time preference.

14.2 The Risk Premium Puzzle

The consumer's time preference is reflected by the marginal rate of substitution of current consumption for future consumption. It can be measured by observing consumption over time. Since the risk premium on equities can also be measured (the 6% referred to above), it is possible to calculate a value for risk aversion.

Mehra and Prescott arrive at a risk aversion value of 26. This is equal to the situation, the example is based on Benartzi and Thaler, in which

Translation of 'De risicopremie op aandelen: Een puzzel?' by M.M.G. Fase and W.F.-J. van de Poll, *Economisch Statistische Berichten*, **81** (December 1996), 1014–1017.

[1] Mehra and Prescott (1985).

[2] See, for example, Blanchard and Fischer (1989, pp. 506–512). A good summary is provided in Jagannathan and McGrattan (1996). The original source is Lucas (1978).

an investment with a 50% probability of a return of 50 000, and the same probability of a return of 100 000, has the same value as a certain return of 51 209.[3] It is highly unlikely that investors are really so risk averse. A risk aversion of about 10 is usually considered acceptable, but it is also argued that a value of around 1 is not uncommon.[4] A risk aversion of 10 is commensurate with an equity premium of just 0.35%, instead of the 6% observed. According to Mehra and Prescott, this is the risk premium puzzle that arises if the equilibrium approach encountered in the literature is accepted.

Mehra and Prescott's finding is an anomaly and is a result that casts serious doubt on a generally accepted academic paradigm of economic theory. This finding has, therefore, been the centre of a great deal of research, particularly in the US.

14.3 In Search of a Solution

The solution to this anomaly is sought from two angles. The first is the theoretical, which tests the validity of the conclusion by refining or reappraising the assumptions used; the second is the empirical, which is concerned primarily with Mehra and Prescott's data on the US. A good example of this approach is Siegel's examination of US and UK data, which in the 19th century was financially more highly developed than the US, using a considerably longer sample period.[5] Nevertheless, the literature pays scant attention to this empirical approach and the debate concentrates mainly on the underlying theory, often using Mehra and Prescott's original data. The literature does sometimes allow a limited expansion to include quarterly or monthly data for the period after World War II and to consider Germany and Japan in addition to the US and UK. The latter led Kocherlakota to state in his outstanding review that the puzzle seemed to be a 'general feature of organized asset markets'.[6] He concluded that the anomaly of the equity premium is still a puzzle, despite the attempts to solve it summarized in his article.

As noted, the literature considers primarily the US. It is therefore open to question whether Kocherlakota's generalization is valid and whether empirical analysis in other countries would be productive. The purpose of this chapter is to consider the situation in The Netherlands using data from roughly the same period as that used by Mehra and Prescott for the US.

[3] See Benartzi and Thaler (1995) and Vorst (1995).
[4] Hansen and Singleton (1983).
[5] Siegel (1992).
[6] Kocherlakota (1996). The quotation is taken from a footnote on page 45.

14.4 The Measurement of Risk Aversion

According to the CCAP model, the expected risk premium is commensurate with the degree of risk aversion. Risk aversion is closely related to impatience in consumption behaviour (in special circumstances, there is a direct relationship between these variables). Risk aversion can be measured by means of the parameters of the utility function. Utility increases as consumption increases, but marginal utility decreases. If the decrease accelerates (that is the second derivative is high), there is a relatively high degree of risk aversion. In risk avoidance, there is a willingness to pay for a large risk with a low probability (for example, taking out fire insurance), whereas in risk-seeking behaviour there is a willingness to pay for a large gain with a small probability (for example, by taking part in lotteries, gambling or other games of chance).

Slightly more formally, the 'relative degree of risk aversion' can be defined by means of the ratio between the second and the first derivative of the consumer's utility: $-\frac{U''(c)}{U'(c)}$.[7] The greater the risk aversion, the greater the risk premium investors will expect. Furthermore, there is a positive relationship in the CCAP model between the risk premium and: the risk premium realized in the past; the correlation between the risk premium and the growth rate of consumption (the impatience of investors); fluctuations in the risk premium; and fluctuations in the growth rate of consumption.

14.5 Risk and Return in The Netherlands

Following Mehra and Prescott's analysis, it was attempted to determine to what extent the level of the equity premium had been a puzzle in The Netherlands over a period of nearly 180 years. The necessary data were compiled through cross-referencing a variety of statistical sources.[8]

Table 14.1 shows the average return on equities, the return on three-month Treasury or equivalent paper (the risk-free rate of interest), the rate of inflation and the risk premium for various (sub)periods between 1828 and 1994. The total return on equities is calculated by adding dividend income to capital gains.

It can be concluded from Table 14.1 that the average equity premium in The Netherlands was considerably lower between 1828 and 1900 than between 1901 and 1994: nearly 4% versus 7%. The low risk premium in the 19th century was due chiefly to the relatively high real, risk-free

[7] See also Mankiw and Zeldes (1991).

[8] For the data used in this chapter, see Poll (1996).

Table 14.1: Return and risk premium in The Netherlands

Period	Return on equities	Risk-free interest rate	Inflation	Risk premium
1828–1900	7.2	3.3	0.3	4.0
1828–1994	9.3	3.7	1.8	5.6
1889–1978	9.3	3.2	2.7	6.1
1901–1939	8.9	2.8	1.5	6.1
1922–1939	5.6	2.4	−1.8	3.3
1901–1994	11.1	4.1	3.0	7.0
1947–1960	15.4	1.9	3.7	13.5
1947–1970	11.6	3.2	3.8	8.5
1947–1994	12.8	5.1	4.2	7.7
1961–1980	7.6	5.9	5.8	1.7
1981–1994	17.8	7.1	2.5	10.7

Notes:
The risk premium is equal to the difference between the real return on equities (nominal return on equities less inflation) and the real risk-free rate of interest (nominal risk-free rate of interest less inflation). The figures are percentages rounded to one decimal place.

return of 3% on average. As a result of the higher rate of inflation in the 20th century, the real risk-free return fell during this period to 1% and the risk premium consequently rose to 7%.

1922–1939 was an interesting period. The fall in the general price level increased the real risk-free return to 4.2%. As a result of the Wall Street Crash in 1929 and the subsequent recession, the average nominal return on equities fell during this period to 5.6%. The deflation, however, meant that the real return was unchanged at around 7.4%, producing a relatively low risk premium of 3.3%.

In the period from World War II to the beginning of the 1960s, the equity premium was relatively high at 13.5% owing to the very high returns achieved on equities during this period. Between 1961 and 1980, by contrast, the risk premium was very low at 1.7%. This was due in part to the two oil crises in 1974 and 1980. After 1980, the equity premium climbed, despite the high risk-free rate of interest, to 10.7%, which contrasts sharply with the record low seen in 1961–1980 but is surprisingly similar to the premium seen in the post-war recovery period of 1947–1960.

Interestingly, the difference between the average real return on equi-

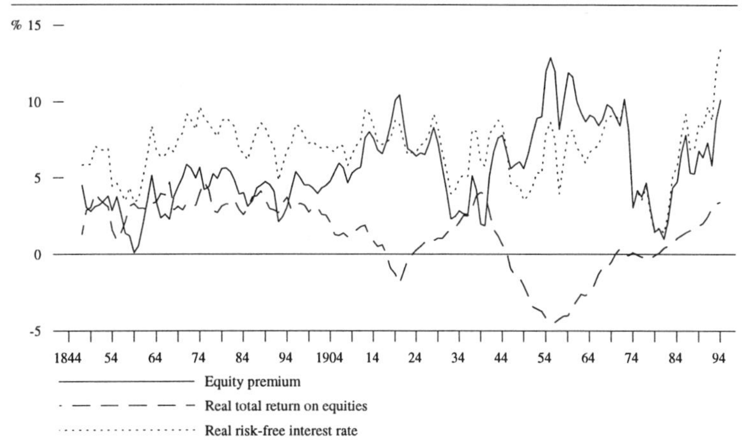

Figure 14.1: Risk-free interest rate, return on equities and equity premium in The Netherlands, 1840–1995 (%)

ties in the 19th and 20th centuries was only one percentage point. The average equity premium in The Netherlands in 1889–1978 was roughly the same as the risk premium that Mehra and Prescott calculated for the US in the same period: 6.1% versus 6.2%.

These findings are presented in a slightly different way in Figure 14.1, which plots the twenty-year moving average of the real return on equities, the risk-free rate of interest and the equity premium. The figure clearly shows the low level of the premium in the 1930s, the high level in the years immediately following World War II, a dip in the premium during the 1970s and an increase in the subsequent years. Figure 14.2, which plots the risk premium as a moving fifty-year average, distinctly shows the upward trend and the variation in the premium.

14.6 A Dutch Puzzle Too

To determine whether the risk premium puzzle also occurs in The Netherlands, in keeping with Mehra and Prescott, calculations were made of the average increase in total consumption and the correlation between the annual increase in consumption and the previously estimated risk premium. Other sampling variables necessary to determine risk aversion were also calculated. Table 14.2 shows the results for the period 1901–1994 (owing to the availability of consumption data) and a number of sub-periods.

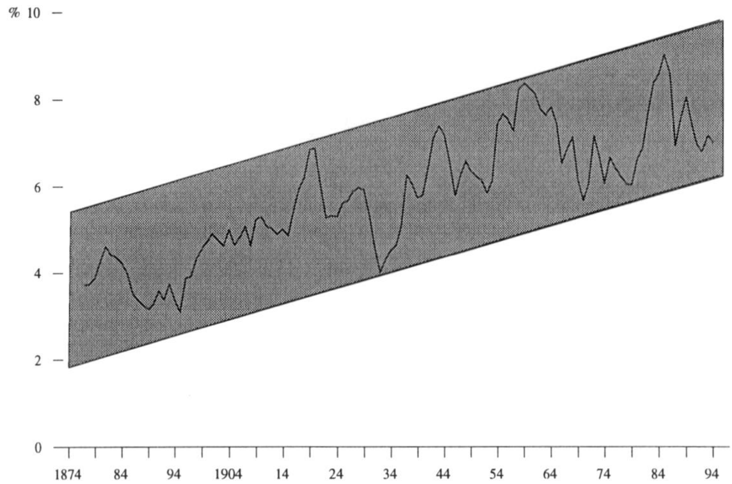

Figure 14.2: Equity premium in The Netherlands, fifty-year moving average (%)

The average total annual increase in consumption of foodstuffs and services throughout the period studied was 1.7%. The relatively high growth rate in 1947–1970 was due mainly to the sharp rise in consumption of services. Table 14.2 also shows that the increase in consumption in 1947–1970 was nearly twice as high as in 1971–1994.

Assuming that there is an adequately positive correlation between the risk premium and the increase in consumption, according to the CCAP model, this would mean that a higher risk premium was expected in the period immediately following World War II. This assumption is supported by the results set out in Table 14.2. Interestingly, the average annual increase in consumption in The Netherlands in 1901–1978 was 1.8%, equal to that in the US as observed by Mehra and Prescott. For the period 1901–1978, the implied degree of risk aversion in The Netherlands was higher than 60. This contrasts sharply with the value of just over 26, calculated by Mehra and Prescott for the US, which, moreover, they considered to be high (if a value of 10 is taken as acceptable and the benchmark value). It can be concluded for The Netherlands, as for the US and the UK, that the level of the risk premium is a puzzle that cannot be explained as long as the CCAP model, with the risk aversion proposed by Mehra and Prescott, is adhered to.

Table 14.2 shows that this conclusion can also be drawn for the sub-periods, with extremely high values for 1947–1994. According to

Table 14.2: Risk aversion in The Netherlands

Period	Risk premium $(r - rf)$	Increase in consumption (g)	Co-variance $\times 10^{-3}$	Cor-relation	Risk aversion
1901–1939	6.1% (0.2)	0.5% (0.04)	1.0	0.14	62.2
1901–1978	6.3% (0.2)	1.8% (0.04)	1.0	0.14	63.3
1901–1994	7.0% (0.2)	1.7% (0.04)	0.7	0.10	102.3
1947–1970	8.5% (0.2)	3.6% (0.03)	1.3	0.19	65.6
1947–1994	7.7% (0.2)	2.7% (0.03)	0.3	0.05	270.8
1971–1994	7.0% (0.2)	1.8% (0.01)	−0.9	0.30	−82.8

Notes:
Risk aversion, using a reduced form of the CCAP model, is calculated as a ratio of the risk premium to the covariance between risk premium and the increase in consumption. The years 1940–1946 were omitted from the analysis. Standard deviations are shown between brackets.

the CCAP model, this means that consumers since World War II have been less inclined to defer their consumption. Consumers are apparently avoiding risks and are averse to strong fluctuations in the increase and absolute level of consumption.

In 1947–1970, the average increase in consumption was a high 3.6%. This was accompanied by a low, but not constant, real risk-free rate of interest. Figure 14.3 shows that in the years following World War II the real risk-free rate of interest trended upwards. According to the CCAP model, this means that the increase in consumption had been adequately anticipated during this period.

14.7 Conclusion

In this chapter, the risk premium on Dutch equities has been measured since 1824 on the assumption that the capital market in The Netherlands in the 19th century, as part of the European capital market, was probably better developed than that in the US. For 1824–1994, the average real total return on equities exceeded 7% and the risk-free rate of interest was approximately 1.5%, producing an average risk premium of more than 5.5%. As a result of the average high real risk-free rate of interest in the 19th century, the premium then was nearly 4%, while in the current century the premium has been nearly twice as high at more than 7%.

By means, in part, of the per capita real increase in consumption

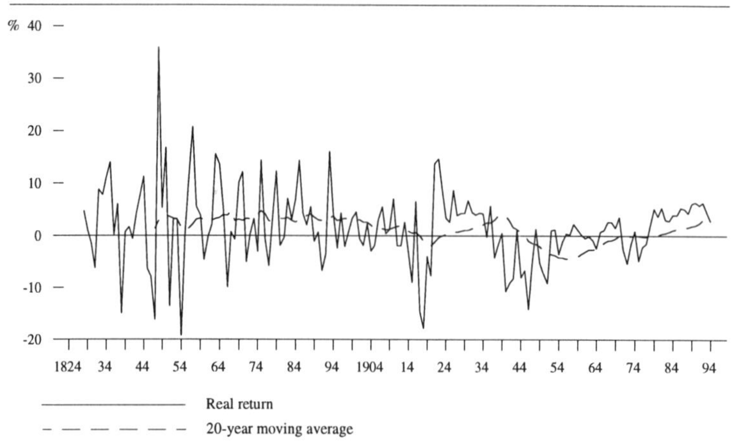

Figure 14.3: The risk-free interest rate in The Netherlands

of foodstuffs and services following the CCAP model, it has been calculated that risk aversion in The Netherlands in the 20th century has been relatively high. It was lower before World War II than after, but considerably higher than the risk aversion value of 10 that many authors consider to be a benchmark value. There is little correlation between the increase in consumption in The Netherlands and the risk premium. In this light, it can be concluded that the equity premium puzzle also exists in The Netherlands, in so far as a risk aversion of 10 can be accepted as a standard.

Contrary to the statements often made in the literature on this subject, this would mean that the puzzle is not an anomaly but at best a consequence of Mehra and Prescott's assumption of what is a normal risk aversion. Perhaps the grounds for adopting the numerical value of 10, customarily used in the formulation of risk aversion based on an ordinal concept of utility, are sufficient. The puzzle therefore loses its urgency. One interpretation of the recurrent empirical finding might be that the puzzle undermines the explanatory power of the CCAP model. To our knowledge, this option has rarely been chosen, which is particularly surprising since it could be concluded — with due respect for the persistency of the facts — that the market apparently demands a high risk premium.

Whatever the case may be, from a practical point of view it is in any event clear that the risk premium in The Netherlands is far from negligible. This has probably encouraged interest in risk-bearing investments in the past twenty years, when the premium was nearly twice as high as for the period studied as a whole and some two percentage points higher than in the twenty year following World War II. Taken over a very long-term, the actual premium in The Netherlands is remarkably stable but there are significant differences between the sub-periods. An interesting question is the extent to which this is due to the characteristics and policy decisions of those periods.

15. The Risk Premium on Equity in Core EMU

15.1 Introduction

The risk premium on equity is the difference between a return on shares and a return on non-risk-bearing investments in, for instance, Treasury paper. For the US, Mehra and Prescott (1985, 1988) have pointed out that according to the Standard & Poor 500 index, the average real return on equity came out at nearly 7% for the period 1889–1978, while the average real return on Treasury paper amounted to less than 1% per annum for the same period, the result being a risk premium of almost 6%. An almost identical result was found by Fase and Poll (1996) for The Netherlands for a similar sample period.

The theoretical basis for determining the risk premium on equity is provided by the so-called consumption-based capital asset pricing or CCAP model, which plays a major role in both current macro-economic theory and modern finance theory (see *e.g.* Romer (1996), Copeland and Weston (1988)). On the basis of several assumptions, discussed in more detail below, this theory predicts a risk premium which should be considerably below the above-mentioned 6%. Mehra and Prescott's finding for the US, as well as Fase and Poll's for The Netherlands, are therefore an anomaly, that is a result which seriously questions a generally accepted scientific paradigm from received economic theory. Perhaps this explains why the results obtained by Mehra and Prescott, going back to Lucas's (1978) CCAP model, attracted much attention, notably in the US.

The attempts made in the literature to explain the observed anomaly move along two lines. The first line of attack entails refinement or adjustment of the assumptions used; that goes especially for the theoretical approach which very often is interesting and imaginative. The second line of attack focuses notably on the data used by Mehra

Translation of 'De risicopremie op aandelen in de Europese Unie' by M.M.G. Fase, *Maandschrift Economie*, **61**(6) (1997), 474–483, is reprinted by permission.

and Prescott for the US, extending to the UK as well. A remarkable example of this is the fascinating data analysis of Siegel (1992), whose sample covers a much longer period of time than Mehra and Prescott's and who also takes into consideration the UK, which in the nineteenth century was a financially much more advanced country than the US. Still, this empirical approach was given barely any serious attention, the analysis concentrating almost exclusively on the theoretical points of departure, using the original data of Mehra and Prescott. A few authors attempted a small digression to quarterly or monthly figures for the period following World War II, including also Germany and Japan, and recently The Netherlands. However, the empirical findings for those countries strongly supported the findings for the US and this led Kocherlakota (1996, pp. 45) in his excellent overview, to conclude that 'It may not be too strong to say that the equity premium and risk free rate puzzle appears to be a general feature of organized assets markets'. Therefore, he comes to the unequivocal conclusion that the anomaly of the equity premium continues to be a puzzle, the amply elaborated theoretical analysis in his review article notwithstanding. As noted, the literature relates almost exclusively to the US. The question therefore arises whether Kocherlakota's generalization is justified, and whether the empirical analysis ought not be extended to other countries. As a matter of fact, the chapter extends the analysis to five countries of the European Union, countries which are, perhaps with the exception of the UK, considered the core EMU countries. These countries are not covered in the empirical examination of the equity premium puzzle by Mehra and Prescott for the US, or by Fase and Poll for The Netherlands. Apart from this empirical analysis, the chapter also presents a survey of the criticism of Mehra and Prescott's analysis, suggesting various intelligent solutions being sought and found — an aspect somewhat underexposed in Kocherlakota — for the equity premium puzzle. This literature centres on the more detailed consideration of the often highly simplified assumptions underlying the models concerned. We use this review of the literature to assess our own findings, and Kocherlakota's conclusion that the equity premium puzzle is a universal phenomenon.

15.2 The 'Equity Premium Puzzle' in the US

The theory, going back to Lucas's (1978) CCAP model, rests on the following assumptions. First, over time consumers strive for utility maximization; second, consumers are to some extent homogeneous; and third, there is a certain correlation — covariance — between the growth of consumption and return on shares. The latter assumption is difficult to understand intuitively, but describes the assumed behaviour of the consumer who also wants to invest. He (or she) desires equally spread consumption over time, which is enabled by saving and dissaving. Consumers require high returns on investment when consumption slows down (and vice versa), and therefore view investment as an insurance against low consumption from income. On the basis of these assumptions, Mehra and Prescott aver that the equity premium in the US should be much lower than the 6% they observe. The expected risk premium of a financial asset i at time t, $\mathrm{E}(r-r_f)$, is, on the one hand determined by the measure of risk aversion on the part of the investor, A, and on the other hand, by the covariance between return on this asset and the marginal substitution rate of consumption. This marginal substitution rate indicates to what extent the consumer prefers future to present consumption. The latter is determined by the growth rate of consumption. The higher the covariance between the growth of consumption and the equity premium, the higher investors expect the risk premium to be, given the risk aversion A and the assumed intertemporal utility function of consumption C per period. This leads to the following basic equation used in all studies:

$$\mathrm{E}(r - r_f) = A \ \mathrm{Cov}\left(r - r_f, \ \frac{C_t}{C_{t-1}} - 1\right). \tag{15.1}$$

which is the starting point of Mehra and Prescott's analysis.

On the basis of this equation and the assumption it contains — identical individual preferences, efficient financial markets and negligible transaction costs — Mehra and Prescott show that this financial and economic equilibrium model is unable to explain the size of the risk premium in the US. Their empirical results are summarized in Table 15.1.

Rewriting equation (15.1) as

$$A = \frac{\mathrm{E}(r - r_f)}{\mathrm{Cov}\left(r - r_f, \frac{C_t}{C_{t-1}} - 1\right)} \tag{15.2}$$

using the results shown in Table 15.1 Mehra and Prescott calculate a relative measure of risk aversion A of 26, whereas a value of 10 is usually considered plausible. They therefore conclude that the risk premium for the period 1889–1979 cannot be higher than 0.35%. However, the risk premium found for the US is over 6%. Mehra and Prescott see this gap as a puzzle. Subsequently a second puzzle emerged, the risk-free puzzle of Weil (1989), with the following background. A high risk aversion means that consumers put present consumption before future consumption. But consumers and investors also prefer a stable consumption pattern.

Table 15.1: Results found by Mehra and Prescott

Average percentage growth of real per capita consumption	1.8%
Real return on Treasury Bills	0.8%
Real total return on S&P 500 (including dividend)	7.0%
Risk premium	6.2%
Covariance (growth of consumption, risk premium)	0.0024

Source: Mehra and Prescott (1985)

Nevertheless, a real risk-free interest rate of no more than 0.8%, at a growth of consumption in the US of 1.8% per year, is ensured.

15.3 The Risk Premium in Core EMU and the UK

In line with the Mehra and Prescott research methodology and their results as shown above, Table 15.2 sets out the main relevant financial statistics for the five EMU countries examined in this chapter. These statistics are averages, calculated for the sample period 1952–1995, and refer to nominal total return on shares and risk-free paper — most often short-term Treasury paper — the inflation rate and the resulting equity premium. The table shows a calculated average equity premium of a little more than 8% for Germany and The Netherlands, with a higher figure of 9.5% for the UK only. For Belgium and France the equity premium is substantially lower. It is noteworthy that over the sample period of more than 40 years, Belgium was the only country where the total return on shares was lower than in the other countries studied. However, for France the nominal return on shares hardly differs from that in Belgium and Germany. We also note that the spread of the rate of return on risk-free assets across countries is much lower than that for the rate of return on shares. If the sample is divided into two equal parts, the first sub-period shows a very high equity premium of 10% for Germany, with a similar pattern for the UK in the second sub-period. Belgium always shows the lower equity premium although in the second sub-period it is about 1.5 percentage points less than in the first sub-period. For The Netherlands, the figures reveal a remarkable stability which is, however, dependent on the sub-period studied as shown by the results of Table 14.1 (see Chapter 14).

An important empirical question concerns the explanation of the remarkable differences between the rates of return among countries shown

Table 15.2: Rates of return, rate of inflation and equity premium (percentages)

	Return on shares	Return on risk-free assets	Rate of inflation	Equity Premium
1952–1995				
Belgium	9.9	6.9	4.0	3.0
France	12.9	7.8	6.4	5.1
Germany	13.8	5.3	3.0	8.5
The Netherlands	13.8	5.5	3.9	8.2
United Kingdom	17.1	7.6	6.1	9.5
1952–1973				
Belgium	7.8	4.1	2.7	3.8
France	7.7	5.4	5.0	2.3
Germany	14.8	4.3	2.5	10.5
The Netherlands	11.8	3.8	3.8	8.0
United Kingdom	12.8	5.0	4.0	7.8
1974–1995				
Belgium	11.8	9.5	5.1	2.3
France	17.2	9.8	6.9	7.5
Germany	12.9	6.3	3.5	6.6
The Netherlands	15.7	7.2	3.9	8.5
United Kingdom	21.5	10.2	8.7	11.3

Note: For Belgium the sample period is 1954–1995; for France 1956–1995.

in Table 15.2. This is important, because these rates of return constitute the basis of our calculated equity premium. Research into the fundamental determinants of national equity returns from a multi-country perspective has lagged behind domestic asset-pricing studies, as noted recently in an interesting paper by Ferson and Harvey (1996). In this paper Ferson and Harvey examine asset-pricing from a global perspective. Therefore, they attempt to explain the rates of return on shares across countries empirically, using country-specific rather than firm-specific attributes like relative valuation ratios, macro-economic performance, interest rate, term structure, the country's credit rating and exposure to economic risks. The statistical results of Ferson and Harvey, based on a cross-section of monthly data for 21 countries including the five countries considered in this chapter, show that most of the country-specific attributes provide substantial explanatory power. The estimation results obtained by Ferson and Harvey for the five countries considered in this chapter, support the rather diverse total rates of return on common stocks shown in Table 15.2. For instance, for Belgium, Ferson and Harvey found a particular influence of the inflation rate, while in the UK, the long-term interest rate has more explanatory power than elsewhere.

To assess the plausibility of the calculated equity risk premium, the most strategic parameter is the implied estimate for risk aversion. This quantity, together with consumption growth, covariance among the latter and equity premium — for reasons of simplicity also shown as correlation coefficient — are set out in Table 15.3.

For the whole sample period, risk aversion is high in all countries, perhaps with the exception of Belgium, a finding that does not substantially change in the two sub-periods. However, calculations not reported here show that the results for the risk aversion are rather sensitive to lagging consumption growth in the covariance with the equity premium. Nevertheless, we may infer that, in terms of Mehra and Prescott's analytical framework, the equity premium puzzle also exists in the EMU countries considered.

15.4 Reactions in the Literature to Mehra and Prescott

Provoked by the research by Mehra and Prescott, numerous authors have attempted to solve the equity premium puzzle by modifying the assumptions of the CCAP model. In order to assess the preliminary conclusion of our data analysis, a brief survey of responses in the literature to Mehra and Prescott's provocative results is appropriate. Rietz (1988) explains the high premium by taking into account the probability of heavy recessions followed by market crashes. Rietz changes Mehra and Prescott's model by adding the probability of a recession attended by sudden large changes in consumption. Rietz concludes that a major fall in consumption is often accompanied by a sharp drop in dividend payments. Shareholders averse to risk will therefore require a higher return, in order to be able to compensate for possible losses.

Constantinides (1990) solves the puzzle by incorporating habit persistence and habit formation into the CCAP model. He observes that every investor behaves in accordance with a certain consumption pattern, and hence is unwilling to reduce his consumption in the future. This is called habit persistence by Constantinides. The utility experienced by

Table 15.3: Risk aversion and the other required estimates

	Equity Premium (%)	Consumption growth (%)	Covariance ($\times 10^{-2}$)	Correlation	Risk aversion
1952–1995					
Belgium	2.8	2.6	0.06	0.19	46
France	5.5	2.7	0.04	0.15	144
Germany	9.1	3.6	0.45	0.51	20
The Netherlands	7.9	2.7	0.13	0.27	60
United Kingdom	9.6	2.3	0.09	0.08	102
1952–1973					
Belgium	4.1	3.5	0.05	0.23	79
France	4.1	3.8	0.07	0.15	63
Germany	13.4	5.5	0.54	0.59	25
The Netherlands	9.0	3.8	0.16	0.33	56
United Kingdom	10.3	2.6	0.01	0.03	1 012
1974–1995					
Belgium	1.7	1.7	0.05	0.16	34
France	6.6	1.9	0.04	0.12	185
Germany	4.8	1.7	0.20	0.39	24
The Netherlands	6.9	1.6	0.08	0.21	84
United Kingdom	8.9	2.0	0.17	0.20	51

Note: For Belgium the sample period is 1954–1995; for France 1956–1995.

investors over a certain period depends on their present consumption level compared to that in the past. This is called habit formation. Here the investor does not take into consideration his future consumption and preference, so that the intertemporal utility function changes into a non-time-separable utility function. An expansion of consumption thus leads to a relatively larger marginal utility increase in the near future. However, the intertemporal utility function used by Mehra and Prescott characterizes the substitution rate of consumption over several periods, so that it is time-separable. As a result of habit persistence and habit formation, the level of consumption is dependent on a minimum survival level. The higher that survival level, the more value the investor attaches to his past consumption, and the lower the variability of consumption growth. Given a low covariance between the growth of consumption and the risk premium, and the assumption of a minimum survival level, the risk premium can be explained in terms of a low aversion to risk.

Mankiw and Zeldes (1991) point out that consumers may not be regarded as a homogeneous group. Only 27.6% of families studied in the US for the period 1970–1984 possessed shares. That is why, by contrast with the model of Mehra and Prescott, Mankiw and Zeldes explicitly assume heterogeneity among consumers in their study, dividing them into two groups: shareholders and non-shareholders. On the basis of their study, Mankiw and Zeldes conclude that as consumers possess more shares, the covariance between the growth of consumption and the share premium will be greater, resulting in a lower risk aversion. Shareholders thus turn out to be less averse to risk than non-shareholders. This partly solves the equity premium puzzle.

Benartzi and Thaler (1995) come to the conclusion that the high risk premium is the result of loss aversion and mental accounting. Loss aversion is understood to mean that investors are more sensitive to loss than to gain. By mental accounting, they mean that individual investors implicitly use methods to assess the financial results of, for instance, investments, transactions or gambling. Such an evaluation may take place daily, every month, once a year or even less frequently. The combination of loss aversion and short evaluation periods is called 'myopic loss aversion' by Benartzi and Thaler. The occurrence of loss aversion means that the evaluation period chosen is not neutral. According to the theory of Mehra and Prescott, investors maximize the expected utility of their future consumption, independently of their time horizon. However, Benartzi and Thaler hold the view that the more often risk-averse investors assess their investment portfolios — evincing a higher degree of myopic behaviour — the more risk they feel they are facing and the higher the equity premium they require. For instance, at an evaluation period of one year, they calculate a risk premium of about 6% for the period 1926–1990. This premium more or less equals the premium calculated by Mehra and Prescott, so that the puzzle is solved. However, if an investment portfolio is assessed only once every twenty years, the risk premium will — according to Benartzi and Thaler — drop to a mere 1%.

Brown, Goetzmann, and Ross (1995) adjust the CCAP model by making allowance for the fact that investors demand a higher premium on shares as a result of the risk that the trade in shares is suspended or terminated. They base their view on the experiences gained in the US over the past century. Of the 36 stock exchanges existing at the beginning of this century, more than half have seen a lengthy interruption of trade as a result of calamities such as war, nationalization or revolution. In order to obtain Mehra and Precott's 6% risk premium, a survival rate of 50% would have been applicable to stock exchanges, according to Brown *et al.* (1995) to stock exchanges. That roughly equals the percentage of stock exchanges surviving into the twentieth century. Introduction of the survival rate into the CCAP model would thus contribute to the explanation of the equity premium puzzle.

In order to explain the high risk premium, Danthine and Donaldson (1996) extend the analysis with the real sector of the economy. They make allowance for adjustment costs for investment, the financial position of enterprises and risk-dispersing labour contracts. In their model, enterprises finance all of their adjustment costs internally, so that the variance in equity decreases and — with a view to maintaining equilibrium within the economy — variance of per capita consumption increases. A larger variance in consumption makes risk-averse investors evince greater demand for risk-free government bonds and smaller demand for shares, so that the expected risk-free return goes down and the expected return on shares goes up. This gives rise to a higher risk premium. The more enterprises are financed from borrowing, the smaller the residual claim on shareholders, making for greater uncertainty as to dividend payments and the expected return on shares. This also leads to a higher risk premium. Finally, risk-dispersing labour contracts may, according to Danthine and Donaldson, cause the variability of consumption by employees — not being shareholders — to decline. Shareholders shield employees from extreme variations in consumption by guaranteeing wage payments, but demand a higher risk premium in return.

Kocherlakota (1996) assumes in his overview that the high risk premium can only be the result of the difference transaction costs in the share and bond markets. That is why investors expect a higher return on shares, *viz.* to compensate for the higher transaction costs.

Transaction costs are also a key element in the recent attempt of Bansal and Coleman (1996) to understand the high equity risk premium analytically. Their approach is to include the monetary element in the usual analytical framework of the CCAP model by considering monetary transaction costs. An important assumption is to consider financial assets other than money to facilitate financial transactions. Numerical exercises, with the parameter representing this ease of financial transactions, show that reasonable values are compatible with the observed equity risk premium, indicating that the model of Bansal and Coleman may also offer a plausible solution for the equity premium puzzle.

15.5 Conclusion

The firmness of a rather sizeable equity premium, observed over time and across countries, supports the hypothesis that this contradicts the CCAP model rather than that the empirical results constitute an anomaly. Moreover, criticism and proposed amendmends in the literature suggest a weakness in the theoretical foundation of the size of the equity premium offered by the CCAP model. This holds, in particular, for the presumed homogeneity of consumer-investors, the frequency of assessing investment portfolios and the fact that financial transactions are diverse in practice. Therefore, we may perhaps conclude that the equity premium puzzle is the result of a particular theory rather than an empirical anomaly.

16. Purchase of Art: Consumption and Investment

Cultural economics is a new and emerging area of research in economics which even has its own journal (*Journal of Cultural Economics*). However, cultural economics has been around a long time as shown by the first writings on economics and art by Galbraith (1960, Chapter 3), Wagenführ (1965) or Baumol and Bowen (1966) in the sixties. Perhaps more important is that these authors — as Becker (1976) from a different perspective — convincingly illustrate the usefulness of economics as a system of thought — a box of tools — to explore questions beyond immediate day-to-day life. Thus, the purchase of a painting, art objects and antiques, or the decision to enrol in a university, become examples of economic decision making. Purchasing an object of art is presumably much like taking up a study: the pleasure derived prevails over the monetary returns it yields. Yet there are those who feel the return on higher education should be taken into account — that is shifting the emphasis from consumption to investment — and indeed, this practice is now both accepted and frequently applied in the field of schooling.[1] In this line of thinking, schooling is seen as an investment in human capital, and the purchase of art an investment that should compete with other portfolio investments on the basis of financial returns. Consequently, the return on art, in particular, paintings, has been subjected to attempts to calculate its financial return without denying the importance of the psychological returns of owning art, that is the benefit of consuming art. This approach regards purchases of art as a possible alternative to investments in, for instance, bonds, shares, gold, real estate and wine, or perhaps, education. The yield on art is determined entirely by price movements in the market. Obviously the art market comprises more than just paintings, which is the focus of this chapter.

Reprinted from *De Economist*, **144**(4) (1996), M.M.G. Fase 'Purchase of art: Consumption and investment', 649–659, ©1996 with kind permission from Kluwer Academic Publishers.

[1] An example of an early plea can be found in Drees (1966, pp. 58–79); an early example is given in Fase (1969, especially pp. 80–82), as well as in Fase (1971), and in Fase (1972c).

Paintings account for almost 90% of the turnover of the international art auctioneers and the Dutch art market is a small fraction of it. In the 1980s, the prices of paintings rose materially. Even after the stock exchange crash of October 1987, prices continued to go up for a long time and art came to be seen as an investment that would keep its value. However, the collapse of art prices in the early 1990s would seem to indicate that the art market, too, is much less predictable and subject to much greater uncertainty than previously supposed.

The art market — rather like the housing market — distinguishes itself from most others in goods and financial assets by the fact that supply is fixed. Of all paintings and drawings — leaving aside contemporary and living painters — there is never more than one copy. This means that the supply (contemporary art apart) is fixed, and the price wholly demand-determined. According to Marshall's (1890, pp. 410–411) well-known classification, the market period is ultra-short, as Jong puts it.[2] This means that the supply of goods on offer is fixed and cannot be expanded at short notice. The supply can, however, shrink when suppliers withdraw their goods, or because works of art are immobilized when they are bought by museums. The art market is thin, imperfect and heterogeneous, choice being made on the basis of the characteristics of art objects. When two paintings put up for sale both meet the collector's specific requirements, the price will usually tip the balance.

16.1 The Price of Paintings and Its Measurement

In recent years, various attempts have been undertaken to augment the transparency of the art market. A potential buyer can enquire at the auctioneer's beforehand what a certain piece is expected to fetch. Furthermore, catalogues of the works of art up for sale often give estimated selling prices. Attending viewing days and auctions may also enhance a person's insight into the price structure of the market, and there are lists of auction prices. However, the prices prevailing in the art trade outside the auction houses, and the value of pieces which have remained unsold at auctions, are difficult if not impossible to trace.

The art market is characterized by uncertainty, not just as to prices, but also as to the quality of an object. There is, first of all, the chance of a painting being faked. In the US alone, there are more than 5 000 paintings by Corot, while Corot is alleged to have painted no more than

[2] See also Jong (1965, p. 270). Delfgaauw (1965, p. 206) prefers the more precise terminology 'infra-short period'.

2 000.[3] The other risk is that of a painting being wrongly attributed. 'The man with the golden helm' has but a fraction of its original value, now that participants in the Rembrandt project have denoted it as being falsely attributed.

The calculation of return is founded on movements in art prices. As ever, an index number is called for, reflecting the peculiarities of the art market. In the literature and the daily practice of the art trade, attention focuses on four methods of measurement in particular. The first is the *geometrical price index*. The calculation of a geometrical price average is based on the assumption that the observed auction prices of individual paintings form a sample from an underlying value distribution of paintings. The price index of the entire set is based on this sample of actual auction prices. For a comparison over time, the set from which the paintings to be auctioned stem, must be established, that is only those paintings accomplished before a certain period and whose creator is no longer alive, are considered to belong to the set. The advantage of employing the geometrical price index is that use is made of all auction data. The drawback is that no distinction is made between various movements in painting. It is furthermore implicitly assumed that the paintings auctioned are invariably equal in quality.

A second method is the *Repeated Sales Regression* (RSR) approach. The RSR method was first developed to measure movements in real estate prices. Where paintings are concerned, the purchase and selling prices of individual works are used to estimate the changes in value of an average painting, or one that may be considered representative over a certain period in time. This method uses only the sales data of a painting that has been sold more than once, the focus being on the price movements of one individual painting. The method works as follows. For each pair of sales, the logarithm of the price relationship is calculated, *i.e.* the logarithm of the price of the later sale minus the logarithm of the price achieved at the first sale. In everyday language, that is more or less the price change as a percentage. With the aid of this percentage, a regression is performed on a set of dummy variables, one dummy variable for each sale.[4] The advantage of using the RSR method is that the increase in value of one painting is measured, so that no adjustment for quality between various paintings is required. The disadvantage, however, is that only a small part of the available sales data can be used.

A third method is the *hedonic price index method.* The hedonic

---

3 Arnau (1961)

4 Note the similarity with the Divisia index number, as described in Divisia (1928, p. 269 and following).

regression method makes adjustments for differences in quality among paintings. The objective features of a painting are recorded (for example the name of the painter, its size, and so on). The hedonic regression method estimates the implicit price of these characteristics, translating them into binary or dummy variables, intended to explain the prices actually realized. The regression coefficients estimated in this manner are the implicit prices of these characteristics. These are then deducted from the effective price of a painting. From the annual averages of these differences, the price of a 'standard painting' can be established. The series of standard prices thus obtained yields a price index. This method has the advantage that all auction data are used, and that the price differences between paintings from different schools are, in principle, distinguished. The problem is that often only few specific characteristics of a painting are known, so that the actual application proves fairly meagre. This is aptly illustrated by a study of Buelens and Ginsburgh.[5]

The final method considered is *Sotheby's Art index*, which concerns antiques and paintings. The paintings are classified in accordance with four categories: old masters, nineteenth-century European paintings, Impressionists and modern art. The composition of the index for each of these four categories is based on a fixed basket of art objects. For the base year 1975, a basket of an average of 30–40 paintings was fixed per category. Grade A paintings from the middle of the market are selected, because, according to Sotheby's, that particular class best reflects the development of the market. On the basis of the prices paid at Sotheby auctions, Sotheby's experts value the paintings in the basket whenever there is an event — such as an auction, a major exhibition or a publication — which will have a clear impact on market prices. The advantage of the Sotheby Art index is that no adjustment needs to be made for differences in the quality of the paintings. Furthermore, a distinction is made between the various painting schools. A drawback is that the prices often reflect the subjective opinions of experts.

Apart from the above-mentioned four index-number approaches, a few other analytical techniques for assessing art price movements are mentioned in the literature. These focus on the efficiency of the art market, behaviour of actors on the art market and the interdependence of art markets, including those measured with Granger causality tests.[6] However, the majority of studies employ price-index numbers as a starting point. The properties of the proposed index-number approaches

---

[5] This method was developed by Buelens and Ginsburgh (1993). See also: Generale Bank (1993, pp. 2–5).

[6] See the survey article by Throsby (1994); Frey and Eichenberger (1995). For the causality approach to the art market the reader may wish to consult Ginsburgh and Jeanfils (1994); for the behavioural approach see *e.g.* Goetzmann (1993).

can be assessed in terms of both form and substance. In the spirit of Irving Fisher, the formal evaluation is applied particularly in theoretical analyses.[7] Three properties seem to be of importance: the extent to which the index has been calculated from actual selling prices; the distinction made as to painting schools; and the degree to which differences in the quality of comparable paintings are taken into account. The four methods considered here clearly make allowance for these properties in varying degrees. The geometrical price index and the hedonic regression approach are supported by actual auction prices.[8] That is not the case for the RSR method and Sotheby's Art index. The distinction by school is made only by the hedonic regression method and Sotheby's Art index. Quality features are explicitly taken into account by the RSR index and Sotheby's Art index, and only marginally by the hedonic regression approach. All in all, the conclusion is that none of the indices discussed meets all requirements.

16.2 A Price Index for Nineteenth-century Paintings: A Case Study

The main shortcoming of Sotheby's Art index, though satisfactory in many respects, is that it is not based on actual auction prices. In order to make up for this major drawback, we have designed an index of our own, following Sotheby's and using actual auction prices. We focus mainly on nineteenth century painting, because this is a class of art where trade is buoyant and sufficient data are available.[9]

Demand for nineteenth-century European paintings is undergoing an interesting development, which is reflected in the prices paid. At the start of the twentieth century, this genre was much in demand, albeit a fluctuating demand. Scottish industrialists were prepared to pay considerable sums for a painting by Jozef Israëls or Jacob Maris. In 1910, for instance, Maris' 'Entrance to the Zuiderzee' made £3 150. In 1924 it was again auctioned, this time for a sum of £2 887, but eight years later, in 1932, it fetched no more than £75. Obviously demand for paintings from that period had slumped. In recent years, nineteenth-century European painting has been basking in renewed popularity among art-lovers. In 1992 Gustave Courbet's 'Flowers on a Bench' was sold in New

[7] Cf. Fisher (1922); see also Fase and Mourik (1986).

[8] In Chanel, Gérard-Varet, and Ginsburgh (1996) it is argued that for paintings the hedonic price index methodology provides a better basis for examining returns and efficiency of the art market.

[9] Taken from Fase and Tol (1994)

York for \$1.54 million. That is a record high for this painter. Another example is that of Jules Dupré's 'Intérieur de Ferme dans le Berry', sold in New York for \$93 500.[10]

We have calculated the price index of nineteenth-century paintings, for the period 1972–1992, using the actual sterling prices paid at the international auctioneers. As pointed out, our index is set up along the lines of Sotheby's Art index, making use of a basket, wholly in the tradition of composite index numbers. In order to be able to utilize all available auction price data, the basket of representative paintings figuring in Sotheby's Art index was replaced by a basket of representative artists. There are 61 of them, and they include C. Springer, I.B.C. Corot, Von Wierus Kowalski and G.H. Breitner. Opting for a representative group of artists largely eliminates differences in quality. The index number is calculated in two steps. First, a price index is calculated for each painter. After that, a composite index of nineteenth-century European paintings is derived from the indices calculated per painter. On the basis of the standard deviation, extremely high or low auction prices are denoted as statistical outliers and ignored in the calculation of the index. The results of the calculation for the period 1972–1992 indicate that, with an index number of 787 (1972=100) in 1989, the market for European paintings peaked. By contrast with other movements, price falls in the following years were moderate. This confirms the increased and persistent demand for nineteenth-century European paintings which, as pointed out above, has manifest itself in recent years.

From the calculated price movements, an average nominal gross return of 10.6% per annum with a spread of about 0.12 results from investing in nineteenth-century European paintings. This figure is on a gross basis, because adjustment for auction costs, taxes, insurance premiums and other handling costs were disregarded.

16.3 Return on Paintings and Other Art Objects in the Literature

The first question which arises in an evaluation of our outcome is how it relates to the findings of other researchers. An overview can be found in the earlier mentioned survey article of Frey and Eichenberger (1995) dealing with financial return on paintings, antiques and collectables with nominal returns ranging between 3.3% for paintings in general and 19% for toy soldiers (real returns vary between −2.3% for antique firearms and 15.8% for watercolour pictures with 0.6% for paintings).

[10] Christies International, Report & Accounts 1992, p. 11.

Table 16.1: Nominal returns on investments in art

Author	Type of index	Period	Type of painting	Average return per annum %	Standard deviation	Coefficient of variation
Fase and Tol	linear composite	1972–1992	19th century	10.6	0.12	0.01
Buelens and Ginsburgh	hedonic	1761–1869	Selection from Reitlinger's list of paintings auctioned at least twice	6.1	0.26	0.04
		1870–1913		12.9	0.52	0.04
		1914–1961		5.5	0.36	0.07
Goetzmann	RSR	1720–1990	Ditto	3.2	0.57	0.18
		1850–1990		6.2	0.65	0.10
		1900–1986		17.5	0.53	0.03
Stein	geometric	1946–1966	Ditto	11.0	0.34	0.03
Sotheby's	linear composite	1975–1992	Total	15.0	0.21	0.01
			Old masters	14.8	0.14	0.01
			19th century	12.8	0.18	0.01
			Impressionists	15.6	0.23	0.01
			Modern	16.4	0.22	0.01

Source: For Fase and Tol (1994): Table 1; for Buelens and Ginsburgh (1993) respectively Goetzmann (1993) calculated respectively derived from the articles mentioned in the text; for Sotheby's from data provided by their research department; for Stein, calculated on the basis of Stein (1977).

We focus on a selection of representative results, set out in Table 16.1. It is worth noting that, according to our price index, the return on nineteenth-century European paintings found by us is some 2 percentage points lower than the corresponding return found by Sotheby's, while the relative spread is equally large. For the other schools, Sotheby's furthermore find a return which is higher, while the relative spread remains the same. Finally, the other studies presented in Table 16.1 show that the longer the period considered, the lower the return.

The second question is how the nominal return on nineteenth-century European art compares with the yield on alternative forms of investment, the UK figuring as yardstick (because our own index is underlain by sterling-denominated auction prices). Table 16.2 shows that, for the period 1972–1992, nominal return on art is lower than the return on other forms of investment, but that in the years 1946–1966 it is considerably higher. This picture is reinforced if the average price rise in the UK is taken into account: for the period 1972–1992 the result is then a real return of about 1% per annum; in the years 1982–1992 it comes out at nearly 3% and in the decades following World War II even at 7.5% per year.

This brings us to the matter of nominal versus real return. A number of the seminal studies on the return on paintings show a clear preference for determining real return. A relevant study often cited is that carried out by Baumol (1986). Baumol made an analysis, for the years 1652–1961, of sales of paintings and of the development of prices in general in the UK, calculating an average real return on art of 0.55% even though, at 0.85%, the median was higher. This return is about 2 percentage points lower than the annual return on government bonds over these three centuries. Authors such as Frey and Pommerehne (1989), who analyzed a slightly longer period, 1635–1987, incidentally come out at a real return of 1½%, reflecting a correspondingly higher rate of return forgone for holding works of art. In their study, Fase and Tol (1994) also found the return on art to be lower than that on other forms of investments. However, over the period 1982–1992, gold and real estate yield a lower return.

One interpretation of this general result, as I pointed out elsewhere,[11] could be that art-lovers being art-consumers do not mind parting with 1–2 percentage points in return for possession of a painting. That is the psychological return on art, the price paid annually for possessing works of art. This conclusion is in line with the outcome of a recent contribution by Pesando (1993). For modern silk-screen prints, and for Picasso paintings, this author comes up — using the RSR approach — with

[11] Fase (1990) and Grauwe (1990).

Table 16.2: Average nominal total return in the UK on a number of investment categories (%)

	1946–1966	1972–1992	1982–1992
Nineteenth-century art	11.0	10.6	8.6
Shares	6.7	14.8	19.2
Bonds	.	11.2	16.0
Gold	1.8	12.9	0.5
Real estate	.	11.8	8.2
Wine (red Bordeaux)	.	.	11.5
Long-term interest rate	4.7	11.5	10.3
Inflation in the UK	3.5	9.5	5.7

Note: For 1946–1966, the Stein index was used; over this period the return on shares is an approximation. For wine, the figure is taken from Boorn, Herst, Koedijk, and Smeets (1996).

Source: IFS; Investment Property Databank.

a real return of 1.5% and 2.1%, respectively, for the years 1977–1992. That is considerably less than the average real return on investments in government bonds or shares of 2.5% and 8.1%, respectively. The period considered coincides almost entirely with that studied by Fase and Tol (1994). A theoretical interpretation of these results is offered by the consumption based asset pricing model, showing that real return on risk-free assets is lower than that on risk-bearing investments. If the theorem is reversed, a low return on art could ensue from the smaller risks involved in investing in paintings. This conclusion is supported by one of the results obtained in the study of Barre, Docclo, and Ginsburgh (1994), pointing out that the prices of paintings, at least for well-known artists, show little randomness, but also co-movements with other markets as those of American stocks.

16.4 Concluding Remarks

This chapter has focused mainly on the financial returns on paintings. In the literature, however, art investment goes beyond paintings and includes objects as antiques, collectables or ancient books. Frey and Eichenberger (1995) have pointed out that a research on art investment is hampered by major problems. These concern the data, which are often biased by the fact that the main source is auctions. A second problem is transaction costs which significantly lower the rate of return but are difficult to register. The third is taxes which differ among countries and art objects. A fourth problem is that the empirical outcomes are partly the result of the approach employed and perhaps less robust than desirable. One final problem is that the set of alternative investment opportunities used for comparison is less clear than often thought. In spite of these problems, it is worthwhile considering investment in art.

The main obstacle to assessing the widespread view that the purchase of paintings or other objects of art would be a good investment, is the absence of a generally accepted method for measuring the increase in the monetary value of these paintings, and of knowledge of handling costs. The best approach is perhaps on the basis of international auction prices. The gross nominal return — that is regardless of handling costs, taxes, and so on — follows directly from the rise in the value observed and according to our calculation over the period 1972—1992 for nineteenth-century European paintings, turns out to have averaged 10.6% measured in sterling. Compared with other forms of investment, except for gold and shares, this does not appear to be an exceptionally high return. Furthermore, we may conclude from the fact that, on the basis of results presented in the literature, returns on art fluctuate fairly heavily. Hence, the investment risk of art is large. An interesting question facing investors is whether the return on, and risk involved in, an investment portfolio would benefit from the addition of investments in art. It is a good omen that the correlation coefficients between return on investment in paintings and that in other assets such as shares, bonds and gold, seems to be low. That would warrant the conclusion that including paintings among portfolio investments offers the possibility of spreading one's risks and augmenting return. This does not necessarily mean, however, that the decision to purchase works of art — like enrolling in school — is mainly motivated by financial considerations. The calculation of returns on investments in art — as when considering other aesthetic or intellectual activities — provides a means to measure the psychological or intellectual value of such enterprises and seems to suggest that purchasing art is also a consumer activity.

Bibliography

Acx, R., O. Lefebvre, E. Peree, M. Quintyn, and R. Schreurs (1986), *Le marché monétaire Belge dans dix ans*, Brussel: Herdisconterings- en Waarborginstituut.

Advokaat, H.G. (1987), 'Over de Belgische geldmarkt over tien jaar', *Bank- en Effectenbedrijf*, **36**, 17–18.

Agmon, T. (1972), 'The relations among equity markets: A study of share price co-movements in the United States, United Kingdom, Germany and Japan', *Journal of Finance*, **27**, 839–855.

Akhtar, M.A. (1983), 'Financial innovations and their implications for monetary policy: An international perspective', Economic Papers 9, BIS, Basel.

Aliber, R.Z. (1973), 'The interest rate parity theorem: A reinterpretation', *Journal of Political Economy*, **81**, 1451–1459.

Almon, S. (1965), 'The distributed lag between capital appropriations and expenditures', *Econometrica*, **33**, 178–196.

Anthony, J.H. (1988), 'The interrelation of stock and options market trading-volume data', *Journal of Finance*, **43**, 949–964.

Argy, V. and Z. Hodjera (1973), 'Financial integration and interest rate linkages in the industrial countries, 1958–71', *IMF Staff Papers*, **20**, 1–77.

Arnau, F. (1961), *The Art of the Faker*, Boston: Little, Brown and Co.

Bakhoven, A.F. (1971), 'De verklaring van het renteniveau in Nederland', *Maandschrift Economie*, **35**, 577–588.

Bansal, R. and W.J. Coleman, II (1996), 'A monetary explanation of the equity premium, term premium, and risk-free rate puzzles', *Journal of Political Economy*, **104**, 1135–1171.

Barre, M. de la, S. Docclo, and V. Ginsburgh (1994), 'Returns of Impressionists, modern and contemporary European paintings 1962–1991', *Annales d'Économie et de Statistique*, **35**, 143–181.

Bartlett, M.S. (1951), 'The effect of standardization on a χ^2-approximation in factor analysis', *Biometrika*, **38**, 337–344.

Baumol, W.J. and W.G. Bowen (1966), *Performing Arts: The Economic Dilemma*, New York: Twentieth Century Fund.

Baumol, W.J. (1986), 'Unnatural value: Or art investment as floating crap game', *American Economic Review*, **76**, 10–14.

Becker, G.S. (1976), *The Economic Approach to Human Behavior*, Chicago: University of Chicago Press.

Benartzi, S. and R.H. Thaler (1995), 'Myopic loss aversion and the equity premium puzzle', *Quarterly Journal of Economics*, **110**, 73–92.

BIS (1986), *Recent Innovations in International Banking*, Basel: BIS, paper prepared by a study group established by the central banks of the G10 countries.

Black, F. (1975), 'Fact and fantasy in the use of options', *Financial Analysts Journal* **31**(4), 36–41 and 61–72.

Blanchard, O.J. and S. Fischer (1989), *Lectures on Macroeconomics*, Cambridge/London: MIT Press.

Bohi, D.R. (1972), 'The international interdependence of interest rates', *Kyklos*, **25**, 597–600.

Bomhoff, E.J. (1983), *Monetary Uncertainty*, Amsterdam: North-Holland.

Boorn, M.J.G. van den, A.C.C. Herst, C.G. Koedijk, and J.L.A.M. Smeets (1996), 'Rendement en risico van Bordeaux-wijnen', *Economisch-Statistische Berichten*, **81**, 490–492.

Bordewijk, H.W.C. (1922), "'Het rentevraagstuk" door mr. L.F.H. Regout', *Economisch-Statistische Berichten*, **7**, 1073–1076.

Box, G.E.P. and G.M. Jenkins (1970), *Time Series Analysis, Forecasting and Control*, San Francisco: Holden Day.

Brady, E.A. (1967), 'A sectoral econometric study of the postwar residential-housing market', *Journal of Political Economy*, **75**, 147–158.

Brainard, W.C. and J. Tobin (1968), 'Econometric models: Their problems and usefulness: Pitfalls in financial model building', *American Economic Review*, **58**, 99–122.

Brits, J.H. and R.M. Oort (1997), 'Budgettaire consequenties indexleningen', *Openbare Uitgaven*, **29**, 84–95.

Brown, S.J., W.N. Goetzmann, and S.A. Ross (1995), 'Survival', *Journal of Finance*, **50**, 853–873.

Brunner, K. and A.H. Meltzer (1972), 'Money, debt, and economic activity', *Journal of Political Economy*, **80**, 951–977.

Buelens, N. and V. Ginsburgh (1993), 'Revisiting Baumol's "Art as floating crap game"', *European Economic Review*, **37**, 1351–1371.

Butter, F.A.G. den, A.M. Dongelmans, and M.M.G. Fase (1977), 'De vraag naar hypothecair krediet en de rentevorming op de hypotheekmarkt', *De Economist*, **125**, 43–74. Reprinted as Chapter 8 in this volume.

Cagan, P. (1965), *Determinants and Effects of Changes in the Stock of Money 1875–1960*, number 13 in Studies in Business Cycles, New York, etc: Columbia University Press.

Campbell, J.Y. and R.J. Shiller (1996), 'A scorecard for indexed government debt', Working Paper 5587, NBER.

Carlson, J.A. and J.M. Parkin (1975), 'Inflation expectations', *Economica*, **42**, 123–138.

Carmichael, J. and P.W. Stebbing (1983), 'Fisher's paradox and the theory of interest', *American Economic Review*, **73**, 619–630.

Centraal Bureau voor de Statistiek (1943), 'Het verloop op langen termijn van de rentestanden', *Maandschrift*, **38**, 117–124.

Centraal Bureau voor de Statistiek (1970), *Zeventig Jaren Statistiek in Tijdreeksen: 1899–1969*, 's-Gravenhage: Staatsuitgeverij.

Chanel, O., L.A. Gérard-Varet, and V. Ginsburgh (1996), 'The relevance of hedonic price indices: The case of paintings', *Journal of Cultural Economics*, **20**, 1–24.

Christiansen, H. and C. Pigott (1997), 'Long term interest rates in globalised markets', Working Paper 175, OECD.

Christ, C.F. (1971), 'Econometric models of the financial sector', *Journal of Money, Credit and Banking*, **3**, 419–449.

Conard, J.W. (1959), *An Introduction to the Theory of Interest*, Berkeley: University of California Press.

Constantinides, G.M. (1990), 'Habit formation: A resolution of the equity premium puzzle', *Journal of Political Economy*, **98**, 519–543.

Copeland, T.E. and J.F. Weston (1988), *Financial Theory and Corporate Policy*, Reading, Mass.: Addison-Wesley.

Copeland, T.E. (1976), 'A model of asset trading under the assumption of sequential information arrival', *Journal of Finance*, **31**, 1149–1168.

Coulbois, P. and P. Prissert (1974), 'Forward exchange, short term capital flows and monetary policy', *De Economist*, **122**, 283–308.

Cramèr, H. (1946), *Mathematical Methods of Statistics*, Princeton, N.J.: Princeton University Press.

Cramer, J.S. (1966), 'Une analyse de budget de famille par composantes principales', *Economie Appliquée*, **19**, 249–268.

Cumby, R. and F.S. Mishkin (1986), 'The international linkage of real interest rates: The Europe-US connection', *Journal of International Money and Finance*, **5**, 5–23.

Danthine, J.P. and J.B. Donaldson (1996), 'Labour contracts, operating leverage and asset pricing', Discussion paper 1353, cEPR.

Deacon, M.P. and A.J. Derry (1994a), 'Deriving estimates of inflation expectations from the prices of UK government bonds', Working Paper 23, Bank of England.

Deacon, M.P. and A.J. Derry (1994b), 'Estimating the term structure of interest rates', Working Paper 24, Bank of England.

Delfgaauw, G.T.J. (1965), *Inleiding tot de Economische Wetenschap*, Wassenaar: Delwel.

De Nederlandsche Bank (1972), 'Enquête kasgeldleningen bedrijven', *De Nederlandsche Bank Quarterly Bulletin* **1972**(1), 32–33.

De Nederlandsche Bank (1984), *MORKMON, een Kwartaalmodel voor Macro-economische Beleidsanalyse*, Monetaire Monografieën 2, Amsterdam etc.: Kluwer.

Dhrymes, P. and P. Taubman (1969), 'An empirical analysis of the savings and loan industry', in I. Friend (ed.), *Study of the Savings and Loan Industry*, Washington: Federal Home Loan Bank Board, pp. 67–182.

Diba, B.T. and H.I. Grossman (1988), 'The theory of rational bubbles in stock prices', *The Economic Journal*, **98**, 746–754.

Divisia, F. (1928), *Économie Rationnelle*, Paris: Doin.

Dodds, J.C. and J.L. Ford (1974), *Expectations, Uncertainty and the Term Structure of Interest Rates*, Londen: Robinson.

Dongelmans, A.M. and M.M.G. Fase (1975), 'Hoofdcomponenten van de rente in Nederland: 1971–1974', *Bank- en Effectenbedrijf*, **24**, 363–369.

Donner, O. (1934), 'Die Kursbildung am Aktienmarkt', *Vierteljahreshefte zur Konjunkturforschung*, **36** Sonderheft.

Dorp, E.C. van (1937), *A Simple Theory of Capital, Wages and Profit or Loss: A New and Social Approach to the Problem of Income Distribution*, London: P.S. King & Son Ltd.

Drees, W. (1966), 'Een redelijke financiering van het wetenschappelijk onderwijs', in E. Tekenbroek, B. Schendstok, and E.L. Berg (eds), *Fiscaal-economische Opstellen*, Alphen a/d Rijn: Samson, pp. 58–79.

Driehuis, W. (1972), *Fluctuations and Growth in a Near Full Employment Economy*, Rotterdam: University Press.

Driehuis, W. (1973), 'Diagnosis and prognosis of cyclical fluctuation on behalf of government and business', *Economic Quarterly Review*, Amsterdam-Rotterdam Bank N.V., **33**, 5–17.

Duisenberg, W.F. (1984), 'Twee monetaire modellen voor Nederland', in H. den Hartog and J. Weitenberg (eds), *Toegepaste Economie: Grenzen en Mogelijkheden*, 's-Gravenhage: Centraal Planbureau, pp. 103–114.

Duisenberg, W.F. (1985), 'Financial innovation and monetary policy; deregulation of The Netherlands capital market', *De Nederlandsche Bank Quarterly Bulletin* 1985(3), 25–30.

Els, P.J.A. van and P.J.G. Vlaar (1996), 'The determination of long-term interest rates in The Netherlands', in *The Determination of Long-term Interest Rates and Exchange Rates and the Role of Expectations*, Volume 2 of *Conference papers*, Basel: BIS, pp. 122–137.

Erp, F.A.M. van, B.H. Hasselman, A.G.H. Nibbelink, and H.R. Timmer (1989), 'A monetary model of the Dutch economy', *Economic Modelling*, **6**, 56–93.

European Monetary Institute (1996), *Annual Report 1996*, Frankfurt: European Monetary Institute.

Fama, E.F. (1966), *Foundations of Finance*, New York: Basic Books.

Fama, E.F. (1984), 'Forward and spot exchange rates', *Journal of Monetary Economics*, **3**, 319–338.

Fand, D.I. (1972), 'High interest rates and inflation in the U.S.: Cause or effect?', *Banca Nazionale del Lavoro Quarterly Review*, **96**, 23–64.

Fase, M.M.G. and E.W. van den Berg (1979), 'Tussen Damrak en de rest van de wereld', *Maandblad voor Accountancy en Bedrijfshuishoudkunde*, **53**, 174–189.

Fase, M.M.G. and A.P. Huijser (1988), 'Financiële internationalisering en de wereldwijde vervlechting van effectenbeurzen', *Economisch-Statistische Berichten*, **73**, 326–332.

Fase, M.M.G., P. Kramer, and W.C. Boeschoten (1990), *MORKMON II: Het DNB Kwartaalmodel voor Nederland*, Monetaire Monografieën, 11, Amsterdam: De Nederlandsche Bank.

Fase, M.M.G. and J.B. Kuné (1974a), 'De vraag naar liquiditeiten in Nederland, 1952–1971', *De Economist*, **122**, 326–356.

Fase, M.M.G. and J.B. Kuné (1974b), 'Price and income expectations in the demand for money', paper presented at ESEM'74, Grenoble. Reprinted as Chapter 1 in M.M.G. Fase (1998) *On Money and Credit in Europe*, Cheltenham etc: Edward Elgar.

Fase, M.M.G. and T.J. Mourik (1986), 'Beursindexcijfers voor Nederland: Inventarisatie en beoordeling', *Economisch-Statistische Berichten*, **71**, 112–117.

Fase, M.M.G. and T.J. Mourik (1990), 'Samenhang omzet op aandelenmarkt en optiemarkt: Een statistische causaliteitsanalyse', WO&E Research Memorandum 9020, De Nederlandsche Bank.

Fase, M.M.G. and M. van Nieuwkerk (1975), 'Anticipated inflation and interest rates in an open economy: A study of the Gibson paradox for The Netherlands', in F. Masera, A. Fazio, and T. Padoa-Schioppa (eds), *Econometric Research in European Central Banks*, Rome: Banca d'Italia, pp. 297–321. Reprinted as Chapter 6 in this volume.

Fase, M.M.G. and W.F.J. van de Poll (1996), 'De risicopremie op aandelen: Een puzzel?', *Economisch-Statistische Berichten*, **81**, 1014–1017. Reprinted as Chapter 14 in this volume.

Fase, M.M.G. and K. Steel (1987), 'On interest rates in Belgium and The Netherlands: A comparative analysis of interest rate developments and financial innovations, 1980–1984', *De Economist*, **135**, 316–319. Reprinted as Chapter 3 in this volume.

Fase, M.M.G. and M. van Tol (1994), 'Het monetaire rendement van beleggen in schilderijen', *Economisch-Statistische Berichten*, **79**, 684–689.

Fase, M.M.G. (1969), *An Econometric Model of Age–Income Profiles*, Rotterdam: Universitaire Press.

Fase, M.M.G. (1971), 'On the estimation of lifetime income', *Journal of the American Statistical Association*, **66**, 686–692.

Fase, M.M.G. (1972a), 'Bond yields and expected inflation: A quantitative analysis of the Dutch experience', *Economic Quarterly Review,* Amsterdam-Rotterdam Bank N.V. **30**(September), 5–10. Reprinted as Chapter 5 in this volume.

Fase, M.M.G. (1972b), 'De samenhang tussen rentestanden in Nederland, 1962–1970', *De Economist*, **120**, 439–478.

Fase, M.M.G. (1972c), 'The distribution of lifetime earnings: A problem of intertemporal aggregation', *Statistica Neerlandica*, **26**, 103–111.

Fase, M.M.G. (1973), 'A principal components analysis of market interest rates in The Netherlands, 1962–1970', *European Economic Review*, **4**, 107–134. Reprinted as Chapter 1 in this volume.

Fase, M.M.G. (1976), 'The interdependence of short-term interest rates in the major financial centres of the world: Some evidence for 1961–1972', *Kyklos*, **29**, 63–96. Reprinted as Chapter 2 in this volume.

Fase, M.M.G. (1981a), 'Financiële activa, rentevorming en monetaire beheersbaarheid: Proeve van een monetair kwartaalmodel voor Nederland', in E. den Dunnen, M.M.G. Fase, and A. Szász (eds), *Zoeklicht op Beleid*, Leiden/Antwerpen: Stenfert Kroese, pp. 43–81.

Fase, M.M.G. (1981b), 'The linkage of stock exchange markets between countries', *Economics Letters*, **7**, 363–369. Reprinted as Chapter 12 in this volume.

Fase, M.M.G. (1981c), *Op het Breukvlak van Macro- en Micro-economie*, Leiden/Antwerpen: Stenfert Kroese.

Fase, M.M.G. (1984), 'The monetary sector of The Netherlands in 50 equations', in J.P. Ancot (ed.), *Analysing the Structure of Econometric Models*, Volume 2 of *Advanced Studies in Theoretical and Applied Econometrics*, 's-Gravenhage: Martinus Nijhoff, pp. 195–228.

Fase, M.M.G. (1990), 'Rembrandt in de ramsj', *Intermediair*, 24-8-1990, 61–62.

Fase, M.M.G. (1992), 'Zeventig jaar rente: De evolutie in theorie en empirie', in M.M.G. Fase and I. van der Zijpp (eds), *Samenleving en Economie in de Twintigste Eeuw*, Leiden/Antwerpen: Stenfert Kroese, pp. 227–250. Reprinted as Chapter 9 in this volume.

Feldstein, M.S. and O. Eckstein (1970), 'The fundamental determinants of the interest rate', *The Review of Economics and Statistics*, **52**, 363–375.

Feldstein, M.S. (1970), 'Inflation, specification bias, and the impact of interest rates', *Journal of Political Economy*, **78**, 1325–1339.

Ferson, W.E. and C.R. Harvey (1996), 'Fundamental determinants of national equity market returns: A perspective on conditional asset pricing', Working Paper 5860, NBER.

Fisher, I. (1907), *The Rate of Interest: Its Nature, Determination and Relations to Economic Phenomena*, New York: Macmillan.

Fisher, I. (1911), *The Purchasing Power of Money*, New York: Macmillan.

Fisher, I. (1922), *The Making of Index Numbers*, Boston: Houghton Mifflin.

Fisher, I. (1925), 'Our unstable dollar and the so-called business cycle', *Journal of the American Statistical Association*, **20**, 179–202.

Fisher, I. (1930), *The Theory of Interest*, New York: Macmillan.

Fisher, I. (1933), 'The debt-deflation theory of great depressions', *Econometrica*, **1**, 337–357.

Frankel, J. (1992), 'Measuring world capital mobility: A review', *American Economic Review*, **82**, 197–202.

Frey, B.S. and R. Eichenberger (1995), 'On the return on art investment return analyses', *Journal of Cultural Economics*, **19**, 207–220.

Frey, B.S. and W. Pommerehne (1989), *Muses and Markets: Explorations in the Economics of the Arts*, Oxford: Basil Blackwell.

Galbraith, J.K. (1960), *The Liberal Hour*, London: Hamish Hamilton.

Generale Bank (1993), 'De rentabiliteit van belegging in kunst', *Bulletin van de Generale Bank*, **335**, 2–5.

Gibson, W.E. (1972), 'Interest rates and inflationary expectations: New evidence', *American Economic Review*, **62**, 854–865.

Ginsburgh, V. and P. Jeanfils (1994), 'Long-term comovements in international markets for paintings', Paper, Université Libre Bruxelles.

Goedhart, C. (1947), *De Rentevorming in de moderne Volkshuishouding*, Leiden/Antwerpen: Stenfert Kroese.

Goetzmann, W.N. (1993), 'Accounting for taste: Art and the financial markets over three centuries', *American Economic Review*, **83**, 1370–1376.

Goldberger, A.S. (1971), 'Econometrics and psychometrics: A survey of communalities', *Psychometrika*, **36**, 83–107.

Gootzeit, M.J. (1991), 'Wicksell's version of Gibson's paradox', *De Economist*, **139**, 62–72.

Gramlich, E.M. and D.M. Jaffee (1972a), 'The behavior of the three sectors together', in E.M. Gramlich and D.M. Jaffee (eds), *Savings Deposits, Mortgages, and Housing: Studies for the Federal Reserve-Mitt-Penn Economic Model*, Lexington etc.: D.C. Heath and Company, chapter 7, pp. 235–286.

Gramlich, E.M. and D.M. Jaffee (1972b), *Savings Deposits, Mortgages, and Housing: Studies for the Federal Reserve-Mitt-Penn Economic Model*, Lexington etc.: D.C. Heath and Company.

Granger, C.W.J. (1969), 'Investigating causal relations by econometric models and cross-spectral methods', *Econometrica*, **37**, 424–438.

Grauwe, P. de and K. Matthews (1988), 'The October 1987 stock market crash: A tale of bubble or fundamentals?', Working Paper 37, Centre for European Policy Studies.

Grauwe, P. de (1989), *International Money*, Oxford: Clarendon Press.

Grauwe, P. de (1990), *De Nachtwacht in het Donker: Over Kunst en Economie*, Tielt: Lannoo.

Greenwald, B. and J. Stein (1988), 'The task force report: The reasoning behind the recommendations', *Journal of Economic Perspectives*, **2**, 3–23.

Griliches, Z. (1967), 'Distributed lags: A survey', *Econometrica*, **35**, 16–49.

Groene, J. de, J.C. Siebrand, and N. van der Windt (1984), 'RASMUS-I, an annual model of the Dutch economy', Research Paper, Macro Economic Policy Group, Erasmus Universiteit.

Gruijters, A.P.D. (1995), *Financiële Integratie en monetair Beleid: Een empirisch Onderzoek naar de Mobiliteit van het Kapitaalverkeer in de geïndustrialiseerde Wereld sinds het Einde van het Bretton-Woods-stelsel*, number 78 in Publication Series, Amsterdam: NIBE.

Hamburger, M.J. (1971), 'Expectations, long-term interest rates and monetary policy in the United Kingdom', *Bank of England Quarterly Bulletin*, **11**, 354–371.

Hansen, L.P. and K.J. Singleton (1983), 'Stochastic consumption, risk aversion, and the intertemporal behavior of asset returns', *Journal of Political Economy*, **91**, 249–266.

Hardouvelis, G.A. (1988), 'Evidence on stock market speculative bubbles: Japan, United States and Great Britain', Research Paper 8810, Federal Reserve Bank of New York.

Harman, H.H.H. (1968), *Modern Factor Analysis*, Chicago: University of Chicago Press.

Haugh, L.D. (1976), 'Checking the independence of two covariance-stationary time-series: A univariate residual cross-correlation approach', *Journal of the American Statistical Association*, **71**, 378–385.

Hernandez-Lopez, M. (1973), 'Les déterminants des taux d'intérêts', *Recherches Économiques de Louvain*, **39**, 19–49.

Hester, D.D. (1969), 'On the dimensionality of market interest rates and price movements', Paper 6956, Social Systems Research Institute, University of Wisconsin.

Hetzel (1992), 'Indexed bonds as an aid to monetary policy', *Federal Reserve Bank of Richmond Economic Review* **78**(1), 13–23.

Hicks, J.R. (1939), *Value and Capital*, Oxford: Clarendon Press.

Hicks, J.R. (1965), *Capital and Growth*, Oxford: Clarendon Press.

Hicks, J.R. (1970), 'Inflation and interest', *Banca Nazionale del Lavoro Quarterly Review*, **94**, 261–275.

Hodjera, Z. (1973), 'International short-term capital movements: A survey of theory and empirical analysis', *IMF Staff Papers*, **20**, 683–740.

Hodrick, R.J. (1987), *The Empirical Evidence on the Efficiency of Forward and Futures Foreign Exchange Markets*, Chur: Harwood.

Hotelling, H. (1933), 'Analysis of a complex of statistical variables into principal components', *Journal of Educational Psychology*, **24**, 417–441, 498–520.

Howe, H. and C. Pigott (1991), 'Determinants of long-term interest rates: An empirical study of several industial countries', *The Federal Reserve Bank New York Quarterly Review* **16**(4), 12–28.

Hsiao, C. (1982), 'Autoregressive modelling and causal ordering of economic variables', *Journal of Economic Dynamics and Control*, **4**, 243–259.

Huang, D. (1966), 'The short-run flows of non-farm residential mortgage credit', *Econometrica*, **34**, 433–459.

Jaffee, D.M. (1972), 'An econometric model of the mortgage market', in E.M. Gramlich and D.M. Jaffee (eds), *Savings Deposits, Mortgages, and Housing: Studies for the Federal Reserve-Mitt-Penn Economic Model*, Lexington etc.: D.C. Heath and Company, chapter 5, pp. 139–208.

Jagannathan, R. and E.R. McGrattan (1996), 'The CAPM debate', *Federal Reserve Bank of Minneapolis Quarterly Review* **19**(4), 2–17.

Jennings, R. and L. Starks (1986), 'Earnings announcements, stock price adjustment, and the existence of option markets', *Journal of Finance*, **41**, 107–125.

Johansen, S. (1991), 'Estimation and hypothesis testing of cointegration vectors in Gaussian vector autoregressive models', *Econometrica*, **59**, 1551–1580.

Jole, A. van (1923), '"Het rentevraagstuk" door mr. L.F.H. Regout', *De Economist*, **72**, 388–395.

Jongh, B.H. de (1921), *Beschouwingen over eenige Effecten- en Credietvormen in hun Betekenis voor de Financiering der Onderneming*, Ph. D. thesis, Nederlandsche Handelshoogeschool, Rotterdam.

Jongman, C.D. (1960), *De Nederlandse Geldmarkt*, Leiden/Antwerpen: Stenfert Kroese.

Jong, F.J. de (1965), *De Werking van een Volkshuishouding: Een eerste Inleiding tot het economisch Denken*, Leiden/Antwerpen: Stenfert Kroese.

Kalchbrenner, J.H. (1971), 'Summary of the current financial intermediary, mortgage and housing sectors of the SSRC-MIT-PENN econometric model', Federal Home Loan Bank Board, Washington DC, (mimeographed).

Kang, H. (1981), 'Necessary and sufficient conditions for causality testing in multivariate ARMA models', *Journal of Time Series Analysis* **7**(2), 95–101.

Keijzer, L.M. and M.E.J. Schuit (1991), 'Rentevergelijkingen in empirische macromodellen: Een overzicht', WO&E Research Memorandum 9121, De Nederlandsche Bank.

Kessler, G.A. (1958), *Monetair evenwicht en betalingsbalansevenwicht*, Leiden: Stenfert Kroese.

Kessler, G.A. (1974), 'Monetaire indicatoren', in V. Halberstadt, G.A. Kessler, J.J. Klant, and C. Goedhart (eds), *Economie in Overleg*, Leiden/Antwerpen: Stenfert Kroese, pp. 277–302.

Keynes, J.M. (1930), *A Treatise on Money*, Volume II, London: Macmillan.

Kirchgässner, G. (1985), 'Die Schweiz im internationalen Zinszusammenhang', *Schweizerische Zeitschrift für Volkswirtschaft und Statistik (Revue Suisse d'Economie Politique et de Statistique)*, **121**, 329–351.

Klaman, S.B. (1961), *The Postwar Residential Mortgage Market*, Princeton: Princeton University Press.

Klein, L. (1956), *A Textbook of Econometrics*, Evanston: Row, Peterson and Co.

Kloek, T. and R. Bannink (1962), 'Principal component analysis applied to business test data', *Statistica Neerlandica*, **16**, 57–69.

Kmenta, J. (1971), *Elements of Econometrics*, New York: Macmillan.

Knoester, A. (1980), *Over Geld en economische Politiek*, Leiden/Antwerpen: Stenfert Kroese.

Kocherlakota, N.R. (1996), 'The equity premium: It's still a puzzle', *Journal of Economic Literature*, **34**, 42–71.

Koning, J. (1974), 'Netherlands company pension funds international portfolio diversification', *European Economic Review*, **5**, 245–262.

Korteweg, P. and P. van Loo (1977), *The Market for Money and the Market for Credit*, Leiden: Nijhoff.

Korteweg, P. (1971), *De monetaire Sector, het Aanbod van Geld en de Instrumenten van de monetaire Politiek*, Leiden/Antwerpen: Stenfert Kroese.

Korteweg, P. (1973), 'Over de beheersbaarheid van de geldhoeveelheid in Nederland', *De Economist*, **121**, 273–299.

Kouri, P.J.K. and M.G. Porter (1974), 'International capital flows and portfolio equilibrium', *Journal of Political Economy*, **82**, 443–467.

Kuipers, S.K., B.W.A. Jongbloed, G.H. Kuper, and E. Sterken (1988), *CESAM, het CCSO Jaarmodel van de Nederlandse Economie*, Groningen: Wolters-Noordhoff.

Lawley, D.N. and A.E. Maxwell (1967), *Factor Analysis as a Statistical Method*, London: Butterworths.

Lawley, D.N. and A.E. Maxwell (1971), *Factor Analysis as a Statistical Method* (2nd ed.), London: Butterworths.

Loo, P.D. van (1983), *A Sectoral Analysis of the Dutch Financial System*, Leiden/Antwerpen: Stenfert Kroese.

Lucas, R.F. (1978), 'Asset pricing in an exchange economy', *Econometrica*, **46**, 1429–1445.

Lutz, F.A. (1940), 'The structure of interest rates', *Quarterly Journal of Economics*, **55**, 36–63.

MacFarlane, H. and M. Brown (1995), 'The inflation risk premium', *UK Strategy and Economics* **2**(6).

Malinvaud, E. (1964), *Méthodes Statistiques de l' Économetrie*, Paris: Dunod.

Manaster, S. and R. Rendleman (1982), 'Option prices as predictors of equilibrium stock prices', *Journal of Finance*, **37**, 1043–1057.

Mankiw, N.G. and S.P. Zeldes (1991), 'The consumption of stockholders and non-stockholders', *Journal of Financial Economics*, **29**, 97–112.

Marshall, A. (1890), *Principles of Economics*, London: Macmillan.

Mehra, R. and E.C. Prescott (1985), 'The equity premium: A puzzle', *Journal of Monetary Economics*, **15**, 145–161.

Mehra, R. and E.C. Prescott (1988), 'The equity premium: A solution', *Journal of Monetary Economics*, **22**, 133–136.

Meiselman, D. (1963), 'Bond yields and the price level: The Gibson paradox regained', in D. Carson (ed.), *Banking and Monetary Studies*, Homewood, Ill.: Irwin.

Meltzer, A.H. (1974), 'Credit availability and economic decisions: Some evidence from the mortgage and housing markets', *Journal of Finance*, **29**, 763–777.

Mishkin, F.S. (1984), 'Are interest rates equal across countries? An empirical investigation of international parity conditions', *Journal of Finance*, **39**, 1324–1357.

Mishkin, F.S. (1992), 'Is the Fisher-effect for real?', *Journal of Monetary Economics*, **30**, 195–215.

Modigliani, F. and R.C. Sutch (1966), 'Innovations in interest rate policy', *American Economic Review*, **56**, 178–197.

Modigliani, F. and R.C. Sutch (1967), 'Debt management and the term structure of interest rates', *Journal of Political Economy*, **75** (Supplement), 569–589.

Mot, E.S., P.J. van den Noord, D.D. van der Schelt-Scheele, and M.A. Koning (1989), 'HERMES – The Netherlands', Final report on the Dutch model, Foundation for Economic Research, Amsterdam.

Mourik, T.J. and C.C.A. Winder (1989), 'Integratie, coïntegratie en foutencorrectie-modellen: Methodiek en toepassing', WO&E Research Memorandum 8919, De Nederlandsche Bank.

Mourik, T.J. (1988), 'Systematic patterns in recent stock returns: An analysis of the efficiency of stock markets', WO&E Research Memorandum 8819, De Nederlandsche Bank, revised 1989.

Muiswinkel, L.F. van (1971), 'Inflatie en rentestand', *De Economist*, **119**, 165–181.

Mundell, R.A. (1968), *International Economics*, New York: Macmillan.

Mundell, R.A. (1971), *Inflation, Interest, and Growth in the World*, Pacific Palisades: Goodyear.

Muth, J.F. (1960), 'Optimal properties of exponentially weighted forecasts', *Journal of the American Statistical Association*, **55**.

Nelson, C.R. (1972), *The Term Structure of Interest Rates*, New York: Harper & Row Ltd.

Nerlove, M. (1972), 'Lags in economic behaviour', *Econometrica*, **40**, 221–251.

Nieuwenburg, C.K.F. and M.F. Koeman (1969), 'Aktuele en berekende kapitaalmarktrente', *Maandschrift Economie*, **33**, 185–189.

Nieuwenburg, C.K.F. and H.J. Leemreize (1974), 'The capital market interest rate in The Netherlands', *Economic Quarterly Review*, Amsterdam-Rotterdam Bank N.V., **36**, 5–16.

OECD (1996), 'Have long-term interest rates in the three major economies become more synchronised?', *Economic Outlook*, **60**, 30–35.

Osborn, D.R. (1984), 'Causality testing and its implications for dynamic econometric models', *The Economic Journal*, **94** (Supplement), 82–96.

Ostas, J.R. and F. Zahn (1975), 'Interest and non-interest credit rationing in the mortgage market', *Journal of Monetary Economics*, **1**, 187–201.

Owen, D.P. (1993), 'Cointegration analysis of the Fisher hypothesis — the role of the real rate and the Fisher identity', *Applied Financial Economics*, **1**, 21–26.

Pesando, J.E. (1993), 'Art as an investment: The market for modern prints', *American Economic Review*, **83**, 1075–1089.

Phelps, E.S. (1970), 'Money wage dynamics and labor market equilibrium', in E.S. Phelps (ed.), *Microeconomic Foundations of Employment and Inflation Theory*, New York: Norton, pp. 124–166.

Pierce, D.A. (1977), 'Relationships — and the lack thereof — between economic time series, with special reference to money and interest rates', *Journal of the American Statistical Association*, **72**, 11–22.

Pierson, N.G. (1912), *Leerboek der Staathuishoudkunde*, Haarlem: Erven F. Bohn.

Pigott, C. (1993), 'International interest rate convergence: A survey of the issues and evidence', *Federal Reserve Bank of New York Quarterly Review*, **18**, 24–37.

Polakoff, M.E. and M.D. Ketchum (1970), *Financial Institutions and Markets*, Boston: Houghton-Mifflin.

Polak, N.J. (1950), *Enige Grondslagen voor de Financiering der Onderneming* (9th ed.), Haarlem: Erven F. Bohn.

Poll, W.F.J. van de (1996), 'Bronbeschrijving gegevens voor onderzoek risico-premie nederlandse aandelen', WO&E Research Memorandum 465, De Nederlandsche Bank.

Porsius, P. (1977), 'Spectral analysis of the structure of interest rates in The Netherlands', *Journal of Monetary Economics*, **3**, 191–215.

Post, J.G. (1973), 'Werkloosheid, inflatie en rentevorming', *Maandschrift Economie*, **37**, 229–241.

Prins, C.J. (1983), 'Enkele determinanten van de rente-ontwikkeling in Nederland', *Economisch-Statistische Berichten*, **68**, 160–162.

Pyle, D.H. (1972), 'Observed price expectations and interest rates', *The Review of Economics and Statistics*, **54**, 275–280.

Regout, L.F.H. (1922), *Het Rentevraagstuk*, 's-Hertogenbosch: Teulings.

Ricketts, N. (1996), 'Real short-term interest rates and expected inflation: Measurement and interpretation', *Bank of Canada Review* 1996(Summer), 23–39.

Rietveld, L. (1993), *Inflatie en de lange Rente: Een empirisch Onderzoek naar de Fisher-hypothese*, Thesis, Erasmus Universiteit Rotterdam.

Rietz, T.A. (1988), 'The equity risk premium: A solution', *Journal of Monetary Economics*, **22**, 117–131.

Ripley, D.M. (1973), 'Systematic elements in the linkage of national stock market indices', *The Review of Economics and Statistics*, **55**, 356–361.

Robinson, J. (1952), *The Rate of Interest and Other Essays*, London: Macmillan.

Roll, R. (1970), *The Behavior of Interest Rates*, New York: Basic Books.

Romer, D. (1996), *Advanced Macroeconomics*, New York etc: McGraw-Hill.

Roos, F. de and W.J. Wieringa (1953), *Een halve Eeuw Rente in Nederland*, Schiedam: HAV Bank.

Rose, D.E. (1972), 'A general error-learning model of expectations formations', Paper presented at the 1972 European Meeting of the Econometric Society in Budapest.

Santoni, G.J. (1988), 'The October crash: Some evidence on the cascade theory', *Federal Reserve Bank of St. Louis Review* **70**(3), 12–33.

Sargent, T.J. (1969), 'Commodity price expectations and the interest rate', *Quarterly Journal of Economics*, **83**, 127–140.

Sargent, T.J. (1972), 'Anticipated inflation and the nominal rate of interest', *Quarterly Journal of Economics*, **86**, 212–225.

Sargent, T.J. (1973a), 'The fundamental determinants of the interest rate: A comment', *The Review of Economics and Statistics*, **55**, 391–393.

Sargent, T.J. (1973b), 'Interest rates and prices in the long run: A study of the Gibson paradox', *Journal of Money, Credit and Banking*, **5**, 385–449.

Sargent, T.J. (1973c), 'Rational expectations, the real rate of interest and the natural rate of unemployment', *Brookings Papers on Economic Activity*, **2**, 429–472.

Sargent, T.J. (1973d), 'What do regressions of interest on inflation show?', *Annals of Economic and Social Measurement*, **2**, 289–301.

Schumpeter, J.A. (1954), *History of Economic Analysis*, New York: Oxford University Press.

Shackle, G.L.S. (1966), 'Recent theories concerning the nature and role of interest', in *Surveys in Economic Theory*, Volume I: Money, Interest and Welfare, London/New York: Macmillan/St. Martin's Press, pp. 108–153.

Shiller, R.J. and J.J. Siegel (1977), 'The Gibson paradox and historical movements in real interest rates', *Journal of Monetary Economics*, **85**, 891–907.

Siegel, J.J. (1992), 'The equity premium: Stock and bond returns since 1802', *Financial Analysts Journal* **48**(1), 28–38.

Sims, C.A. (1972), 'Money, income and causality', *American Economic Review*, **62**, 540–552.

Smith, L.B. and G.R. Sparks (1973), 'Institutional mortgage lending in Canada 1954–1968: An econometric analysis', Research Study 9, Bank of Canada.

Smith, L.B. (1969), 'A model of the Canadian housing and mortgage markets', *Journal of Political Economy*, **77**, 795–816.

Smith, L.B. (1970), 'Housing and mortgage markets in Canada', Research Study 6, Bank of Canada.

Société Générale de Banque (1973), *La bourse en Belgique et la gestion de portefeuille*, Brussel: Société Générale de Banque.

Sommermeijer, W.H. (1962), 'Componentenanalyse van eindexamencijfers', *Statistische en Econometrische Onderzoekingen*, 86–104.

Sparks, G.R. (1967), 'A model of the mortgage market and residential construction activity', in *American Statistical Association Proceedings*, pp. 77–85.

Sparks, G.R. (1974), 'Econometric estimation of constrained demand functions for assets', Technical Report 2, Bank of Canada.

Spek, J. van der (1971), 'Een eeuw lonen en prijzen (1870–1970)', *Sociale Maandstatistiek*, **19**, 418–423.

Spencer, R.W. (1973), 'Strong credit demands, but no 'crunch' in early 1973', *Federal Reserve Bank of St. Louis Review* **55**(6), 2–10.

Spolander, M. and M. Kuismanen (1994), 'Measuring inflation expectations in Finland: A survey data approach', Discussion Paper 21/94, Bank of Finland.

Steel, K., A. Vleminckx, and R. Schreurs (1986), 'Securitisatie op de international financiële markten', Rotterdamse Monetaire Studies 22, Erasmus University Rotterdam.

Stein, J. (1977), 'The monetary appreciation of paintings', *Journal of Political Economy*, **88**, 1021–1035.

Sterken, E. (1990), 'DUFIS: An econometric model of the Dutch financial system', Technical Report, Rijksuniversiteit Groningen, Groningen.

Stevers, T.A. (1963), *Renteverschillen en Renteniveau*, Rotterdam/'s-Gravenhage: Nijgh & Van Ditmar.

Stokman, A.C.J. (1990), 'Aspecten van de rentestructuur', WO&E Research Memorandum 9027, De Nederlandsche Bank.

Stone, R. (1947), 'On the interdependence of blocks of transactions', *Journal of the Royal Statistical Society*, **9**, 1–32.

Tesar, L.L. and I.M. Werner (1992), 'Home bias and the globalisation of securities markets', Working Paper 4218, NBER.

Theil, H. (1962), 'Best linear index numbers of prices and quantities', *Econometrica*, **28**, 464–480.

Thornton, H. (1802), *An Enquiry into the Nature and Effects of Paper Credit of Great Britain*, Londen: J. Hatchard.

Throsby, D. (1994), 'The production and consumption of the art: A view on cultural economics', *Journal of Economic Literature*, **32**, 1–29.

Tiao, G.C. and G.E.P. Box (1981), 'Modelling multiple time series with applications', *Journal of the American Statistical Association*, **76**, 802–816.

Tiao, G.C. and R.S. Tsay (1983), 'Multiple time series modelling and extended sample cross-correlations', *Journal of Business and Economic Statistics*, **1**, 43–56.

Tinbergen, J. (1932, December), 'Prijsvorming op de aandelenmarkt', *De Nederlandsche Conjunctuur*, 12–23.

Tinbergen, J. (1939), 'The dynamics of share-price formation', *The Review of Economics and Statistics*, **29**, 153–160.

Vercruysse, P., J. Lavry, and J. Pirard (1971), *Taux d'intérêt en Belique: Contribution à une étude économétrique*, Brussel: Société Générale de Banque.

Vermaat, A.J. (1966), *De Controverse tussen de 'Loanable Funds' Theorie en de 'Liquidity Preference' Theorie*, Ph. D. thesis, Vrije Universiteit, Amsterdam.

Verrijn Stuart, C.A. (1917), *Inleiding tot de Beoefening der Statistiek*, Volume III, Haarlem: Bohn.

Visco, I. (1975), 'Anticipated inflation and the nominal rate of interest: Further results', *Quarterly Journal of Economics*, **89**, 303–310.

Visser, H. (1980), *Monetaire Theorie*, Leiden/Antwerpen: Stenfert Kroese.

Vlaar, P.J.G. (1996), 'Wie wil er indexleningen uitgeven?', *Economisch-Statistische Berichten*, **81**, 855–857.

Volker, P.A. (1980), 'Interest rate harmonisation among selected industrial countries 1961(1)-1970(12)', *European Economic Review*, **14**, 361–376.

Vorst, A.C.F. (1995), 'De tijdshorizon van beleggers', *Economisch-Statistische Berichten*, **80**, 14.

Vries, H. de (1971), *Landbouw en Bevolking tijdens de Agrarische Depressie in Friesland (1878–1895)*, Agronomisch-historische Bijdragen 7, Wageningen: Veenman & Zonen.

Vuchelen, J. (1975), 'A monetary model for Belgium', in P. Frantzen (ed.), *Current Problems of Financial Intermediaries*, Rotterdam: University Press, pp. 27–76.

Wagenführ, H. (1965), *Kunst als Kapitalanlage*, Stuttgart: Forkel.

Weil, P. (1989), 'The equity premium puzzle and the risk free rate puzzle', *Journal of Monetary Economics*, **24**, 401–421.

Yohe, W.P. and D.S. Karnosky (1969), 'Interest rates and price level changes, 1952–1969', *Federal Reserve Bank of St. Louis Review* **51**(12), 18–38.

Zellner, A. (1979), 'Causality and econometrics', *Carnegie Rochester Conference Series on Public Policy*, **10**, 9–54.

Name Index

Subject Index